# BUILDING STONE ATLAS OF SUSSEX

**Roger Cordiner and Anthony Brook**

*A record of a once great industry*

# BUILDING STONE ATLAS OF SUSSEX

A comprehensive cartographic guide to the building stones of Sussex

## ROGER CORDINER

## and

## ANTHONY BROOK

Foreword by Brian Short

Emeritus Professor of Historical Geography, University of Sussex

# CREDITS

Research and Building Stone Survey    Roger Cordiner and Anthony Brook

Design    Roger Cordiner and Anthony Brook

Photographs    Roger Cordiner, unless stated otherwise.
Image enhancements in Photoshop Elements

Maps and Diagrams    Roger Cordiner
Images constructed in Paint Shop Pro.

Cover Design    Roger Cordiner

Desk Top Publishing    Roger Cordiner, in Serif Page Plus X9

Published for    Roger Cordiner and Anthony Brook by
Verite CM Limited
Worthing, West Sussex, UK.
www.Veritecm.com

Copyright    © Roger Cordiner and Anthony Brook 2017

ISBN Number    978-1-910719-49-7

Contact and Sales    rogercordiner@gmail.com
anthony.brook27@btinternet.com

**Above**

Remains of Bramber Castle Gatehouse (1073 AD). A core of chalk and flint has a coating of coursed flints.

**Title Page Background Image**

Wall in the Chichester Cathedral Precinct displaying at least 18 Types of building stone. The rubble-stone has been recycled from former Medieval and Roman buildings.

# FOREWORD

**I**n his masterful book, *The pattern of English building*, Alec Clifton-Taylor introduced many of us to the way in which the geology of our country has been used alongside traditional materials to make some of our most interesting and revered buildings. First published in 1962 his book ran to several editions and stimulated public interest to the extent that the BBC screened a series of his programmes in 1978, based around six towns – of which Chichester was one. Since then many others have made the connections between the visual record of our past and the environment within which our buildings are set. Distinctive regional patterns have been sought, and the aesthetics of Alec Clifton-Taylor's historical approach have been married to a more scientific analysis through the more developed study of geology. Prior to the Second World War, French geographers came to use the term *pays*, particular countrysides marked by their village patterns, farming types, food, wine, even dialect – and especially their local architecture, so related as it was to the surrounding and available stone.

In this publication Roger Cordiner and Anthony Brook have immersed themselves in the traditions of these forerunners but bring to this analysis a keen appreciation of Sussex geology. Whereas, for example, Gallois, in his British Regional Geology monograph on *The Wealden District* (1965), could only muster one paragraph on building materials, we are now offered a full treatment of the interrelationships between Sussex medieval churches and their building stones. As such this volume will be an indispensable adjunct to the recent *Buildings of England* volume by the late Nicholas Antram on East Sussex (2013), with its contribution on building stone by Bernard Worrsam, as well as complementing the excellent Sussex parish churches website by John Allen (http://www.sussexparishchurches.org/). The distribution maps allow us a quick appreciation of the use of particular stones in different parts of the county, both east and west, but the format also offers great detail where possible. The fact that we are told that a wall in the Chichester Cathedral Precinct has at least 18 types of building stone, and that it is probably made of rubble from former Roman buildings, hints at the rich detail on offer.

The authors have also distinguished between the locally-available stone from the different regions of Sussex and those imported both from outside the county and from the Continent. They recognise too that there will be debate about some of the contents, about the identification and use of some stone, but the fact that the material is now so clearly displayed for us will surely move the study of building stone in Sussex forward. Packed with detail, this will be a sourcebook for years to come.

**Brian Short**
**Emeritus Professor of Historical Geography**
**University of Sussex**

# CONTENTS

# CONTENTS

## Note

The background panel colour for each building stone chapter matches that of its Stratigraphic Group as shown in the column on the left of the page.

The Marlipins in Shoreham-by-Sea, dating from the 13th c., which may have been a customs house, is possibly the oldest complete secular building in England. The frontage is a chequer-work pattern of Caen Stone and Flint.

# ACKNOWLEDGEMENTS

The authors would like to thank all those who have helped and guided us as we traversed the Sussex countryside in search of Medieval parish churches; to the members of public who helped us find the way; to churchgoers and village residents who care for their ancient buildings and welcomed us inside; to the parish clergy and church wardens who gave their time to talk to us; to bus drivers who set us down and picked us up in places where few had stopped before; and to landlords and staff of the many village pubs conveniently located close to the churches, who served us such welcoming ale.

We would particularly like to thank Susan Cordiner for many hours of work proof-reading the text. Special thanks go to Chris Powell, Managing Director, Verite, CM. Ltd of Worthing for his advice and excellent work in publishing this Atlas.

A considerable amount of research has been carried out by the authors to make this Atlas an accurate and reliable guide to the building stones of Sussex. In a multi-disciplinary study such as this there is considerable debate about the identification, naming, origin and historic use of some building stones: many of these problems are referred to in the text. The authors are solely responsible for any errors and omissions and would welcome your observations and comments.

**Roger Cordiner and Anthony Brook.**

**Worthing, November 2017.**

Sundial carved from Hastings Sandstone. Withyham Church.

# PREFACE

A survey of the building stones of West Sussex was originally begun on a part time basis by Roger Cordiner in 2001. He later worked with Roger Birch, then Head of Geology at Collyer's College, Horsham to complete the work. This led to the publication of their book *Building Stones of West Sussex* (2014).

Roger Cordiner and Anthony Brook decided in 2014, that because of the large number of building stone types used in Medieval times in both East and West Sussex, there was a need for a survey of their distribution which would best be illustrated in an Atlas of maps. A database of the building stones present in all Medieval churches of West Sussex had already been compiled; this was extended to cover the Medieval churches of East Sussex and Brighton and Hove. The survey of East Sussex, completed in the autumn of 2015, was carried out on foot visiting and recording the building stones in up to 4 churches in a day. This was greatly facilitated by the wealth of local footpaths, many of which converge on the churches, as they were used in the past by parishioners. Each traverse was planned with the help of 1:50,000 and 1:25,000 scale Ordnance Survey maps. The guide to Sussex in the *Buildings of England* series by Pevsner, Nairn and Antram (see bibliography) was indispensable in locating and researching the history of the Medieval parish churches, as well as numerous other stone-built buildings.

This Atlas illustrates the distribution of 41 types of building stone used in Sussex in Medieval times. The distribution of each type is clearly apparent on the maps and can be related to factors such as geology, geography, transport, trade and finance.

The Atlas is a unique record of a once great industry as revealed in the remaining stone-built fabric, furnishings and memorials of ancient churches. The quarries from which the building stone was extracted have long gone, with only one now in full-time production: Philpots Quarry at West Hoathly, 8km north of Haywards Heath.

The Atlas reveals an important facet of the proud heritage of Sussex which until recently has been largely ignored. It will be a considerable asset to all those with an interest in the ancient stone buildings of Sussex; to conservators, architects, planners, geographers, geologists, historians, archaeologists and all those with a regard for the ancient stone buildings of Sussex.

Wall adjoining the precinct of Chichester Cathedral displays at least 18 different building stones, as listed below in stratigraphic order. A greater number of different building stones were used in Chichester in Roman and Medieval times than anywhere else in Sussex.

| Indigenous Building Stones | Imported Building Stones |
| --- | --- |
| Roman Brick | Bembridge Limestone |
| Travertine | Quarr Stone |
| Erratics | Ryde Stone |
| Mixon Stone | Calcaire Grossier |
| Bognor Rock | Ventnor Stone |
| Flint (Field Flint) | Purbeck Marble |
| Chalk | Caen Stone |
| Lavant Stone | |
| Malmstone (Grey Malm) | |
| Carstone (Ferruginous Sandstone) | |
| Sussex Marble | |

# SUSSEX in 1575

A coloured extract showing Sussex from Christopher Saxton's map (1575) of the counties of South East England. This map portrays the late-Medieval landscape of Sussex, showing towns and villages with symbols for parish churches and other religious buildings. The river systems and woodlands of the High Weald are emphasised but the map does not show the network of roads and tracks, as this would have been of value to the Spanish who were threatening to invade at the time.

# INTRODUCTION

This Atlas presents a comprehensive guide to the building stones used in West and East Sussex from *c*. 950 to 1840 AD. The ancient buildings of Sussex, in particular the parish churches, display a wider range of building stones than in any other comparable area of the British Isles with the probable exception of London. 43 types and numerous varieties are described and illustrated; the distribution of each is mapped revealing its 'building stone landscape'.

The Atlas maps have been compiled from a survey of 302 extant Medieval parish churches, together with Chichester Cathedral, 14 ruined and 'lost' churches and 5 ruined religious houses. A further 22 Medieval churches in adjacent counties but close to the border of Sussex are also included on the maps to give enhanced coverage. Because of their religious and cultural significance the majority of parish churches have survived, often being enlarged over the centuries, whilst many other religious, military and civic buildings have been demolished. Churches have continued as revered buildings in the landscape in some cases for a thousand years and therefore preserve a unique record of local history within their stonework.

An important result of the building stone survey is the recognition that parish churches generally display a greater number of building stone types than are present in other ancient buildings within their parish.

During Medieval times building stone was a very useful but often expensive commodity so that as buildings needed repair, were enlarged, or new buildings erected, any source of available stone became a valuable resource. Building stone in the walls of ancient buildings was often appropriated from other structures or recycled from previous phases of building. The Romans introduced building with stone into Sussex so that the ruins of their buildings provided a rich store of material well into Norman times. Large amounts of stone were recycled from former buildings in Roman Chichester (Noviomagus) for use in the construction of churches and walls in the city and its hinterland. The fabric of the earliest stone-built churches, dating from the Late-Saxon period, was often at least partially built of recycled Roman building stone.

Post-Medieval stone buildings tend to be constructed of a single type of building stone such as Hastings Sandstone, Hythe Sandstone or Flint. The building of the railways led to the cheap import of building stones from outside Sussex, with the result that after the mid-19th century many stone quarries were forced to close with the result that fewer buildings were constructed of local stone.

Building stones are derived from rocks which are cohesive enough for construction purposes. Ashlar is the best quality stonework, where blocks of stone are square-cut, carefully prepared and laid in courses, while rubble-stone consists of irregularly-shaped blocks, often quarry waste. Ashlar is usually cut to size in the quarry soon after the rock has been extracted when it is soft and easily sawn and carved. Blocks of ashlar are normally stored for a year or more, over which time the rock releases water and salts known as 'quarry sap' and a hard skin develops on the stone surface. Ashlar was more expensive than rubble-stone which probably cost little more than carriage from the quarry. Rubble-stone, due to the irregular shape of the blocks, required larger amounts of mortar than ashlar to bed the building stone into a wall. Ornamental stone, such as Purbeck Marble and true marble, which could be sharply carved and polished for use in memorials commanded the highest price of all building stones. These elite building stones were used for memorials and ornamental stonework in high-status buildings where finance was more readily available.

In their outcrop across Sussex, Cretaceous and Tertiary strata contain numerous beds of harder rock, most of which have been used in the past for building stone. The major source of higher-quality building stone was sandstone from the Lower Cretaceous strata in the High Weald and from the Lower Greensand cuesta. There is little good building stone suitable for ashlar on the coastal plain of West Sussex, which meant that during Medieval times considerable amounts of building stone needed to be imported from the Isle of Wight, Dorset, Devon and the Continent. It was shipped to Sussex ports, and estuaries such as those at Chichester, Pevensey and Rye (see map page 9).

The building stone distribution maps are mainly based on the survey of the exterior and surrounding walls of Medieval parish churches. South-facing exterior walls tend to show the cleanest and more easily identified stonework, while those that face north tend to be damp and colonised by lithophyllic algae and lichen. Building stone in the interior of ancient churches is often more difficult to identify due to a surface covering of paint, dust and dirt, although memorials, fonts and ledgers may show clean, well-polished surfaces.

The architectural style of stonework is a general guide to dating masonry of ancient parish churches, although it must be borne in mind that building stone was often recycled from redundant or ruined buildings.

## Rocks used for Building Stone

Building stone can be obtained from igneous, sedimentary and metamorphic rock, with each of them often providing stone for specific uses such as ashlar, roofing and infill. The indigenous building stones of Sussex are almost exclusively from sedimentary rock, mainly sandstone and limestone, although a very small amount of igneous and metamorphic, erratic and exotic rocks have been used.

Each of the three classes of rock have been a source of building stone over the ages:

**1. Igneous rocks,** such as granite and basalt, formed from molten magma which cooled and solidified either deep beneath the Earth's surface or was extruded as volcanic lava. These rocks tend to be very hard and difficult to cut and shape. Because they are composed of a mass of interlocking crystals they are very resistant to weathering as water does not penetrate easily into them. Since the development of diamond sawing and polishing in the 19th century many igneous rocks have been used for ornamental stonework.

**2. Sedimentary rocks** have been formed from the erosional products of pre-existing rocks. The materials of which they are composed have passed through a cycle of weathering, erosion, transport and deposition, with the particles being deposited in water or on land in layers (see diagram below). Some sedimentary rocks have been wholly or partly formed by precipitation of salts such as rock salt and gypsum ( e.g. Alabaster), or from biogenic remains, mainly fossil shell material (e.g. Sussex Marble).

**3. Metamorphic rocks** have been formed from pre-existing rocks by heat and/or pressure deep beneath the Earth's surface. Gneiss, formed at high temperatures and pressures shows well-developed banding. Schist, formed at lower temperatures and pressures is rich in mica minerals which form a coarse planar structure. Slate, formed at higher pressures, is fissile and can be cleaved into thin slabs for roofing. Marble, a metamorphosed limestone, is much used for ornamental work, sculptures and memorials.

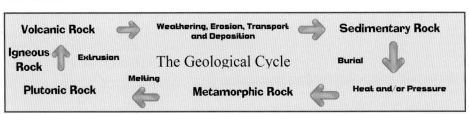

## Naming of Building Stones

In the past quarrymen and stonemasons had an intimate knowledge of the properties of the stone beds they worked. Names were given to individual beds often describing their use or appearance: the Purbeck Limestone of Dorset for instance includes over 20 different named beds. There is no accepted convention on the naming of building stones so that one type of building stone may have a number of different names. The traditional names often go back hundreds of years and generally relate to the locality or town close to where the rock was quarried followed by the word 'Stone'. The name when followed by 'Rock' is generally regarded as the geological name for a rock; confusingly this is sometimes used for building stones e.g. Bognor Rock. Some building stones including Chalk, Flint and Carstone have a single designation, the same as the rock name from which they are obtained. A particular building stone 'Type' as defined below, may have several different names: for example Hythe Sandstone is often called Midhurst, Petworth or Pulborough Stone, denoting the area where it was quarried and/or used. Some building stone Types notably 'The Greensands' are very similar, so they are difficult to identify and may be wrongly named. Popular, descriptive names are commonly used for some building stones e.g. 'Featherstone' for Quarr Stone or 'Streaky Bacon Stone' for Ancaster Stone.

## Types and Varieties of Building Stone

Any classification of varied natural products such as building stones is fraught with problems. The name of a building stone 'Type' may be derived from the place or area where the stone was quarried or used (i.e. Sussex Marble); the geological strata (Formation name) from which it was extracted (i.e. Hastings Sandstone, Weald Clay Sandstone); a traditional name (Malmstone, Carstone); or a geological rock type (Chalk and Flint). Some geological Formations which crop out over a wide area include numerous Types of building stone: the Upper Greensand in southeast England includes Reigate Stone, Malmstone, Ventnor Stone and Eastbourne Stone.

Many 'Types' of building stone occur in a number of distinct 'Varieties'. These can be building stones from the same quarry or from the same geological Formation in a different locality, but they are distinct as they display unique physical and chemical properties. Hastings Sandstone includes numerous named 'Varieties' many of which have important properties and uses e.g. Tilgate Stone which was formerly crushed for road metal and also used for paving.

# SUSSEX PARISH CHURCHES - dating from 950-1550 AD

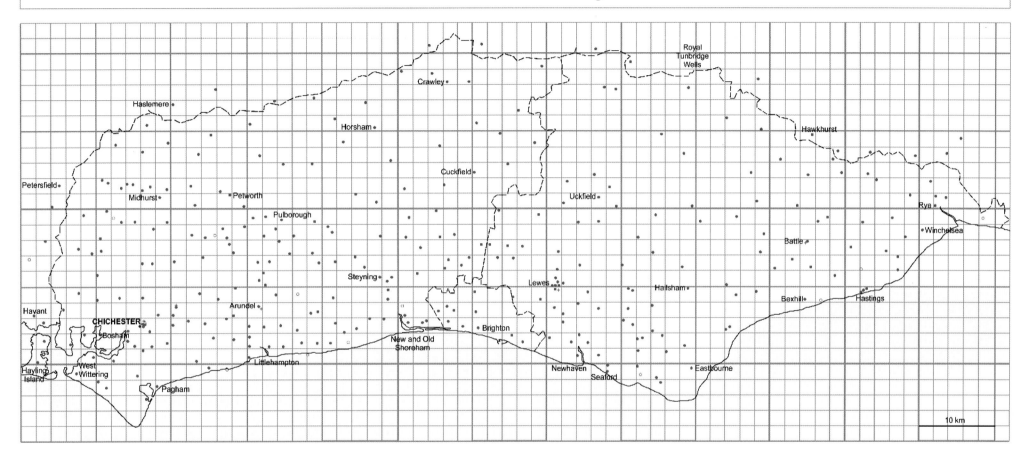

## Explanation of the Atlas Maps

The Atlas maps are divided into 2km-side grid squares based on the Ordnance Survey National Grid. The maps portray the distribution of building stones in 302 extant Medieval parish churches and 22 beyond but close to the border of Sussex. Also included are 14 ruined and 'lost' Sussex churches where some building stone still exists, or where there are records of building stone use. The building stones of Chichester Cathedral, Chichester, Boxgrove, Arundel and Lewes Priories, and Battle Abbey, each designated by a cross on the map above, are also recorded on the Atlas maps.

Coloured grid squares indicate the presence of the named building stone within the fabric of the churches and/or the churchyard walls located within the squares. Each map also shows the county boundary, the coastline and if relevant the outcrop of the strata from which the building stone was quarried. A complete list of all the churches and religious houses recorded on the maps is given in the Appendix pages 122-124.

## The Medieval Building Stone Landscape

The building stone distribution maps are based on the building stone Types used during Medieval times from *c*. 950 AD to The Reformation in 1537. This was the period in Sussex, especially in Norman times, when the greatest use was made of both indigenous and imported building stones in a now almost-forgotten major industry. The distribution of each type of building stone defines the 'Building Stone Landscape' for that stone. Medieval stonework especially in Chichester and near former Roman Villas may include recycled Roman building stone. An example of this is the use of Grey Malmstone in church walls in the Chichester area, although generally the identification of Roman building stone is problematic. Important post-Medieval building stones such as Portland Stone, as used between the mid-16th to mid-19th centuries, are also recorded.

In Sussex construction in stone began soon after the Roman Invasion in 43 AD. A settled society was established by the late-1st century with the development of the city of Chichester, the building of Fishbourne Roman Palace and numerous Roman villas in the southern part of Sussex. The Romans initiated the building stone industry to the extent that during their occupation all the major building stones, both indigenous and imported, were used. Apart from parts of the city walls of Chichester and walls of Pevensey Roman Fort, no original Roman stonework is now present above ground level, much of it having been recycled for later work. Reused stone was incorporated into subsequent Medieval buildings, particularly in the Chichester area, leading to considerable challenges in dating stonework.

## Building Stone Resources of Sussex

Sussex is underlain by sedimentary rocks which range from Lower Cretaceous to Quaternary in age: the older beds of sandstone e.g. Hastings Sandstone and Hythe Sandstone crop out in the north and east while younger beds of Flint and Chalk occur in the south. The older rocks which underlie the higher land of the High Weald, the greensand and chalk cuestas, were relatively easy to quarry and provided the most important indigenous resources for building stone. Flint nodules derived from the chalk and Quaternary flint deposits, such as beach gravel, were used in over half the Medieval churches of Sussex.

## The Main Medieval Building Stones recorded in Sussex Churches

The list below shows the most widely-used Medieval building stones present in 316 Sussex churches, together with Chichester Cathedral. The church total includes 302 extant and 14 ruined and 'lost' churches.

### Indigenous Building Stone

| | Number of Medieval churches |
|---|---|
| Flint (all varieties) | 189 |
| Hastings Sandstone | 174 |
| Hythe Sandstone | 125 |
| Horsham Stone-slate | 114 |
| Chalk and Chalk Calcrete | 109 |
| Sussex and Charlwood Marble | 102 |
| Eastbourne Stone | 72 |
| Erratics | 56 |
| Malmstone | 54 |
| Carstone | 43 |
| Lavant Stone | 43 |
| Woolwich and Reading Ironstone | 40 |
| Sarsen Stone | 34 |
| Mixon and Hounds Stone | 30 |

### Imported Building Stone

| | |
|---|---|
| Caen Stone | 152 |
| Purbeck Marble | 104 |
| Quarr Stone | 66 |
| Bembridge Limestone | 40 |

**Note**
Relatively few Medieval memorials have survived so that ornamental stone such as Marble is underrepresented.

# THE DOMINANT BUILDING STONES OF SUSSEX

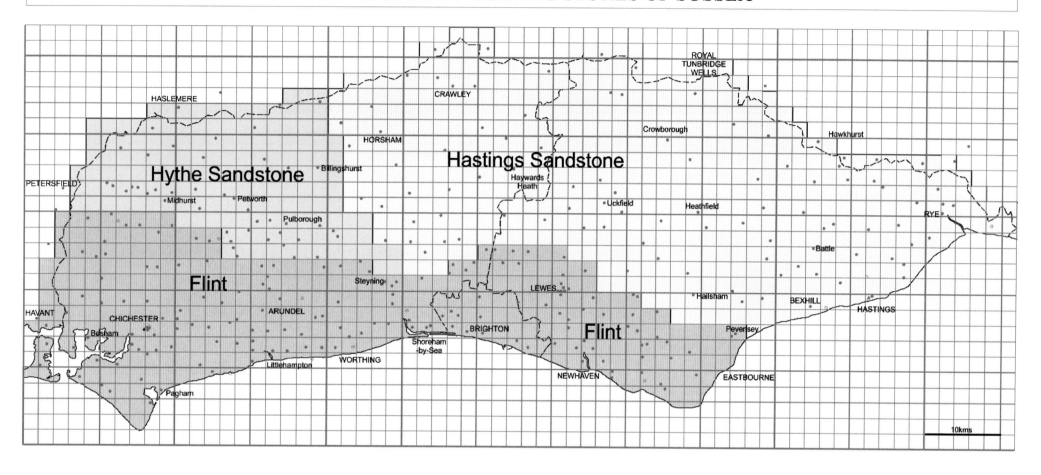

The 'Building Stone Landscape' of Sussex is dominated by three major building stone Types:

**Flint**
**Hythe Sandstone**
**Hastings Sandstone**

The map illustrates the main area of use of each of these building stones. Flint has generally been used as rubble-stone nodules that require ashlar or brick dressings to stabilise the corners, and door and window apertures of buildings.

Three further building stones are dominant over relatively restricted areas:

**Malmstone** -Along the Upper Greensand Bench in West Sussex.
**Eastbourne Stone** -In the Eastbourne area.
**Mixon Stone** -In the Manhood Peninsula, south of Chichester.

Many Medieval churches on the coastal plain of south-west Sussex e.g. in Chichester, and in the ports of Shoreham, Pevensey and Rye, display 15 or more different building stones.

5

# GEOLOGY OF INDIGENOUS SUSSEX BUILDING STONES

The geological structure of Sussex is dominated by the elongated dome of the Weald Anticline, which has a width of *c.* 50 km between the opposing chalk escarpments of the North and South Downs. The axis of the Weald Anticline extends across the northern part of Sussex rising in the west in the Petersfield-Alton area of Hampshire and trending east and then south-east to the English Channel through the Hastings area (see block diagram page 7). It continues as the Weald-Artois Anticline beneath the English Channel into northern France, where it plunges south-east beneath the Boulonnais.

Cretaceous, Palaeogene (Tertiary) and Quaternary sedimentary rocks with a total thickness of *c.* 2km crop out across Sussex. The oldest rocks exposed at the surface belong to the Purbeck Group, which straddles the Jurassic-Cretaceous boundary. The Purbeck strata occupy three small inliers north-west of Hastings where they consist of *c.* 130m of shale with beds of limestone, deposited in brackish and marine conditions. The limestone was used to a small extent as a local building stone but was mainly burnt for lime. Thick beds of gypsum at the base of the Purbeck Group have been extensively mined since the early 20th century.

The Purbeck Group is overlain by up to 400m of mainly alluvial and fluvial sands, sandstones and clays of the Hastings Group. Strata of this Group underlie the High Weald where the harder sandstone beds such as the Top Ashdown Sandstone and Ardingly Sandstone were widely quarried in the past to provide good-quality building stones. The overlying Weald Clay Group consists of terrestrial and freshwater clay and silt, with minor, thin sandstone beds, the best known of which is Horsham Stone-slate. Sussex Marble, an important ornamental stone, is a freshwater shelly limestone which occurs in several thin beds. The overlying Lower Greensand and Selborne Groups are both marine and include important building stones: Hythe Sandstone, Malmstone and Eastbourne Stone. The Upper Cretaceous is represented by up to 500m of chalk belonging to the Chalk Group, which has provided both Chalk and Flint for building. Lavant Stone, a gritty phosphatic limestone within the upper part of the chalk (White Chalk Subgroup), crops out over a very limited area near Mid Lavant, north of Chichester, where it was quarried in Roman and Medieval times.

Tertiary (Palaeogene) sands and clays overlie the chalk with a slight angular unconformity, the missing strata representing a time interval of *c.* 15 million years. Tertiary strata crop out in the south-west of Sussex, flanking the northern margin of the Hampshire Basin Syncline, which extends westward across the northern part of the Isle of Wight. Thin beds of hard stone within the predominantly clay-and-sand strata have been used locally for building stone, most notably Mixon Stone and Bognor Rock.

Quaternary (Superficial) deposits, many of them products of periglacial conditions during cold Stages of the Pleistocene within the past 2.6 million years, include solifluction deposits, brickearth (derived from wind-blown dust), and alluvium which fills the lower valleys and estuaries. Solifluction and beach deposits have provided large quantities of Flint for building on the coastal plain. Travertine has, and continues to be formed around a few calcareous springs at the foot of the South Downs escarpment.

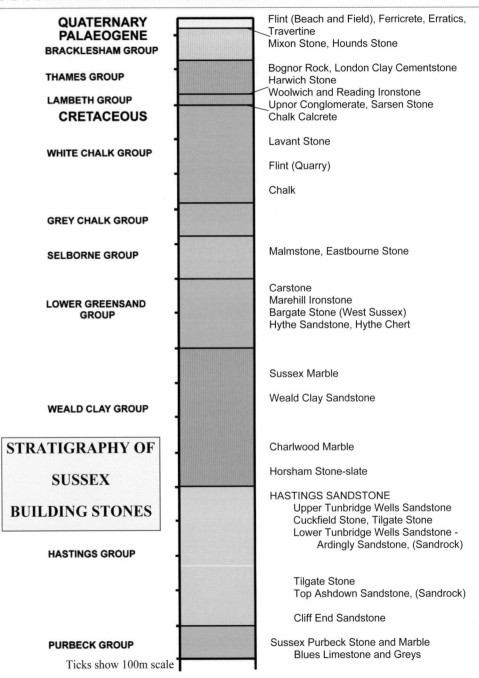

**STRATIGRAPHY OF SUSSEX BUILDING STONES**

QUATERNARY
PALAEOGENE
BRACKLESHAM GROUP — Flint (Beach and Field), Ferricrete, Erratics, Travertine / Mixon Stone, Hounds Stone

THAMES GROUP — Bognor Rock, London Clay Cementstone / Harwich Stone

LAMBETH GROUP — Woolwich and Reading Ironstone / Upnor Conglomerate, Sarsen Stone

CRETACEOUS — Chalk Calcrete

WHITE CHALK GROUP — Lavant Stone / Flint (Quarry) / Chalk

GREY CHALK GROUP

SELBORNE GROUP — Malmstone, Eastbourne Stone

LOWER GREENSAND GROUP — Carstone / Marehill Ironstone / Bargate Stone (West Sussex) / Hythe Sandstone, Hythe Chert

WEALD CLAY GROUP — Sussex Marble / Weald Clay Sandstone / Charlwood Marble / Horsham Stone-slate

HASTINGS GROUP — HASTINGS SANDSTONE / Upper Tunbridge Wells Sandstone / Cuckfield Stone, Tilgate Stone / Lower Tunbridge Wells Sandstone - Ardingly Sandstone, (Sandrock) / Tilgate Stone / Top Ashdown Sandstone, (Sandrock) / Cliff End Sandstone

PURBECK GROUP — Sussex Purbeck Stone and Marble / Blues Limestone and Greys

Ticks show 100m scale

# BIRD'S EYE VIEW OF THE WEALD

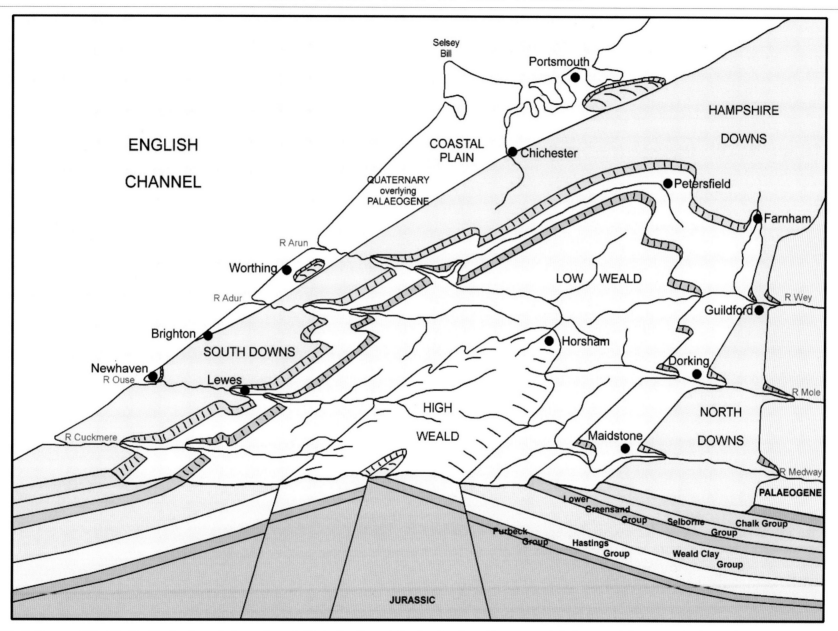

Geological block diagram of The Weald with view towards the south-west, illustrating its westerly-plunging dome-like structure. The foreground shows a geological section from Beachy Head to east of Maidstone, a distance of about 65km. The main escarpment-forming strata of the Chalk and Lower Greensand have been eroded back from the central core of the anticline to reveal older rocks such as those belonging to the Purbeck Group, which form three inliers in the High Weald north of Battle. Progressively younger strata crop out towards the margins of the Weald Anticline.

# HISTORIC USE OF BUILDING STONE IN SUSSEX

Building with stone was introduced into Sussex by the Romans soon after their invasion in 43 AD, for villas, civic, and religious buildings. Within a few years they were making considerable use of local stone, including Mixon Stone from Selsey, Hythe Sandstone from Pulborough, and Flint and Chalk from the Sussex Downs, coastal plain, and beaches. Numerous buildings were constructed of stone in Chichester (Noviomagus), at Fishbourne Roman Palace and other villas including those at Bignor, Southwick and Barcombe. Ashlar, carefully-shaped and finished stonework, required higher-quality building stone than was generally locally available, which led to the importation of building stone from the Isle of Wight, Dorset and Normandy. Large amounts of local flint were used in the construction of Chichester city walls in the late-3rd century and the walls of Pevensey Fort in the 4th century.

After the Roman army was withdrawn in 410 AD building in stone ceased for over 500 years until the establishment of a more settled and prosperous society in late-Saxon times. In the mid-10th century building stone started to replace the wooden fabric of the many small churches; some of this stone was probably recycled from nearby Roman buildings, the ruins of which would have been prominent features in the landscape. Former Roman quarries were reopened and new ones excavated to provide building stone. The Late-Saxon church at Worth near Crawley was built of Hastings Sandstone quarried from the outcrop to the south. Superior building stone suitable for ashlar including Quarr Stone from the Isle of Wight and Caen Stone from Normandy began to be used. These more expensive building stones were mainly used for dressings, columns and arches, and carved stonework where finance was available, such as at Chichester, Bosham, Sompting Abbots, Bishopstone and Arlington.

After their Conquest in 1066 AD the Normans embarked upon a large-scale building programme of castles, churches, and religious institutions. Considerable amounts of ashlar were required for their sturdily-built, Romanesque-style stonework. Flint was an important building stone on the Sussex Downs and Coastal Plain, as at Lewes and Bramber Castles, and large ashlar blocks of Hythe Sandstone were used at Arundel Castle. Chichester Cathedral, begun c. 1076 AD, and Lewes Priory in the following year, required large quantities of imported Caen Stone and Quarr Stone, but by the mid-12th century supplies of Quarr Stone had ceased. At this time a more ornate architectural style was introduced with richly-carved ornamental stone arches in Caen Stone, as illustrated at Steyning and New Shoreham churches.

The demand for building stone fluctuated greatly during the Middle Ages as new construction projects were started and older buildings improved and/or enlarged. Towards the end of the 12th century, at the transition to the Gothic, Early-English architectural style, many churches were built or remodelled. Battle and Bayham Abbeys, built of Hastings Sandstone, represent fine examples of religious buildings of the early-13th century. The transition to the Early English Style, as seen at New Shoreham church, made considerable use of Caen Stone. Flint was used in abundance when and where other stone was unavailable, although large amounts of lime mortar were required to bed-in the irregularly-shaped nodules.

During later Medieval times Horsham Stone-slate became increasingly important for roofing and paving but always remained expensive because of the difficulties of transporting heavy stone slabs overland across the Weald from the quarries in the Horsham area. Purbeck Marble had been imported from Dorset as a decorative stone in Roman times; large amounts were used in Chichester Cathedral in the 13th century for shafts and ornamental capitals. Sussex Marble was utilized in smaller quantities as it is more prone to decay and probably difficult to transport from quarries in the Low Weald north of Petworth. As an elite stone it had specialized uses for fonts and memorials in churches, particularly in those locations where it could be transported by barge down the major rivers.

The Decorated (Gothic) architectural style was introduced from the early-14th century in churches e.g. Winchelsea, built c. 1300, possibly the finest example of this period in Sussex. Church window tracery of this period, usually carved in Eastbourne Stone, is preserved at Warbleton, Wartling and Etchingham. The Perpendicular (Gothic) style, introduced from the mid-14th century, is well represented by the solid ashlar-built 'Pelham Towers' of churches in the East Sussex High Weald, including East Hoathly, constructed of Top Ashdown Sandstone. In West Sussex, Poynings and Amberley churches were remodelled at this period with the use of much flint rubble.

The extensive oak forest of The Weald provided sturdy timbers for many large Wealden-style, timber-framed houses built during the 15-16th centuries. Stone-built houses were more expensive and flaunted the wealth of their owners, such as the Ironmasters of the Weald: Gravetye Manor near East Grinstead, built in 1598 of Ardingly Sandstone with a Horsham Stone-slate roof, is a fine example of this period. In West Sussex large country houses located along the 'greensand bench' including Petworth, Cowdray and Parham were built largely of Malmstone and Hythe Sandstone.

Because of their ruinous condition by the early 19th century many ancient Sussex parish churches had to be extensively rebuilt in Victorian times. They were often greatly-remodelled and enlarged but usually show evidence of previous construction incorporating at least some of the earlier stonework. Considerable building in vernacular stone was carried out during the 19th century, but increasing amounts of building stone were imported after the 1840s. With the establishment of the railways large quantities of imported Jurassic limestones including, Clipsham Stone and Bath Stone for ashlar and quoins, were brought in by rail.

After the First World War few Sussex quarries continued in production due to lack of manpower and increasing imports of building stone. Local building stone became increasingly difficult to source except by using recycled material from older buildings. Hastings Sandstone (Ardingly Sandstone from Philpots Quarry, West Hoathly), and to a lesser extent Hythe Sandstone, are still obtainable in limited quantities for specialist projects and renovation work.

# NAVIGATION AND COASTLINE *c.* 1000 AD

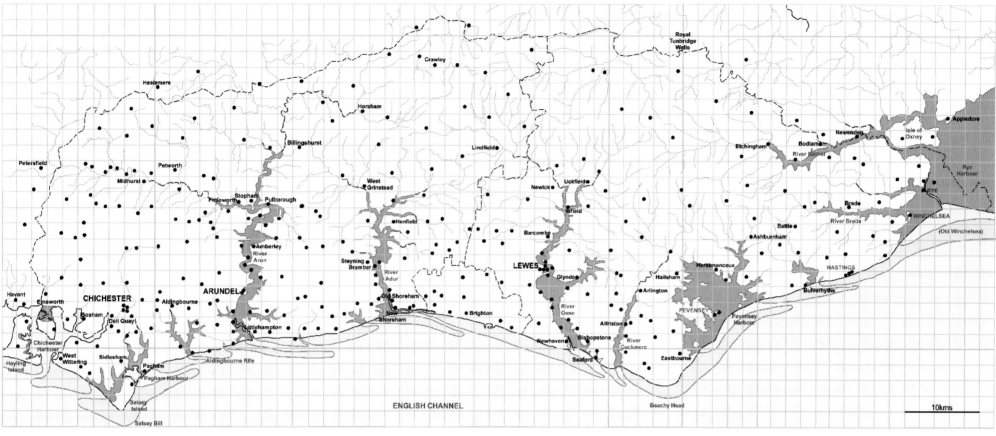

## Key

- Medieval settlements shown by the location of parish churches.
  A selection of settlements, especially those along navigable waterways, are named.
  Larger towns named in upper case.
  The Cinque Ports (Pevensey, Hastings, Winchelsea and Rye) are shown in red

- Upper reaches of rivers which were probably navigable by rafts and other shallow-draught vessels at least during part of the year.

- Former estuaries which silted-up and were reclaimed after Norman times.

- Land lost to the sea since early Norman times. Shingle bars flanked the low-lying coastal areas west of Brighton and at Pevensey and Rye.

From the Iron Age until the 13th century rising sea level flooded the incised valleys along the Sussex coast creating estuaries along the lower courses of the main rivers. These became progressively silted-up during later Medieval times, and the land reclaimed. Less alluvium accumulated in Chichester and Pagham Harbours which have remained as marine inlets to this day. At the beginning of the second millennium the coastline extended at least 1km further south, much of it flanked by extensive shingle banks. During Medieval times Sussex was relatively isolated from the rest of England, with the Weald Forest to the north and Rye Harbour to the east. Access by sea into coastal areas was relatively easy, so that much building stone for building projects was imported and transshipped by barge and raft up the estuaries and navigable rivers.

# THE MAIN BUILDING STONES IN MEDIEVAL CHURCHES OF SUSSEX

## HYTHE SANDSTONE

Stedham Church tower built 1673.

## CAEN STONE and QUARR STONE

Chichester Cathedral. Building began *c.* 1076 with its dedication in 1108. A major fire in 1114 led to rebuilding which was mainly completed by 1184. Much of the building stone in the walls consists of a random pattern of Caen and Quarr Stone ashlar. The Caen Stone weathers to a lighter colour.

**Left**

## HASTINGS SANDSTONE

Old Ore Church ruins, Hastings. The church dates from the 12th century.

**Right**

## FLINT

Southease Church built of Field Flint dates from Late-Saxon times with later 12th to 14th century work. The round tower is one of only three in Sussex, the others being in Lewes (St Michael's) and Piddinghoe.

# STONE QUARRYING IN SUSSEX

Stone quarrying in Sussex began when flints were mined on the South Downs during the Early Neolithic Period, *c.* 4,000 BC. Numerous quarries were established in the Roman period to supply stone for their building projects. Quarrying began again in Late-Saxon times with numerous new quarries opened in the Norman period to supply stone for their great building programme. Stone quarrying continued to supply building projects in the later Medieval times, but most quarries had closed by the early 20th century.

**Above**

A hand operated-crane or drag-line being used to extract a large block of Top Ashdown Sandstone.
Mountfield Quarry 1815, depicted by Thomas Hearne (1744-1817) .

**Right**

An illustration of the quarry in the Cuckfield Stone at Whitemans Green where Gideon Mantell first discovered the fossil bones of the dinosaur which he named *Iguanodon*. This view from his book *Illustrations of the Geology of Sussex* (1827) shows Mantell with his geologist friends, Charles Lyell and William Buckland (all wearing top hats), excavating a fossil on a visit in March 1824

This quarry was one of many in the Cuckfield area in the 18th-19th centuries. It was opened-up to supply crushed Tilgate Stone for the Brighton-to-London Turnpike road which passed through the area.

**Above**

Photograph showing a working quarry at Nutley, (1904) in Top Ashdown Sandstone. Extraction and preparation of building stone was carried out manually, including winching the large blocks of stone out of the quarry with a hand-operated crane.

The photograph shows that methods of quarrying changed little from Medieval times until the early 20th century. Quarrying was very labour intensive, with the use of simple tools such as winches, crowbars, hammers, chisels, picks and shovels.
(Unknown photographer).

| Age | Berriasian |
| --- | --- |
| | Lower Cretaceous |
| **Lithostratigraphy** | Durlston and Lulworth Formations |
| | Purbeck Group |

## Geology

The Purbeck Group crops out in three partly fault-bounded inliers within the High Weald of East Sussex near Brightling, Mountfield and Whatlington. The Group is *c.* 130m thick, and consists of limestone, shale, sandstone and gypsum beds, which were deposited in freshwater and brackish coastal lagoons about 140 million years ago. The Jurassic-Cretaceous boundary lies near the base of the Purbeck Group so that the upper strata exposed in East Sussex, belonging to the Durlston Formation, are of Lower Cretaceous age. The basal 20m of the Purbeck Group, belonging to the Lulworth Formation, consist of four beds of gypsum and anhydrite separated by thinner beds of shale. The gypsum is of economic importance and has been mined at the Mountfield and Brightling Mines since 1876.

In the 18th and 19th centuries the limestone beds were mainly mined for lime production, while the flaggy, calcareous sandstone beds were used to a minor extent for paving.

Carved capitals (below) and part of a pillar (right) constructed of Blues Limestone. This ornamental stone is a grey-blue shelly (*Unio*) limestone which takes a good polish.

Photographs by Roger Cordiner are reproduced by kind permission of Historic England. Battle Abbey Museum.

## Building Stone
## Names and Varieties -

Sussex Purbeck Stone, Sussex Purbeck Limestone, Greys.
Sussex Purbeck Marble, Blues Limestone.
Sussex Purbeck Sandstone and Flagstone.

The Greys and Blues Limestones provided a small amount of building stone for local use in the past. The Blues Limestone is a blue-grey, freshwater limestone packed with shells of the fossil bivalve *Unio*. It is a fine ornamental stone which takes a high polish, being used for capitals, columns and bases at Battle Abbey. Greys Limestone was used for walling and lime production, and the flaggy sandstone beds for paving and tomb slabs.

## Historic Use

| Norman | Battle Abbey (polished capitals, columns and bases). |
| --- | --- |
| Late Medieval | Mountfield Church (walling stone). |
| Post Medieval | Bateman's (calcareous sandstone paving). |

Sussex Purbeck Limestone paving at Bateman's, near Burwash, the former home of Rudyard Kipling.

Rubble blocks of shelly Sussex Purbeck Limestone were used in the walls of Mountfield Church, dating from 12-13th centuries.

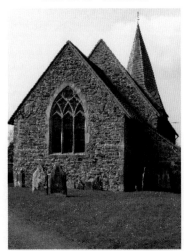

**Stratigraphic column (left margin):**

Superficial Deposits
Bracklesham Group
Thames Group
Lambeth Group
White Chalk Subgroup
Grey Chalk Subgroup
Selborne Group
Lower Greensand Group
Weald Clay Group
Hastings Group
Purbeck Group

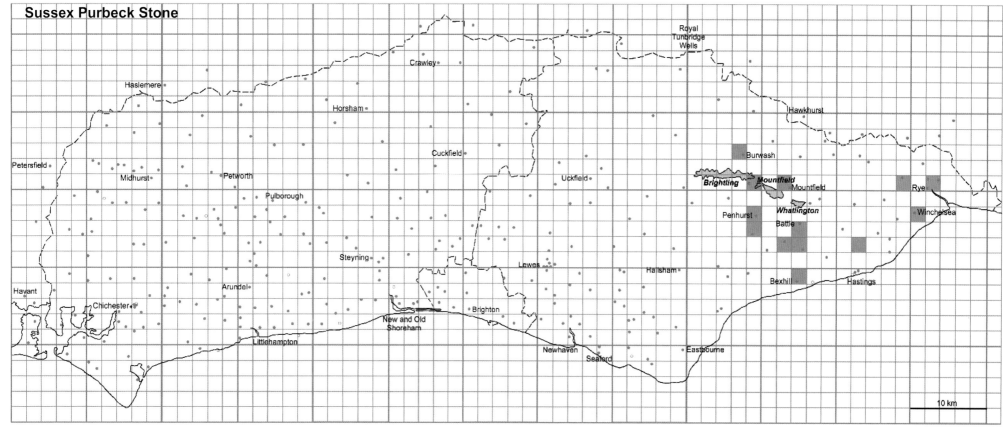

**Sussex Purbeck Stone**

## Distribution of Sussex Purbeck Stone

Sussex Purbeck Stone use, including limestone and sandstone varieties, is mainly limited to an area in central East Sussex near the Purbeck Inliers from which the stone was obtained. This building stone has been recorded in thirteen Medieval churches as well as Battle Abbey, where Blues Limestone, used for columns, capitals and bases, was probably obtained from the outcrop at Netherfield 5km to the north-west.

Except at Mountfield Church where it is the main building stone, Sussex Purbeck Stone was mainly used for higher-value work such as flooring, ledgers, tombstones and carved capitals. Its outcrop in a relatively inaccessible area in the heart of the High Weald in East Sussex meant it was difficult to access and transport, and so was only used as a minor building stone in the local area extending south to the coast at Bexhill. The distribution of this stone is probably more extensive than shown, as the interior of a number of churches was not accessible at the time of the survey.

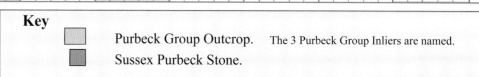

**Key**

Purbeck Group Outcrop.    The 3 Purbeck Group Inliers are named.

Sussex Purbeck Stone.

## East Sussex and Dorset Purbeck Stone and Marble

Purbeck Limestones from East Sussex and Dorset are similar, while Purbeck Marble is sometimes confused with Sussex Marble, so care has to be taken in their identification. East Sussex Purbeck Marble has a distinctive blue-grey colour and like Purbeck Unio Marble is packed with fossil shells of the freshwater bivalve, *Unio*.

In Medieval times Purbeck Marble was much easier to obtain, with a ready supply coming by sea from Dorset. It was used throughout Sussex from the early-13th c. for ornamental stonework including ledgers, altars and fonts; and for columns, shafts, capitals and bases in Chichester Cathedral, Battle Abbey and Winchelsea Church.

Superficial Deposits

Bracklesham Group

Thames Group

Lambeth Group

White Chalk Subgroup

Grey Chalk Subgroup

Selborne Group

Lower Greensand Group

Weald Clay Group

Hastings Group

Purbeck Group

| | |
|---|---|
| **Age** | Berriasian-Valanginian |
| | Lower Cretaceous |
| | |
| **Lithostratigraphy** | Hastings Group |
| | Tunbridge Wells Sand Formation |
| | Wadhurst Clay Formation |
| | Ashdown Formation |

## Geology

The strata of the Hastings Group consist of up to 400m of sand, sandstone, siltstone, and clay with ironstone concretions. They were deposited by rivers and in lakes over a vast plain which extended across South East England and beyond during the early part of the Lower Cretaceous (145-125Ma). Much later, some 15Ma ago, Alpine folding pushed the region of the Weald into a major anticline which, as it was worn down, revealed the older strata in the central area (see page 7).

The Hastings Group strata crop out around the core of the Weald Anticline or Dome along a 35km wide belt of land extending from Horsham in the west to Hastings in the east. Exposures are generally poor except along the coast at Hastings where the sandstone forms 120m high cliffs. Two sandstone beds, Ardingly Sandstone and Top Ashdown Sandstone, provide the best building stone. They are relatively resistant to weathering and occasionally form rocky outcrops such as at Uckfield and West Hoathly.

## Building Stone
## Names and Varieties -

Hastings Sandstone - Sussex Sandstone, Wealden Sandstone, Forest Stone.
     Hastings Sandstone includes numerous varieties (see page 16).
     Ardingly Sandstone and Top Ashdown Sandstone are the best quality ashlar building stones.

## Building Stone Stratigraphy (see stratigraphic column on page 6)

Upper Tunbridge Wells Sandstone
Cuckfield Stone
Lower Tunbridge Wells Sandstone - includes:
     Ardingly Sandstone (used for ashlar)
Ashdown Sandstone - includes:
     Top Ashdown Sandstone (used for ashlar)

Tilgate Stone concretions occur within both the Cuckfield Stone and Wadhurst Clay.

## Historic Use

| | |
|---|---|
| Roman | Pevensey Castle. |
| Late Saxon | Worth (pilasters) & Beckley Chs. (herring-bone work). |
| Norman | Battle Abbey and Hastings Castle. |
| Late Medieval | 'Pelham Church Towers', e.g. Chiddingly Church. Camber Castle. |
| Post Medieval | Sackville College and Gravetye Manor. |
| Victorian | Lancing College Chapel, Christ Church-St. Leonards. |

East gate to Pevensey Castle.
3rd c. Roman archway in Hastings Sandstone.

Battle Abbey Gatehouse dates from 1338AD when the Abbey was give a licence to crenellate.

Camber Castle built 1549-53 with Hastings Sandstone, on the orders of Henry VIII as a defence against a possible French invasion.

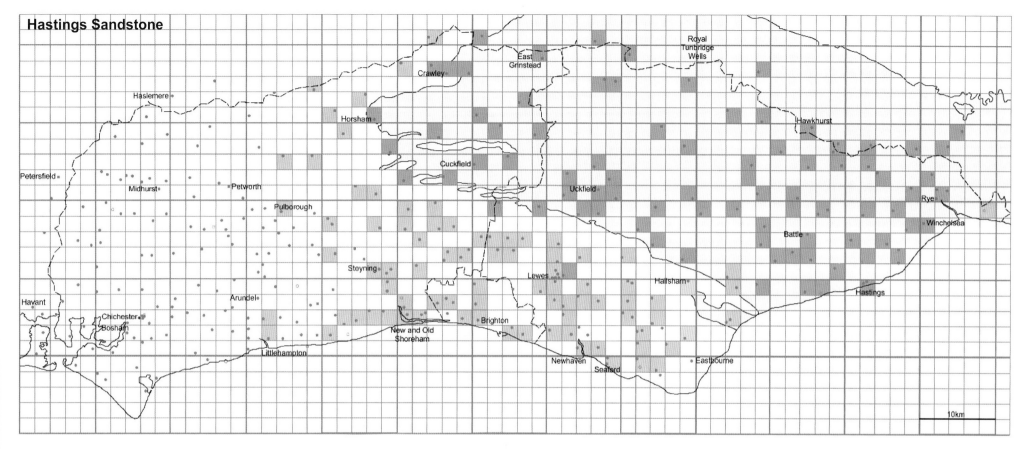

Hastings Sandstone

## Distribution of Hastings Sandstone

The use of Hastings Sandstone as the main building stone in Medieval churches closely defines the area of outcrop of the Hastings Group from which it was obtained. Every Medieval church in the High Weald is constructed of this building stone. It was used in conjunction with other building stones in a belt about 8km wide around the margin of the Hastings Sandstone outcrop. The distribution of Hastings Sandstone in the south of Sussex shows a concentration of stone use in churches adjacent to the Rivers Adur, Ouse and Cuckmere. These rivers and their upper tributaries acted as route-ways for the transport of building stone south from the High Weald.

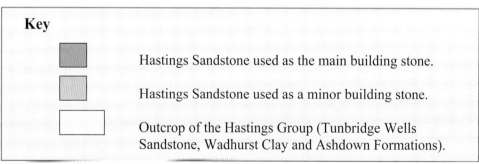

**Key**

Hastings Sandstone used as the main building stone.

Hastings Sandstone used as a minor building stone.

Outcrop of the Hastings Group (Tunbridge Wells Sandstone, Wadhurst Clay and Ashdown Formations).

### Hastings Sandstone Ashlar

In the western part of the High Weald, west of Heathfield, the best quality Hastings Sandstone ashlar was obtained from the Ardingly Sandstone; in the eastern part Top Ashdown Sandstone provided the best quality ashlar ( see map on page 19).

# SANDSTONE VARIETIES

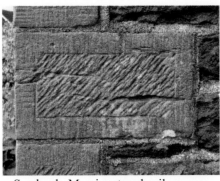

Sandrock. Massive, tough, silver-grey sandstone. Warnham Church.

Ferruginous sandstone rubble. Wadhurst Church.

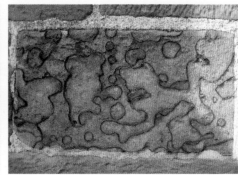

Liesegang-banded sandstone with convolute structure. Battle Church.

Grey to buff massive sandstone with carving of 'The Green Man'. Little Horsted Church.

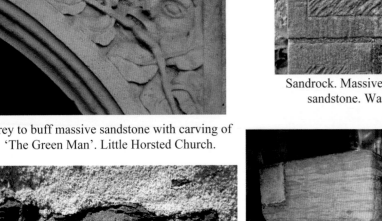

Siderite ironstone concretion. Hailsham Church.

Ochre, flaser-bedded sandstone. Kingston Bucci Church.

Tilgate Stone paving setts, Rye.

Banded sandstone. Bolney Church.

Finely-bedded, flaggy sandstone. Icklesham Church.

Close-up of sphaerosiderite (spherulitic siderite) sandstone. Herstmonceux Church.

Bivalve sandstone with sections of the river mussel *Unio*. Kingston-near-Lewes Church.

Close-up of sandstone with layers of grit. Frant Church.

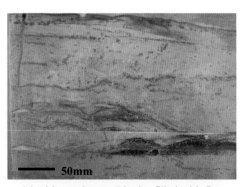

Lignitic sandstone. Ripples filled with fine lignite particles. Warnham Church.

## Varieties of Hastings Sandstone

The list below briefly describes the most important varieties of Hastings Sandstone which have been used for building stone. They occur in beds throughout the Hastings Group and are therefore not diagnostic of any particular Formation.

1. Sandrock - Massive, well-cemented silver-grey sandstone.
   This is the best quality ashlar from the Ardingly Sandstone and Top Ashdown Sandstone. Used for quoins and dressings in most churches of the High Weald.

2. Massive brown, buff, ochre, pale-grey and off-white fine-grain sandstone.
   This is the commonest variety of Hastings Sandstone. It has mainly been used for rubble-stone wall infill between quoins.

3. Finely-bedded, often cross-bedded, laminated sandstone displaying sedimentary structures including contorted bedding. This variety is particularly common in the east part of the outcrop, e.g. Iden and Peasmarsh churches.

4. Ochre, flaser and lenticular-bedded sandstone with sand-filled ripples.
   This variety occurs interbedded with Sandrock. Excellent examples of flaser-bedded ashlar are visible in the walls of Lancing College Chapel.

5. Brown-and-grey banded sandstone, with alternating soft and hard sand beds.
   A relatively uncommon variety. Used in the east wall of Bolney Church.

6. Massive sandstone with brown-to-red Liesegang bands caused by iron staining.
   A very striking building stone; notably used at Hartfield, Etchingham and Battle churches.

7. Tilgate Stone. Pale, massive-to-laminar, hard calcareous sandstone.
   Mostly used in the past for road-stone and paving setts, e.g. in Lewes and Rye.

8. Sphaerosiderite (spherulitic siderite)-spotted sandstone packed with 5mm-size spherical nodules. A relatively common building stone used as isolated rubble blocks.

9. Dark-brown siderite concretion (iron ore) mainly derived from the Wadhurst Clay Formation. Isolated rubble blocks used in church walls in the High Weald, e.g. at Wadhurst Church.

## Historic Use of Hastings Sandstone

The earliest recorded building in sandstone from the Hastings Group was in Roman times: finely-bedded laminar blocks of ferruginous Tunbridge Wells Sandstone were used in the main walls of Pevensey Fort. Within the High Weald, Ashdown Sandstone was used in the construction of buildings associated with iron smelting.

Building with stone did not begin again until Late-Saxon times when a number of small churches were constructed, many of which most likely replaced wooden structures. One of the few remaining examples in the High Weald which shows building from this period of history is the church at Worth. Pevsner (1965 p. 641), in his book on the buildings of Sussex, describes this church as, '..one of the most powerful of Anglo-Saxon churches, large in scale and powerful in conception'.

After the Norman Conquest huge amounts of stone were required for the massive building programme of castles, churches and religious houses. Bolney, Horsted Keynes and Hellingly churches show stonework of this period, but generally little has survived without later alteration and rebuilding.

During the 13th-15th centuries many parish churches in the High Weald were built using Hastings Sandstone, with the building stone sourced from nearby quarries. Especially notable are the sturdily-constructed, castellated 'Pelham Church Towers' of sandrock ashlar, as seen at East Hoathly Church.

Numerous large grand houses including Ashburnham House and Brightling Park were built in Tudor to Stuart times with money derived from the Wealden iron industry. After the Dissolution of the Monasteries in 1537 large amounts of stone from redundant religious buildings became available, such as from Lewes Priory and Battle Abbey.

Many country houses within the High Weald were built in the 18th and 19th centuries of Hastings Sandstone as high quality stonework added prestige to the buildings. Although some cottages in this area were built of stone most are of brick, some with the vernacular white weatherboarding typical of the eastern part of the Weald. Building stone was never used in the High Weald on a large scale for housing so there are no stone-built villages as in Dorset or the Cotswolds. At the outbreak of the First World War most working quarries in the High Weald ceased operating and few reopened afterwards, so that very little construction in Hastings Sandstone has been effected since 1914.

Late-Saxon chancel arch, Worth church.

Norman double-light window with baluster shaft. Fletching church.

Late-11th century doorway reset during Victorian renovation. Wivelsfield church.

Sackville College 1617-19, East Grinstead. Jacobean almshouses built by the second Earl of Dorset.

Bodiam Castle dates from 1385. By the 18th century it was a ruin but was restored in the 19th to early 20th century.

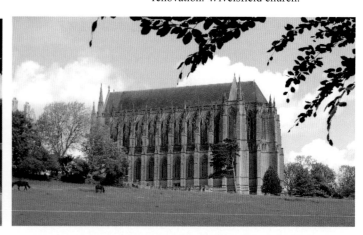

Lancing College Chapel, built on a grand scale, was constructed between 1868-1911. It was originally planned to have a spire.

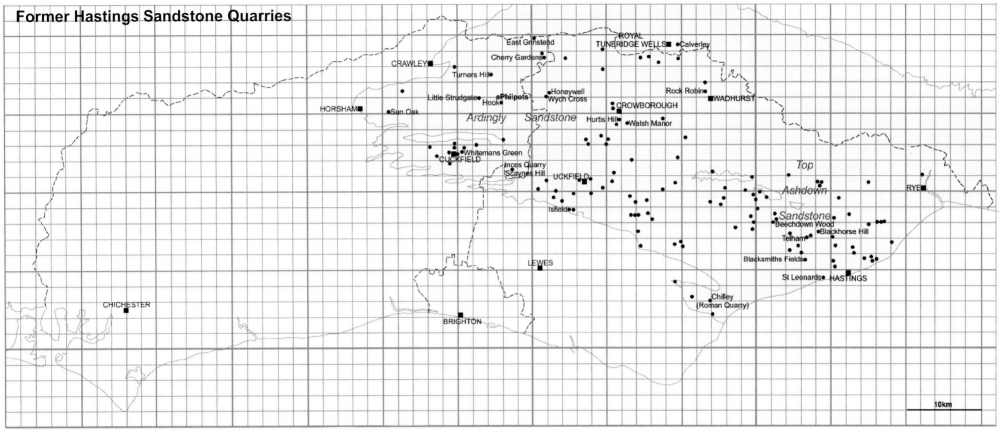

**Former Hastings Sandstone Quarries**

East Grinstead
ROYAL TUNBRIDGE WELLS ■ • Calverley
Cherry Gardens
CRAWLEY ■
Turners Hill
Honeywell
Rock Robin
Little Strudgate
Hook
**Philpots**
Wych Cross
WADHURST ■
HORSHAM ■
• Sun Oak
*Ardingly Sandstone*
CROWBOROUGH
Hurtis Hill
• Walsh Manor
• Whitemans Green
CUCKFIELD
Inces Quarry
Scaynes Hill
UCKFIELD
*Top*
*Ashdown*
RYE ■
Isfield
*Sandstone*
Beechdown Wood
• Blackhorse Hill
Telham
Blacksmiths Fields
LEWES
St Leonards • HASTINGS
Chilley
(Roman Quarry)
CHICHESTER
BRIGHTON ■

10km

## Key

Hastings Group outcrop.

● Quarry sites with the name where known, recorded in Geological Survey Map Memoirs.

● Philpots Quarry near West Hoathly, the last large operating quarry in Hastings Sandstone (Ardingly Sandstone), is shown in bold.

'Ardingly Sandstone' and 'Top Ashdown Sandstone' shown on the map in red, designate the main areas of quarrying of these higher-quality building stones. Ardingly Sandstone was particularly quarried around Cuckfield, East Hoathly, East Grinstead, Crowborough and Uckfield, while Top Ashdown Sandstone was quarried to the north of Hastings.

**Philpots Quarry**

View looking north across Philpots Quarry near West Hoathly where Ardingly Sandstone is worked beneath an overburden of Grinstead Clay. The clay capping has protected the Ardingly Sandstone from weathering so that its natural cement has been preserved, making it a good-quality building stone. This is the only building stone quarry in Sussex still in full-time production.

19

# 3 HORSHAM STONE and HORSHAM STONE-SLATE

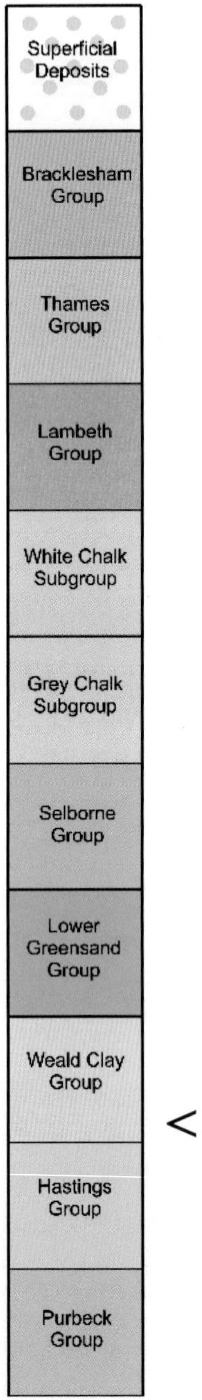
Superficial Deposits
Bracklesham Group
Thames Group
Lambeth Group
White Chalk Subgroup
Grey Chalk Subgroup
Selborne Group
Lower Greensand Group
Weald Clay Group
<
Hastings Group
Purbeck Group

| | | |
|---|---|---|
| **Age** | Barremian | Lower Cretaceous |
| **Lithostratigraphy** | Horsham Stone Beds 1a and 1b<br>Weald Clay Group | |

## Geology

Horsham Stone and Horsham Stone-slate are derived from two beds of sandstone which occur near the base of the Weald Clay Group. Horsham Stone-slate, a slightly-calcareous, laminated sandstone, used for roofing and paving, is found towards the top of each sandstone bed.

Horsham Stone crops out in an arcuate pattern around the north, west and south of Horsham where it underlies a low cuesta. To the south and west of Horsham, in the vicinity of Christ's Hospital, the strata have a very gentle dip where Horsham Stone underlies an extensive plateau. The northern outcrop dies out to the east in the Crawley area and the southern outcrop continues to near Bolney.

## Building Stone

### Varieties

Horsham Stone (building or walling stone).
Horsham Stone-slate (roofing/paving stone) -also known as Horsham Slab or Ripplestone.

## Historic Use

| | |
|---|---|
| Roman | Bignor Roman Villa (Horsham Stone-slate roof). |
| Norman | Sedgwick Castle (former hunting lodge). |
| Late Medieval | Horsham Church, Cuckfield Church (roofs).<br>Itchingfield Church (walls and roof). |
| Post Medieval | Parham House (Horsham Stone-slate roof).<br>Steyning (Horsham Stone-slate roofs on *c.* 30 houses). |
| Victorian | Slinfold Church (rebuilt 1860), Southwater Church (1849). |
| Modern | Buildings in Horsham Park (reused stone-slate on roofs).<br>Houses at Budgenor (near Midhurst), and Midhurst. |

Cleaved, roughly-cut blocks of Horsham Stone in the south wall of Slinfold Church. This stone breaks into tabular blocks and weathers to an ochre-brown colour.

West Grinstead Church has a large Horsham Stone-slate roof. Horsham Church has the largest Horsham Stone-slate roof in Sussex.

Large, smooth slabs of Horsham Stone-slate paving and church walls of Horsham Stone. Slinfold Church.

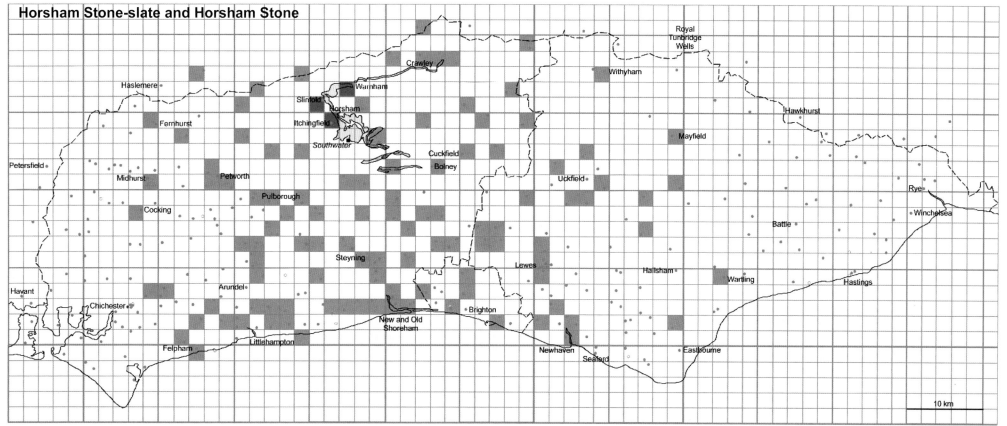

**Horsham Stone-slate and Horsham Stone**

## Distribution of Horsham Stone and Horsham Stone-slate

Horsham Stone-slate is an unique Sussex building stone which is ideal for roofing and paving, and was used widely across the central area of Sussex, south to the coast. Overland transport of this heavy stone from the quarries situated around Horsham was difficult in Medieval times so that stone for use in the south of Sussex was most likely transported down the Rivers Arun, Adur and Ouse. Use of this stone for roofing was almost certainly more extensive than shown; when churches fell into disrepair the heavy Horsham Stone-slate was often replaced with roofing tiles.

The lower part of the Horsham Stone beds consist of massive, finely bedded, rich-ochre to brown sandstone, which weathers to a rich-brown colour. This sandstone was used in churches and cottages located near quarries in the Warnham, Slinfold and Itchingfield areas.

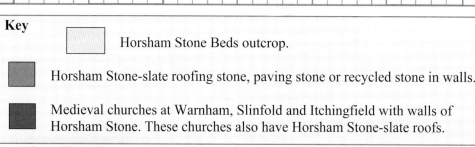

**Key**

- Horsham Stone Beds outcrop.
- Horsham Stone-slate roofing stone, paving stone or recycled stone in walls.
- Medieval churches at Warnham, Slinfold and Itchingfield with walls of Horsham Stone. These churches also have Horsham Stone-slate roofs.

Stained glass window in Southwater Church (1849), showing Easted's Farmhouse (*c.* 1485), displaying a Horsham Stone-slate roof. Records show the church was built of Horsham Stone from Stammerham Quarry. The dressings are in Hastings Sandstone from Sun Oak Quarry near Horsham.

Former quarry site with discarded slabs of Horsham Stone-slate. Finches Wood near Sedgwick Park, south of Horsham.

Iguanodon footprint in an excavated slab of Horsham Stone. Lower Broadbridge Farm Quarry, Horsham.

**Right**

Roadside exposure of Horsham Stone south of Nuthurst, showing flaggy sandstone.

**Right**

Horsham Stone rubble with fossil burrow structures. Cottage wall Slinfold.

Excavated slabs of Horsham Stone and Stone-slate. Lower Broadbridge Farm Quarry, Horsham.

Vertical views of Horsham Stone-slate (Ripplestone) paving.
Left, linear ripples, Slinfold Church.
Right, Trough cross bedding, Shipley Church.

3m long slab of Horsham Stone-slate. Tithe Stone, Warnham churchyard.

# BUILDINGS

Modern housing with Horsham Stone walls and facing at Budgenor near Midhurst.
The stone came from Lower Broadbridge Farm Quarry, Horsham.

Priest's House dating from 15th century with Horsham Stone-slate roof. Itchingfield churchyard.

Modern buildings in Horsham Park with roofs of reused Horsham Stone-slate.

Horsham Stone tower dating from the 15th century. Warnham Church.

Horsham Stone-slate roof.
The Priest's House, West Hoathly Museum.

Horsham Stone-slate seat.
Clayton churchyard.

Horsham Stone-slate roof to lych-gate.
East Preston Church.

23

| Age | Barremian |
| --- | --- |
| | Lower Cretaceous |
| **Lithostratigraphy** | Beds 3, 5 and 7 |
| | Weald Clay Group |

## Geology

The Weald Clay consists of up to 400m of fluviatile, lacustrine and terrestrial clay, and minor sandstone and limestone beds. These rocks were laid down across an extensive plain which covered South East England during Lower Cretaceous times. Sand and sandstone strata are best developed in West Sussex in the Billingshurst and Horsham areas, where they occur in 4 separate beds and groups of beds, each up to *c.* 2m in thickness, within the Weald Clay. They are numbered 1, 3, 5 and 7; the lowest is Bed 1, the Horsham Stone. In some places the sand beds have been cemented with calcite to form hard sandstone layers. Bed 5a (Andrews Hill Sandstone) near Billingshurst has provided stone-slate similar to Horsham Stone-slate.

## Building Stone

Weald Clay Sandstone building stone is a flaggy, finely-bedded and often cross-bedded sandstone which naturally splits into tabular blocks. The laminar sandstone lends itself to herringbone work, seen at Wisborough Green and West Grinstead churches. Bed 5a in the Rudgwick to Billingshurst area has provided stone-slate for roofing although Weald Clay Sandstone was mainly used for walling stone.

## Historic Use

| | |
| --- | --- |
| Medieval | Billingshurst, Wisborough Green and Shipley churches |
| Post Medieval | Paving at Wisborough Green Church. |
| | Quarried and used in the Wisborough Green and |
| | Billingshurst area in the 18th to early-19th centuries. |

Superficial Deposits

Bracklesham Group

Thames Group

Lambeth Group

White Chalk Subgroup

Grey Chalk Subgroup

Selborne Group

Lower Greensand Group

Weald Clay Group

Hastings Group

Purbeck Group

Finely-bedded, cross-bedded sandstone rubble, set upside down in relation to the strata.
Rudgwick Church.

Tabular sandstone blocks laid in herringbone work which is often regarded as Late-Saxon.
Wisborough Green Church..

Carefully-laid, tabular sandstone blocks.
South wall of Shipley Church.

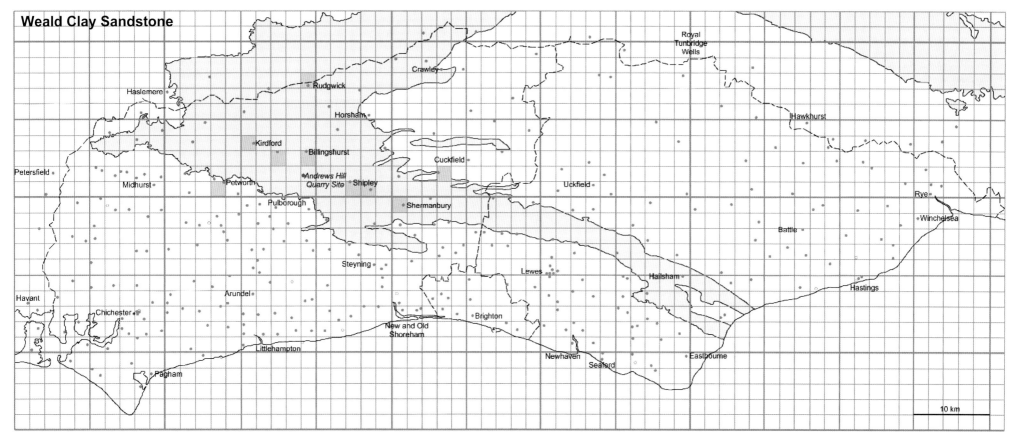

10 km

## Distribution of Weald Clay Sandstone

Weald Clay Sandstone distribution in Medieval churches closely follows the occurrence of the more compact sandstone beds within the Weald Clay of West Sussex. The sandstone beds die out towards the east, so that this stone was not used in East Sussex.

Much of the building stone appears to have been quarried from the Andrews Hill Sandstone (Bed 5a), from its outcrop south of Billingshurst: it is known to have been worked in this area in the early 19th century. Its use follows the outcrop of this sandstone in the area from Rudgwick and Wisborough Green to Billingshurst and Shipley. This sandstone was only quarried on a small scale, being recognised in only 9 churches dispersed around the Billingshurst area.

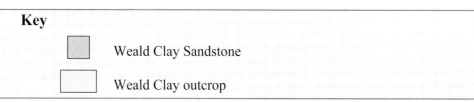

**Key**

Weald Clay Sandstone

Weald Clay outcrop

Herringbone work in the north wall of West Grinstead Church. This style of stonework is often regarded as typical of the Late-Saxon period, although it could be later, as tabular stone lends itself to this arrangement.

Superficial Deposits

Bracklesham Group

Thames Group

Lambeth Group

White Chalk Subgroup

Grey Chalk Subgroup

Selborne Group

Lower Greensand Group

Weald Clay Group

Hastings Group

Purbeck Group

| | |
|---|---|
| **Age** | Barremian    Lower Cretaceous |
| **Lithostratigraphy** | Large Paludina Limestone, Beds 4 and 6<br>Small Paludina Limestone, Bed 2<br>Weald Clay Group |

**Building Stone Varieties -** (Place names reflect where the stone was quarried and used)

**Large Paludina Limestone,** Winklestone
   Petworth Marble
   Laughton Marble
   Bethersden Marble (Kent)

**Small Paludina Limestone**
   Charlwood Marble

## Geology

Sussex Marble is a freshwater limestone packed with fossil shells of the river snail *Viviparus,* formerly known as *Paludina*. It was deposited in shallow lakes which spread across the Wealden landscape on three occasions. Beds 4 and 6 contain the large *Viviparus* (c. 20mm), the latter bed formerly quarried as Sussex or Petworth Marble in the area north of Petworth, and as Laughton Marble near Laughton in East Sussex. Bed 2 displays the small *Viviparus* (c.10mm), and was quarried as Charlwood Marble, in the area west of Charlwood, along the West Sussex-Surrey border. The limestone is composed of a matrix of small calcite crystals with varying amounts of clay and iron minerals which give it a variety of green, blue-grey and brown colours. Sussex Marble beds vary up to 40cm in thickness and were quarried in shallow pits or delves along valley sides.

Sussex Marble is not a true marble but a shelly limestone which takes a high polish. It was a high-value decorative stone, often utilized for memorial slabs, altars, ledgers and fonts, but rarely used for carving because it is easily fractured. This stone was also used for walling and paving, although it generally deteriorates in wet conditions. Much Sussex Marble was burnt for lime to improve the clay soils of the Weald; it was also used as a flux in the Wealden iron furnaces.

## Historic Use

| | |
|---|---|
| Roman | Small amounts at Fishbourne Palace and Southwick Villa. |
| Norman | Rudgwick, Ifield and Slaugham Church fonts,<br>Lewes Priory gateway (adjacent to Southover Church). |
| Late Medieval | Warminghurst, Street and Laughton Church walls.<br>Chichester Cathedral, shafts. Boxgrove Church, bases. |
| Post Medieval | Petworth House Marble Room. Petworth Church floor. |

14th century tower of Laughton Church constructed of Laughton Marble

Charlwood Marble paving slabs. Charlwood Church.

Polished Petworth Marble floor tiles. Petworth Church.

Norman font of Sussex Marble. New Shoreham Church.

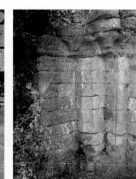
Laughton Marble in the remains of the gateway to Lewes Priory. Southover Church.

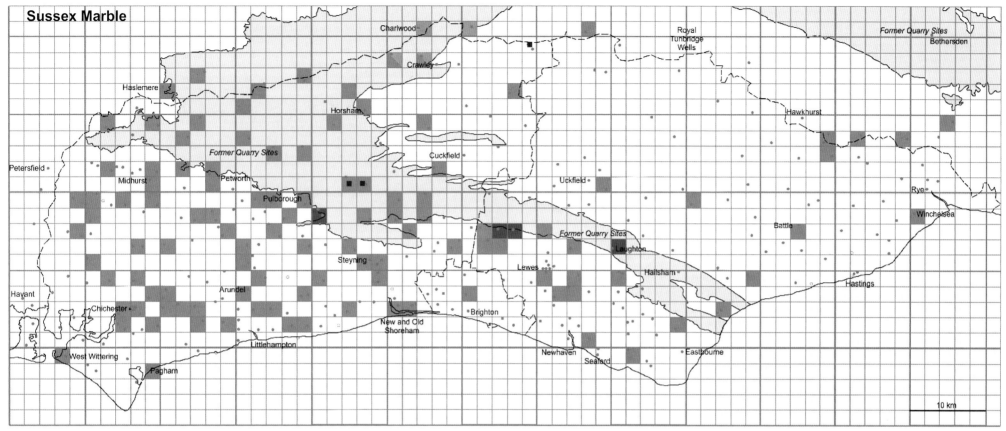

Sussex Marble

## Distribution of Sussex Marble

Sussex Marble was quarried in four main areas in the Low Weald, located near Petworth, Billingshurst, Laughton and Bethersden (in Kent). Quarries north of Petworth were the most productive in Sussex, supplying Petworth Marble throughout West Sussex.

Although it was a high-value decorative stone Sussex Marble was never used to the same extent as Purbeck Marble, mainly due to its more fragile structure and the difficulties of transport out of the Weald. Sussex Marble displays a relatively even distribution in Medieval churches across West Sussex, but has a much more sporadic distribution in East Sussex, with little recorded in the High Weald. Two concentrations are found in East Sussex, one in the south-west which can be related to quarrying in the Laughton area, and the other close to the eastern border of the county where it was obtained from quarries in the Bethersden area of Kent.

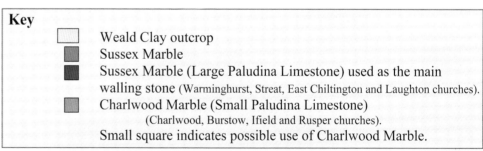

Key

Weald Clay outcrop

Sussex Marble

Sussex Marble (Large Paludina Limestone) used as the main walling stone (Warminghurst, Streat, East Chiltington and Laughton churches).

Charlwood Marble (Small Paludina Limestone)
(Charlwood, Burstow, Ifield and Rusper churches).

Small square indicates possible use of Charlwood Marble.

## Charlwood Marble (Small Paludina Limestone)

Charlwood Marble is similar to Purbeck Marble and therefore easily misidentified. It is a common building stone at Charlwood, Surrey close to the West Sussex border, where it is the main building stone in the church. It was utilized for paving and walling in Charlwood village but little has been used elsewhere.

Superficial Deposits

Bracklesham Group

Thames Group

Lambeth Group

White Chalk Subgroup

Grey Chalk Subgroup

Selborne Group

Lower Greensand Group

Weald Clay Group

Hastings Group

Purbeck Group

| Age | Aptian |
| | Lower Cretaceous |
| **Lithostratigraphy** | Hythe Formation |
| | Lower Greensand Group |

## Geology

The Hythe Formation outcrops in a 0.5 to 2km wide belt of land extending across Sussex from Eastbourne in the east to Rogate in the west, along the southern side of the Weald. The Formation consists of harder sandstones in the west in the Rogate-to-Haslemere area which form a prominent escarpment around the western margin of the Weald Dome. Cherty and glauconitic sandstones make up the greater part of the Formation with minor beds of sand, silt, clay, chert and fuller's earth. Sandstones predominate in West Sussex where the Formation has been extensively quarried for freestone, making it the main building stone across much of the west and south-west of West Sussex.

Hythe Formation sandstone was deposited in a warm shallow sea which spread across South East England about 120Ma. Fossil shells are generally poorly preserved but cylindrical burrow structures, including *Planolites* and *Macaronichnus,* are abundant and often infilled with chert or glauconite.

## Building Stone
### Alternative Names

Midhurst, Petworth, Pulborough and Fittleworth Stone. Greensand, Lower Greensand.

### Varieties

1. Brown knobbly sandstone packed with chert-rich nodules.
2. Massive, ochre to brown ferruginous sandstone.
3. Minor varieties include white siltstone; white to blue-grey, finely-bedded cherty sandstone; and soft green glauconitic sandstone.

### Historic Use

| | |
| --- | --- |
| Roman | Fishbourne Roman Palace. |
| Late Saxon | Woolbeding, Selham and Sompting Abbots churches. |
| Norman | West Chiltington, Stopham and Lurgashall churches. |
| | Arundel Castle. |
| Late Medieval | Trotton church. |
| Post Medieval | Petworth House, Cowdray House (ruins), |
| | Stedham church. |
| Georgian and Victorian | |
| | Midhurst, Petworth and Pulborough (houses & walls). |

17th century farmhouse with walls and dressings of Hythe Sandstone. Note the drystone wall. Woolbeding.

Petworth House, begun in 1688, is mainly built of Petworth Stone from former quarries in the adjacent Park and at Byworth 1.5km to the south-east. The central part of the frontage is of Portland Stone.

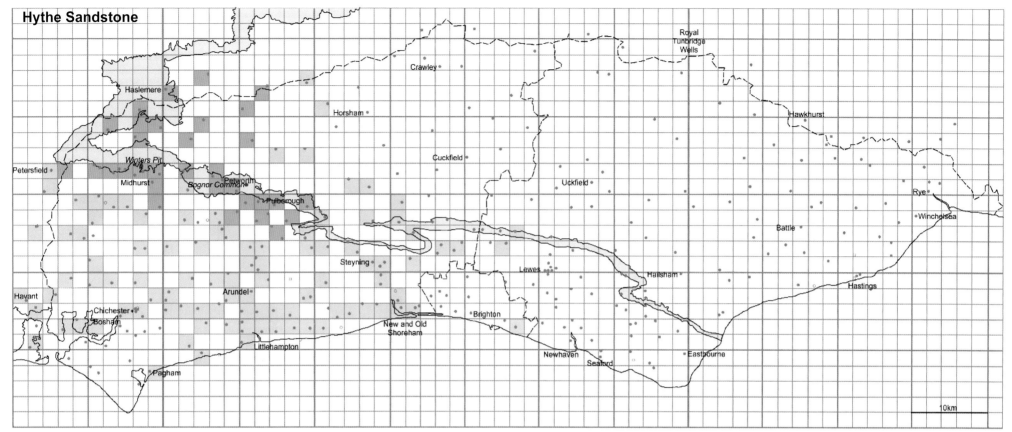

**Hythe Sandstone**

## Distribution of Hythe Sandstone

Hythe Sandstone is one of the three major vernacular building stones of West Sussex, its use concentrated in the south and west of the county (see map on page 5). Although the Hythe Formation crops out across the south-west part of East Sussex the strata in this area consist mainly of loosely-consolidated sand and silt unsuitable for building stone. Hythe Sandstone was commonly utilized as the sole building stone in the construction of Medieval churches along and close to the outcrop of the Hythe Formation, particularly in the Pulborough, Petworth and Midhurst areas. Large supplies of this building stone were extracted from numerous small quarries located along the Lower Greensand dip slope and either transported overland, or by barge down the Rother, Arun and Adur Rivers for use in buildings situated on the chalk downs and coastal plain.

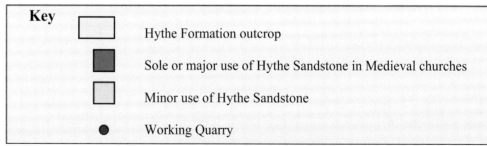

**Key**

Hythe Formation outcrop

Sole or major use of Hythe Sandstone in Medieval churches

Minor use of Hythe Sandstone

● Working Quarry

## Post-Medieval Use of Hythe Sandstone

A revival in the use of Hythe Sandstone took place from the 18th to early 20th century when many houses and cottages in Midhurst, Petworth and Pulborough were constructed of this massive ochre and brown sandstone. Small amounts of this building stone are still quarried at Winters Pit, Easebourne and Bognor Common Quarry, Fittleworth (shown on the map).

Knobbly-texture sandstone. Massive, moderately-consolidated sandstone weathering to a very rough surface. The sandstone is packed with small chert-rich nodules, which have formed within fossil burrow structures.
Pulborough Church quoin.

Massive, grey sandstone ashlar, weathering to brown.
Victorian work with a rock-faced finish.
Easebourne Church.

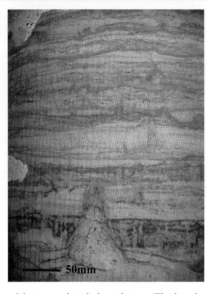

Liesegang-banded sandstone. The bands, caused by ferruginous water percolating through the rock, have picked out bedding structures such as the 'sand volcano' (bottom centre). Broadwater Church column.

Massive, brown sandstone with 15cm long *Planolites* burrow structure preserved in iron oxide. This sandstone shows 'salt and pepper' texture, the 'salt' being the minute hollows produced by weathered-out sponge spicules, and the 'pepper' the dark-coloured glauconite grains.
House wall, Petworth.

Blue-coloured, cherty, bedded sandstone. The rock consists of alternating finely-bedded and thicker bioturbated layers.
Stopham Church.

Hard, finely-bedded cherty sandstone. This rock shows well-preserved, scalloped, cross-bedding structure.
House wall, Petworth.

Banded sandstone showing alternating beds of green glauconite-rich and white quartz-rich layers.
Stopham Church.

Finely-bedded, dark-green, glauconitic sandstone and contrasting pale-grey sandstone.
Cottage wall, Tillington.

Arundel Castle, Norman entrance gate.
It appears that the builders ran out of ashlar
after completing the lower part,
finishing the work with flint.

Medieval tomb slab.
Stedham Church.

Stopham Bridge which crosses the
River Arun above its confluence with
the Rother, dates from 1442.

Carved capital below the chancel
arch showing Late-Saxon moulding.
Selham Church.

Crocket capital, and column, carved
in Hythe Sandstone. Tillington
Church.

High quality building in Hythe Sandstone.
Somerset Lodge, Petworth, a merchant's house
constructed in 1653.

Cowdray House ruins, Midhurst, dating
from the 1520s, was destroyed by fire in
1793. Hythe Sandstone with contrasting
pale-coloured Malmstone quoins.

Headstop sculpture with a
king's head below the west
door arch,
Tillington Church.

Swan Bridge, Pulborough, built in 1950 to carry the A29 over
the River Arun, possibly the last major project in Hythe
Sandstone. It was constructed close to the site where the
Roman road, Stane Street, crossed the river.

**Quarries in Hythe Sandstone recorded in the Domesday Book, 1086 AD.**

| Locality | Value | |
| --- | --- | --- |
| Stedham | 6s | 8d |
| Iping | 9s | 4d |
| Grittenham (near Tillington) | 10s | 10d |
| Bignor * | 4s | 0d |

*Recorded as a molaria (quernstone) quarry. This probably refers to the quernstone quarry at Lodsworth, which dates back to the Iron Age. It is located 11km north-west of Bignor.

**Above and Below**

The remains of a quarry in Fittleworth Wood. Numerous quarries operated in this area in the 19th to early 20th centuries. The photograph above shows an abandoned hand-operated winch.

Four quarries are recorded in West Sussex in the Domesday Book, with none in East Sussex. They all appear to be in Hythe Sandstone and indicate the importance of this building stone in Late-Saxon to Early-Norman times. These quarries may date back to Roman times.

**Above**
Working quarry at Winters Pit, Easebourne.

**Below**
Recent workings for rubble stone at the site of the Iron Age, quernstone quarry at Lodsworth.

Former quarry at Codmore Hill, Pulborough, showing massively-bedded Hythe Sandstone.

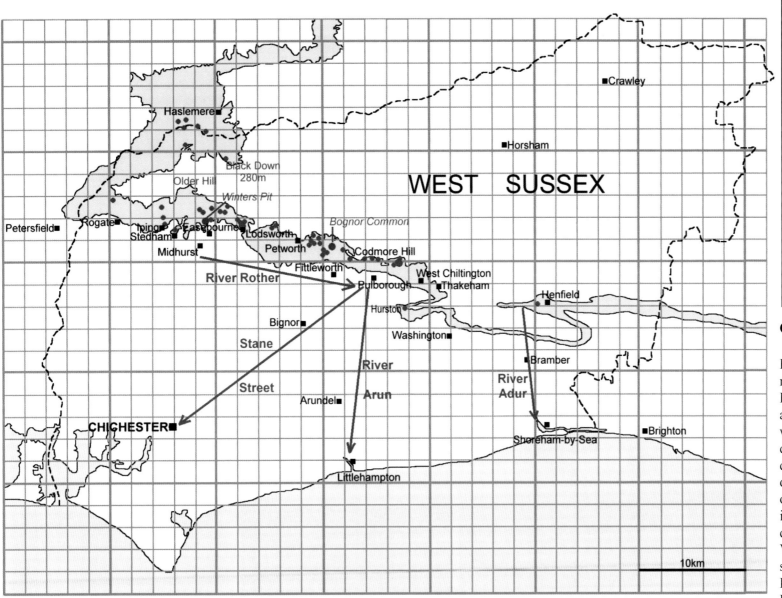

**Key**

Hythe Formation outcrop

● Former quarries

● Working quarries

● Iron Age and Roman quarries

■ Selected towns and villages

Arrows indicate Medieval transport routes for Hythe Sandstone south towards the coast down the Rivers Rother, Arun and Adur and along the Roman Road, Stane Street, towards Chichester.

## Quarrying

Hythe Sandstone was quarried from massive sandstone beds within the Hythe Formation along its outcrop across the central part of West Sussex, west of Henfield. The earliest known quarry was that at Lodsworth where quernstones were manufactured on site during the Iron age. Quarries were opened-up in Roman times particularly in the Pulborough area and numerous quarries operated along the Rother Valley in Medieval times. The dip slope of the Hythe Formation in the Pulborough, Fittleworth, Petworth and Easebourne (Midhurst) areas shows evidence of intensive quarrying in the 18th to mid-20th centuries.

| Superficial Deposits |
| Bracklesham Group |
| Thames Group |
| Lambeth Group |
| White Chalk Subgroup |
| Grey Chalk Subgroup |
| Selborne Group |
| Lower Greensand Group |
| Weald Clay Group |
| Hastings Group |
| Purbeck Group |

| **Age** | Aptian | Lower Cretaceous |
|---|---|---|
| **Lithostratigraphy** | Hythe Formation | |
| | Lower Greensand Group | |

## Geology

Chert is the general name for crypto-crystalline silica, where the silica is in the form of aggregates of microscopic quartz crystals. Hythe Sandstone, particularly in the Pulborough to Rogate area, includes beds of cherty sandstone, chert-rich nodular sandstone and lenses of massive chert up to *c.* 50cm in thickness. Chert from the Hythe Formation is a very tough, mainly grey rock with a sub-conchoidal or occasionally splintery fracture. Occasionally translucent amber-coloured chert is present, as seen at Rudgwick Church.

Beds of massive chert grade into cherty sandstone packed with very fine opaline-silica sponge spicules, from which the silica in the chert beds was most likely derived. In weathered rock these have been dissolved to form minute cylindrical holes, which with a scattering of dark glauconite grains gives a 'salt and pepper' texture. Chert beds within the Hythe Formation are generally considered to have formed by replacement of original limestone or calcareous sandstone by silica, soon after the strata were deposited.

## Building Stone
### Alternative Names
  Whinstone, Hornstone.

Hythe Chert is a minor building stone which was only available in relatively small quantities. It is a tough, massive grey rock, which has been used as scattered blocks of rubble-stone in Hythe Sandstone walls, although some buildings in Petworth contain roughly cut blocks. Cherty sandstone, cut into small blocks was formerly utilized for paving setts due to its hard-wearing properties.

## Historic Use

| Late-Saxon | Lurgashall Church (string courses) |
| Medieval | Stopham, Coates, Rogate and Rudgwick Churches |
| Victorian | United Reformed Church, Petworth, |
| | House and garden walls, Petworth |

Roughly-shaped blocks of Hythe Chert. Garden wall, Petworth.

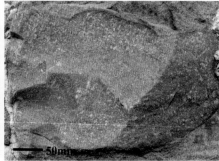

Hythe Chert rubble showing sub-conchoidal fracture surface. House wall, Midhurst.

Hythe Chert paving setts. Petworth.

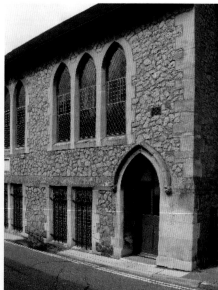

United Reformed Church, Petworth *c.* 1850. Mosaic-work of Hythe Chert with Hythe Sandstone dressings.

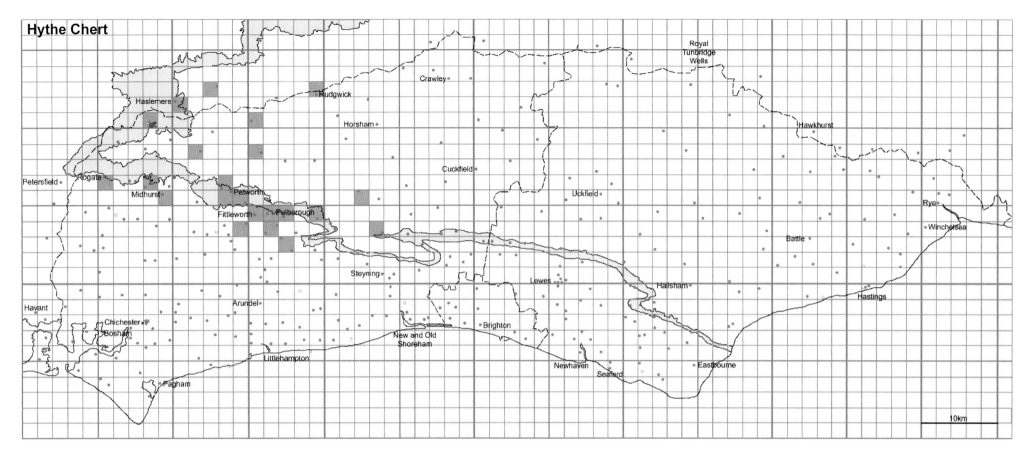

Hythe Chert

## Distribution of Hythe Chert

Hythe Chert building stone is a minor building stone which was only used as the main construction material in a few walls and buildings in Petworth, where this rock is relatively common in the nearby Hythe Formation outcrop.

The distribution of Hythe Chert in Medieval churches is concentrated along and close to the outcrop of the Hythe Formation in the area between Pulborough and Rogate, and north to Haslemere and Chiddingfold in Surrey, reflecting the local abundance of this rock in the Hythe Formation. Small amounts of this building stone are also present in Medieval churches situated on the Low Weald in the north-west of West Sussex, as at Rudgwick. Chert beds in the Hythe Formation die out to the east of Pulborough, and are absent in East Sussex.

**Key**

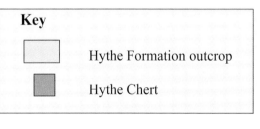

Hythe Formation outcrop

Hythe Chert

Hythe Chert setts used for ornamental paving.
Midhurst.

35

| Superficial Deposits |
|---|
| Bracklesham Group |
| Thames Group |
| Lambeth Group |
| White Chalk Subgroup |
| Grey Chalk Subgroup |
| Selborne Group |
| Lower Greensand Group |
| Weald Clay Group |
| Hastings Group |
| Purbeck Group |

| | |
|---|---|
| **Age** | Aptian     Lower Cretaceous |
| **Lithostratigraphy** | Bargate Beds (West Sussex) |
| | Easebourne Member (West Sussex) |
| | Bargate Member (south-west Surrey) |
| | Sandgate Formation |
| | Lower Greensand Group |

## Geology

Bargate Stone is a marine sandstone from the basal strata of the Sandgate Formation. The building stone beds are best developed in South West Surrey where they were formerly quarried on a large scale. Flaggy, calcareous sandstone of the same age in the Midhurst area of West Sussex was only quarried to a very minor extent. Surrey Bargate Stone has a rich honey colour, and occurs in 10–15cm thick beds. Varieties include; sandstone with numerous small vughs or holes, sandstone with comminuted fossil shells, cherty sandstone, conglomerate with black chert pebbles, and grey chert concretions and beds. Vertical joint planes in the rock are often lined with crystalline calcite.

In the Midhurst area of West Sussex a further variety of Bargate Stone has been quarried from the lower part of the Easebourne Member. Here it occurs as a tough flaggy calcareous sandstone, together with calcareous sandstone concretions known as doggers.

## Building Stone
### Varieties
Bargate Stone (Surrey), West Sussex Bargate Stone.

The common building stone quarried in South West Surrey is a rich ochre-coloured sandstone which was cut into brick-size blocks, as seen in 19-20th century church walls, including St John's Roman Catholic Church, Horsham and St Richard's Church, Aldwick. In the Midhurst area of West Sussex minor use has been made of tough, flaggy, calcareous sandstone for walling and paving slabs.

## Historic Use

| | |
|---|---|
| Late-Saxon | Godalming Church (Surrey). |
| Norman | Guildford Castle (Surrey). |
| Medieval | Chiddingfold Church (Surrey). |
| Post Medieval | Loseley Hall 1562-68 (Surrey). |
| 19-20th century | St George's Church, Worthing and St Richard's Church, Aldwick. |

**Left**

Flaggy beds of Bargate Stone in the Easebourne Member at the base of the Sandgate Formation are exposed in a sunken lane at Rotherbridge 1.5km south-west of Petworth.

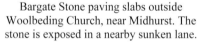

Brick-size blocks of Bargate Stone from south-west Surrey in a wall of St Richard's Church, Aldwick, built 1933.

Bargate Stone paving slabs outside Woolbeding Church, near Midhurst. The stone is exposed in a nearby sunken lane.

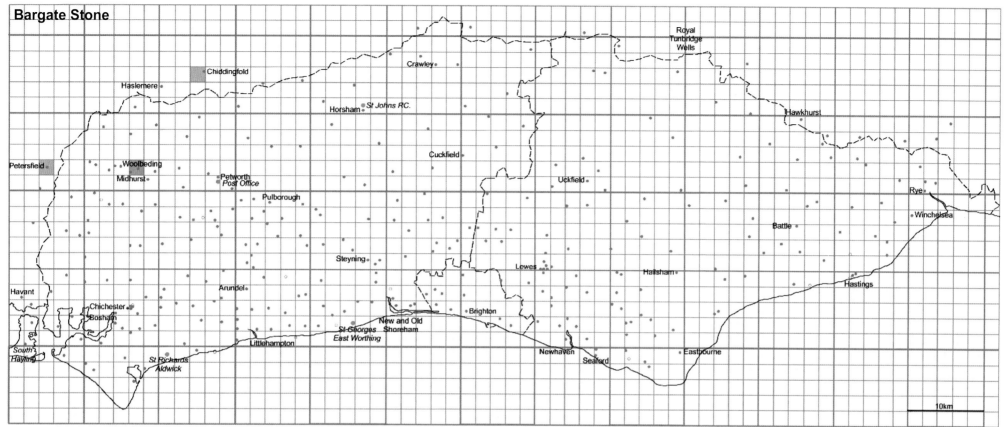
Bargate Stone

## Distribution of Bargate Stone

Surrey Bargate Stone was an important Medieval building stone in South West Surrey especially in the Guildford area, its use extending as far south as Chiddingfold, 2km north of the West Sussex border, and Petersfield in Hampshire. The lack of penetration of this building stone southward into West Sussex in Medieval times was probably due to the problems and expense of transporting heavy stone across the clay terrain of the Low Weald. Other building stones including Hythe Sandstone and Weald Clay Sandstone were more readily available in the north-west of West Sussex. From the mid-19th century building stone was easily transported long distances by rail, which led to the use of Bargate Stone in a few buildings scattered across West Sussex.

West Sussex Bargate Stone had very minor use for paving and walling in the area close to where it was quarried near Woolbeding (Midhurst) and Tillington.

**Key**

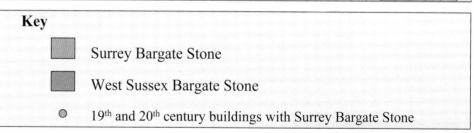

Surrey Bargate Stone

West Sussex Bargate Stone

○   19th and 20th century buildings with Surrey Bargate Stone

20cm-thick bed of Bargate Stone at Winters Pit, Easebourne near Midhurst. Here the stone is a tough, flaggy, calcareous sandstone.

Superficial Deposits

Bracklesham Group

Thames Group

Lambeth Group

White Chalk Subgroup

Grey Chalk Subgroup

Selborne Group

< Lower Greensand Group

Weald Clay Group

Hastings Group

Purbeck Group

| Age | Aptian Lower Cretaceous |
|---|---|
| **Lithostratigraphy** | Pulborough Sandrock Member |
| | Sandgate Formation |
| | Lower Greensand Group |

## Geology

The Pulborough Sandrock Member crops out in a narrow belt of country in West Sussex from Rogate in the west to West Chiltington and Parham in the east. This Member consists of up to 20m of beds of fine-grained, cross-bedded sand together with more consolidated beds of ferruginous sandstone and siltstone. In the Pulborough area up to 50cm of iron-oxide cemented sand and siltstone, at the top of the Member, has been used locally as a minor building stone.

Ferruginous siltstone varieties of Marehill Ironstone show a variety of textures from massive to open and flaky. Like Carstone, this rock has suffered secondary cementation due to percolation of iron-rich water.

A bed of ferruginous siltstone (ironstone), packed with moulds and casts of fossil shells occurs within the Pulborough Sandrock outcrop between Pulborough and Midhurst.

## Building Stone
**Alternative Names** -
Marehill Ironstone, Pulborough Sandrock
**Varieties** -
Massive, red-brown ferruginous sandstone. (Paler than Carstone, and unlike Carstone does not contain quartz grit. Pulborough cottage walls)
Brown ironstone packed with fossil shell moulds and casts of bivalves and brachiopods. (Parham Park Estate walls)
Dark-brown ferruginous siltstone with an open 'milk-flake' texture. (Wiggonholt Farm and garden walls).
Dark-brown siltstone with an onion-skin texture. (Greatham Church)

Much of the Marehill Ironstone seen in old buildings is probably a byproduct of sand extraction in the Sandgate Formation in the Pulborough area.

## Historic Use

| | |
|---|---|
| Norman | Stopham and Greatham Churches. |
| Late Medieval | Wiggonholt Church. |
| 17th century | Egdean Church. |
| Early 19th century | Parham Park Estate Wall. (from quarry in Parham Park) |

Marehill Sandrock Mine, Pulborough. In the early 20th century this mine produced fine moulding sand from the Pulborough Sandrock. Marehill Ironstone, a hard, laminated ferruginous siltstone forms the mine roof.

Marehill Ironstone rubble in a garden wall near Wiggonholt Church. This ferruginous siltstone has a 'milk-flake' texture.

Fossiliferous, ferruginous siltstone packed with moulds of fossil brachiopods and bivalves. Parham Park Estate wall.

50mm

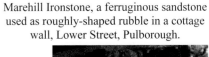

Marehill Ironstone, a ferruginous sandstone used as roughly-shaped rubble in a cottage wall, Lower Street, Pulborough.

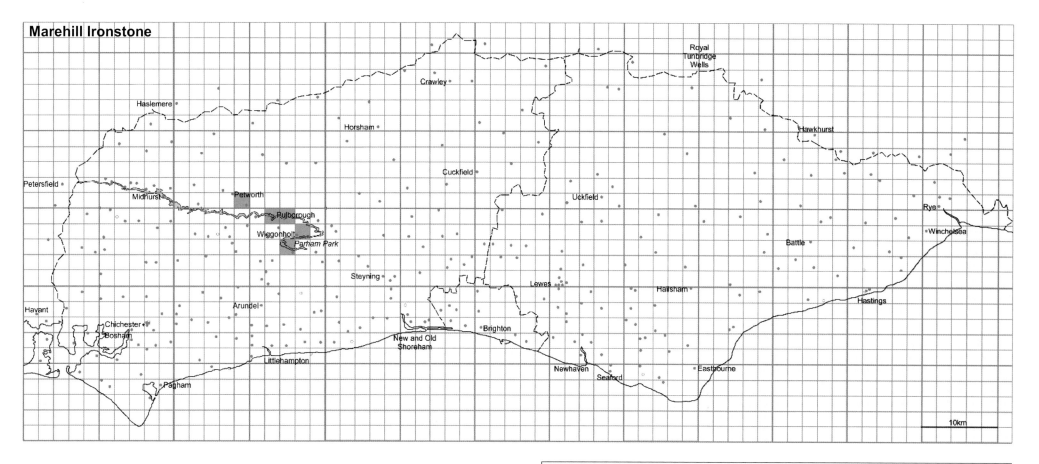

**Marehill Ironstone**

10km

## Distribution of Marehill Ironstone

Marehill Ironstone is a minor rubble building stone which has only been used close to its outcrop in the area between Petworth and Parham in West Sussex. A number of distinctive varieties reflect the local rock type.

40mm

20mm

Left:
Onion skin weathering.
Greatham Church.

Right:
Fossiliferous ironstone.
Park Farm,
Pulborough.

### Key

Outcrop of Pulborough Sandrock Member

Marehill Ironstone

## Identification of Marehill Ironstone

The Pulborough Sandrock Member includes a number of varieties of ferruginous sandstone and siltstone, some of which are similar to Carstone and ferruginous varieties of Hythe Sandstone. Deep-red to red-brown ferruginous sandstone is the commonest variety as displayed in cottage walls in Pulborough. Unlike Carstone it is not gritty and is of a brighter colour. Ferruginous siltstone with 'milk-flake' and onion-skin texture, and fossiliferous ferruginous siltstone (ironstone), are unique building stone varieties.

| Age | Aptian | Lower Cretaceous |
|---|---|---|
| **Lithostratigraphy** | Folkestone Formation | |
| | Lower Greensand Group | |

Left side column (geological column):

- Superficial Deposits
- Bracklesham Group
- Thames Group
- Lambeth Group
- White Chalk Subgroup
- Grey Chalk Subgroup
- Selborne Group
- Lower Greensand Group <
- Weald Clay Group
- Hastings Group
- Purbeck Group

## Geology

The Folkestone Formation (Folkestone Sand) consists of cross-bedded sands with thin layers of ferruginous sandstone and grit known as Carstone. It crops out in a narrow belt of country across south-central West Sussex from Rogate in the west to Keymer in the east and extends into East Sussex as far as Streat, where it dies out. This Formation underlies a number of heathland plateaux in the west of West Sussex including Ambersham and Iping Commons.

Carstone is a tough, dark-brown, quartz sandstone and grit, strongly cemented by iron-oxides and hydroxides. This rock occurs as concretions and layers up to 15cm thick within the sand beds. It was formed when iron-rich water percolated down through the sand and was impeded by thin clay beds beneath the base of each cross-bedded unit. This lead to the cementation by iron-oxides of the coarse, gritty, basal sand beds.

## Building Stone

**Alternative Names -**

Ironstone and Ryestone.

Iron Grit - a bed of ferruginous sandstone up to 30cm thick at the base of the overlying Gault Formation in the Washington area.

Carstone is minor rubble building stone in Medieval churches, probably originally obtained from the surface of heathlands which overlie the Folkestone Sand, as on Iping and Ambersham Commons. It was either used as rubble stone or roughly-cleaved, brick-size blocks

## Historic Use

| Roman | Fishbourne Roman Palace, Bignor and Funtington Roman Villas. |
|---|---|
| Norman | Burton Church (herringbone work). |
| Late Medieval | Stopham and Coates churches. |
| 18th c. to mid 20th c. | Cottage walls in Fittleworth. |

In the 18th to mid-20th centuries larger quantities of this building stone became available as a by-product of sand quarrying, when it was used in houses and cottages as cleaved brick-size blocks, and also for paving setts. It was also commonly used for 'nailhead' galleting in Hythe Sandstone and Malmstone walls.

**Left**    Carstone paving setts. Thakeham Church.

**Below**    Carstone galleting in a Hythe Sandstone farm cottage wall, Minstead near Midhurst. Carstone galleting was referred to as 'Tuppenny nails' by Gilbert White (1789).

19th century cottages in Fittleworth built of roughly-shaped, brick-size, Carstone blocks.

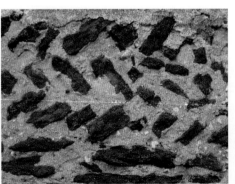

11th century herringbone work. Burton Church near Duncton.

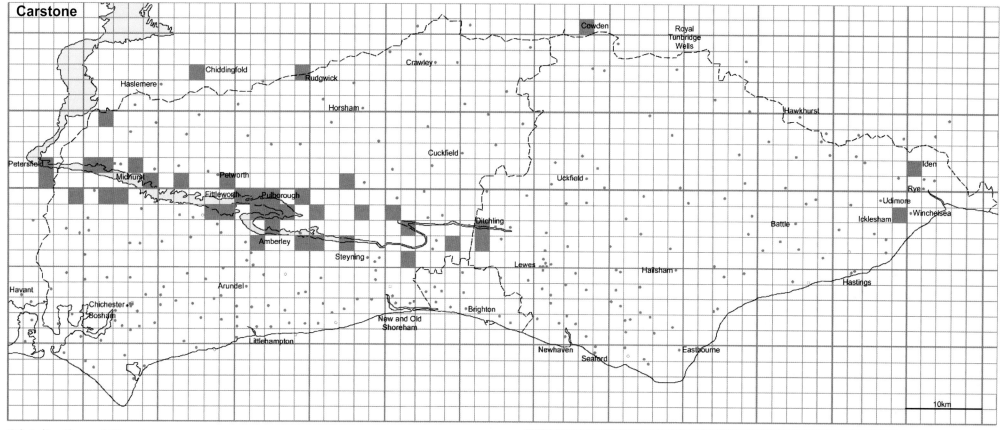

**Distribution of Carstone**

Carstone is present as scattered pieces of rubble-stone in numerous Medieval parish churches located in a zone within *c*. 4km of the Folkestone Formation outcrop between Petersfield and Ditchling. A few cottages and farmhouses dating from the 18th to mid-20th century, as at Fittleworth, have walls entirely constructed of Carstone.

**Carstone and Ironstone Building Stone on the West Sussex Coastal Plain**

Scattered rubble blocks of ferruginous sandstone and siltstone are present in Medieval church walls on the West Sussex Coastal Plain. This building stone is provisionally identified as ironstone from the Woolwich and Reading Formations (see page 64), on the basis that it is finer grained than Carstone and does not contain yellow-stained quartz pebbles. Ironstone rubble in the walls of Medieval churches in the Chichester area may be recycled material from former Roman buildings.

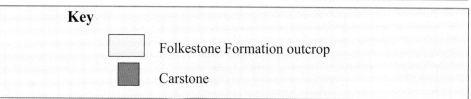

**Key**

| | Folkestone Formation outcrop |
| | Carstone |

**Carstone in the East of East Sussex**

Carstone rubble in the walls of Icklesham and Iden churches in the far east of East Sussex was probably brought along the coast from the Folkestone Formation outcrop at its type locality on the foreshore at Folkestone, 35km to the east-north-east.

**Folkestone Stone**, a gritty, cherty, glauconitic sandstone also comes from the Folkestone Formation at Folkestone and has only been identified from a single rubble block at Udimore Church.

| Age | Albian | Lower Cretaceous |
|---|---|---|
| **Lithostratigraphy** | Upper Greensand Formation | |
| | Selborne Group | |

**Superficial Deposits**

**Bracklesham Group**

**Thames Group**

**Lambeth Group**

**White Chalk Subgroup**

**Grey Chalk Subgroup**

**Selborne Group** <

**Lower Greensand Group**

**Weald Clay Group**

**Hastings Group**

**Purbeck Group**

## Geology

The Upper Greensand Formation crops out in a belt across West Sussex from the Hampshire border at Buriton to the East Sussex border near Clayton. It is absent throughout most of East Sussex, but reappears between Beachy Head and Eastbourne, where strata similar to those in the Isle of Wight have been quarried for Eastbourne Stone.

The strata consist of marine sandstone, siltstone and clay beds containing varying amounts of colloidal silica and glauconite. The upper part of this Formation provides a variety of cohesive stone beds, known in West Sussex and East Hampshire as Malmstone, which form a low cuesta or bench below the chalk escarpment. Springs issuing from the Malmstone have provided a reliable supply of water for the 'spring-line' villages located along the outcrop, such as Elsted and Cocking.

## Building Stone

Malmstone is the name both of the rock and the building stone from the Upper Greensand Formation in West Sussex and East Hampshire. It is sometimes referred to by builders as 'Clunch'.

**Varieties** - (Illustrated on page 45)

| | |
|---|---|
| White Malmstone | Massive, white calcareous siltstone. |
| Grey Malmstone | Massive, grey to green-grey siltstone. |
| Blueheart (Amberley Blue) | Massive, pale blue-grey siltstone with sub-conchoidal fracture, weathering brown. |
| Malmstone 'Marble' | Flaggy calcareous siltstone with large fossil burrow structures. It takes a good polish and was used for paving and ledgers. |
| Laminated, dark-green glauconitic siltstone | Poor-quality rubble, rarely used. |

## Historic Use

| | |
|---|---|
| Roman | Bignor Roman Villa, Chichester (reused Roman rubble). |
| Late-Saxon | Elsted Church. |
| Norman | Amberley Castle. |
| Late-Medieval | Barlavington and Sullington Churches. |
| Tudor | Parham House. |
| Victorian | Duncton Roman Catholic Church (1866). Storrington Church, (1876 rebuilding). |

Amberley Castle, dating from 12-13th c., was formerly a residence of the Bishops of Chichester. The main walls are of Blueheart (Amberley Blue), which weathers to a brown surface.

Cottage at Cocking constructed of roughly-shaped, brick-size White Malmstone blocks with brick dressings.

11th c. herringbone work with infilled arcades all in White Malmstone. Elsted Church.

Cottages in Amberley with walls of Amberley Blue rubble.

## Distribution of Malmstone

**Malmstone** building stone in Medieval churches is concentrated in 2 areas:
1. Along and adjacent to the outcrop across the south-central part of West Sussex.
2. In the south-west of West Sussex, centred around Chichester.

**White Malmstone** is the predominant variety used along and adjacent to the western part of the Upper Greensand outcrop west of Cocking, where it is the common building stone in villages such as South Harting, and Buriton, just over the border in Hampshire. Blueheart or Amberley Blue is the common variety in the area between Duncton and Washington and is particularly abundant in Amberley and Storrington.

**Grey Malmstone** in numerous Medieval churches and other ancient buildings in the Chichester area may be reused building stone from former Roman buildings in Chichester. Grey Malmstone is also present in church walls in the lower Adur Valley.

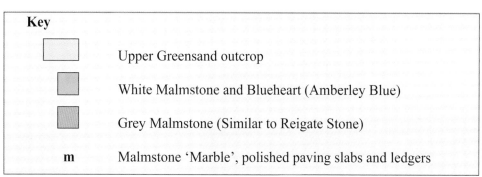

**Key**

| | |
|---|---|
| | Upper Greensand outcrop |
| | White Malmstone and Blueheart (Amberley Blue) |
| | Grey Malmstone (Similar to Reigate Stone) |
| **m** | Malmstone 'Marble', polished paving slabs and ledgers |

**Reigate Stone** from the Upper Greensand of Surrey (page 94), is similar to Grey Malmstone with which it is easily confused: Reigate stone often contains small scattered grains of muscovite, which are generally absent in Grey Malmstone. Malmstone and Reigate Stone are regarded as separate building stone Types due to their geographical occurrence and historic use.

# MALMSTONE BUILDINGS

Cowdray House, Midhurst. A castellated Tudor House, partly destroyed by fire in 1793, is built of Hythe Stone with contrasting White Malmstone quoins.

Duncton Roman Catholic Church built in 1866 with cleaved blocks of Blueheart.

Barn constructed of brick-size Malmstone blocks with brick dressings. The building stone is a mix of Grey Malmstone and Blueheart. The stone is rather soft and shows considerable weathering. Bepton Farm.

The south wall of Barlavington Church is built of Blueheart blocks which show a brown-weathered outer skin.

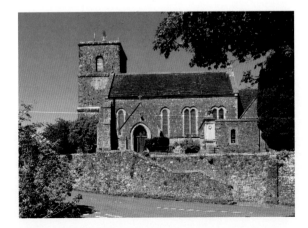

Storrington Church, dating from the 11th century, shows considerable rebuilding with Blueheart in the 18th and 19th centuries.

Parham House, south facade. A fine Tudor mansion dating from 1577, constructed of Blueheart with a Horsham Stone-slate roof.

Parham House dovecote is constructed of Blueheart.

# VARIETIES OF MALMSTONE

## WHITE MALMSTONE

**Above** Weathered stonework, South Harting Church.
**Right** Cottage wall, South Harting.
White Malmstone is an important building stone in villages along the western part of the Upper Greensand outcrop.

## GREY MALMSTONE

**Left and Above**

Old garden wall, and city walls (southern sector), Chichester. Soft, grey to blue-grey, massive siltstone similar to Reigate Stone. This building stone is prone to weathering in exposed positions, which causes surface flaking. It was used mainly in the Chichester area where it is probably reused Roman building stone.

## MALMSTONE 'MARBLE'

Floor slabs displaying large fossil burrow structures. Trotton Church.

## BLUEHEART or AMBERLEY BLUE

**Above** Cottage wall, Amberley.
**Right** Storrington Church wall.
Grey to blue-grey tough, massive, cherty siltstone with a sub-conchoidal fracture. The surface weathers to form a light-brown surface crust.

## GLAUCONITIC SILTSTONE

Laminated, glauconitic siltstone and poorly-consolidated Grey Malmstone rubble. Wall adjacent to Amberley Church.

| Superficial Deposits |
| --- |
| Bracklesham Group |
| Thames Group |
| Lambeth Group |
| White Chalk Subgroup |
| Grey Chalk Subgroup |
| Selborne Group |
| Lower Greensand Group |
| Weald Clay Group |
| Hastings Group |
| Purbeck Group |

| **Age** | Albian     Lower Cretaceous |
| --- | --- |
| **Lithostratigraphy** | Upper Greensand Formation<br>Selborne Group |

## Geology

The Upper Greensand strata are well developed across West Sussex where they provide several of varieties of Malmstone building stones (Chapter 11). This Formation is absent across most of East Sussex but reappears in a narrow outcrop along the foreshore between Eastbourne and Beachy Head, where the strata bear similarities with those of the Upper Greensand of the Isle of Wight. At Cow Gap Steps below Beachy Head the Upper Greensand comprises 9m of glauconitic silt and sand with several thin limestone beds. The top 60cm immediately below the Glauconitic Marl at the base of the Grey Chalk Subgroup is a calcareous, glauconitic sandstone freestone, which was probably the source of the building stone. The surface of this stone often reveals sections of long, straight, fossil serpulid tubes and burrow structures.

## Building Stone

Eastbourne Stone, sometimes referred to as Bourne Stone, is a soft, massive, green-grey, glauconitic sandstone which in the past was obtained from foreshore quarries at Eastbourne. It comes from the same geological Formation as Ventnor Stone from the Isle of Wight with which it is virtually identical. This stone could be obtained in large blocks which, on exposure, develop a hard surface crust; once this flakes off the stone is prone to weathering. The soft, massive texture of Eastbourne Stone made it easy to carve, so that it was commonly used for moulded window and door architraves.

**'Eastbourne Marble'** - A light-grey limestone within the Upper Greensand at Eastbourne has been used for polished paving-stones in Eastbourne Church.

## Historic Use

| | |
| --- | --- |
| Roman | Pevensey Roman Fort walls, Eastbourne Roman Villa. |
| Late-Saxon | Bishopstone Church. |
| Norman | Lewes Castle, Eastbourne and Westham churches. |
| Late Medieval | Willingdon and Pevensey churches. |
| Victorian | Rubble stone in house and garden walls in Eastbourne. |

Buttress showing weathered ashlar.
Eastbourne Church.

Window tracery in a flint wall.
East Dean Church.

Polished floor slabs displaying long, straight burrow structures. Eastbourne Church.

Roman stonework in the walls of Pevensey Roman Fort. Roughly-hewn blocks laid between string courses of brick.

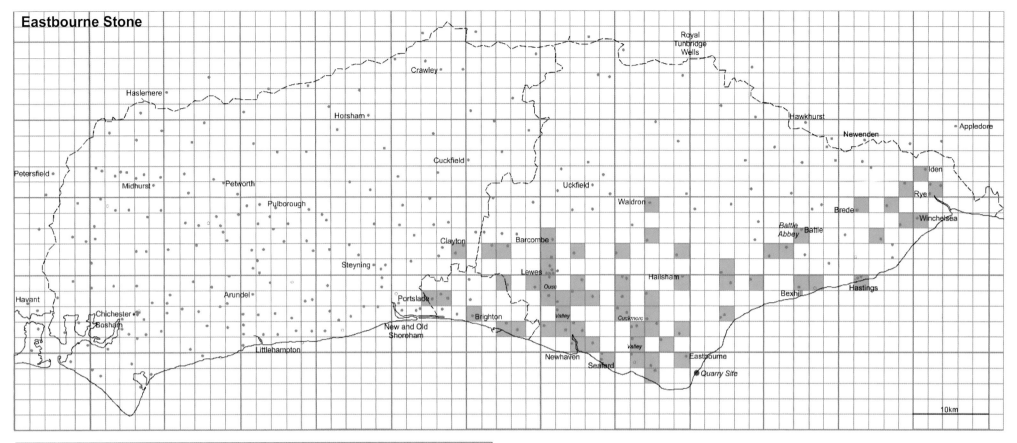

Eastbourne Stone

## Key

Eastbourne Stone

## Distribution of Eastbourne Stone

Eastbourne Stone has been used as a building stone in Medieval churches across the southern part of East Sussex extending from Brighton in the west to Rye in the east, but has only been used as the major building stone in Eastbourne and Willingdon Churches. Probable use of this building stone extended westwards as far as the West Sussex-Brighton and Hove border, as proposed in the following section. Eastbourne Stone shows a concentration in Medieval churches along the Ouse and the Cuckmere valleys, with a lesser concentration in the area around Rye. This indicates shipment of this building stone from the foreshore quarries at Eastbourne along the coast and up the navigable rivers such as the Ouse.

## Eastbourne Stone and Ventnor Stone

The Upper Greensand building stones, Eastbourne Stone and Ventnor Stone from the Isle of Wight, are the same age and are very similar in appearance and fossil content. They are considered to be different building stone 'Types' as they were quarried from widely separated areas. Both of these building stones are relatively-soft, massive, glauconitic sandstones, displaying long, straight, fossil serpulid tubes.

Massive green, glauconitic sandstone building stone used in Medieval churches in coastal areas of West Sussex has long been considered to be Ventnor Stone from the Isle of Wight (page 92). The boundary between the areas of use of Ventnor and Eastbourne Stones in this Atlas has been drawn at the West Sussex-Brighton and Hove border on the basis of the distribution pattern of these building stones.

47

| | |
|---|---|
| **Age** | Upper Cretaceous |
| **Lithostratigraphy** | Divided into 9 Chalk Formations<br>White Chalk and Grey Chalk Subgroups<br>Chalk Group |

**Superficial Deposits**

**Bracklesham Group**

**Thames Group**

**Lambeth Group**

**White Chalk Subgroup** <

**Grey Chalk Subgroup**

**Selborne Group**

**Lower Greensand Group**

**Weald Clay Group**

**Hastings Group**

**Purbeck Group**

## Geology

Chalk is a soft, white-to-grey limestone which was deposited across wide areas of northwest Europe during the Upper Cretaceous Epoch (*c.* 100 to 66 Ma.), when sea levels were considerably higher than today. Chalk is composed of calcite mud within which are myriads of minute calcite platelets, the fossil skeletons of *coccolithophores*, free-floating calcareous algae that thrived in the Cretaceous sea.

The Chalk Group, up to 400m thick, underlies the South Downs where it crops out in a belt some 10km wide along the southern margin of the Weald. The chalk strata dip gently to the south forming a cuesta with a wide dip-slope incised by a network of dry valleys. The steep, north-facing chalk escarpment rises to a height of about 200m above sea level.

## Building Stone
**Varieties -**
    Chalk - Lavant Stone (p. 52), Chalk Calcrete (p. 50),
    Chalk Breccia (Coombe Rock) (p. 50).
    'Clunch' is a term sometimes used by builders for chalk infill in walls.

Chalk is a relatively-soft, porous, very fine-grained limestone which can easily be carved and cut for ashlar. It is best suited for use in the interior of buildings, or in the exterior fabric where it can be protected from the elements, because repeated wetting and drying leads to its disintegration. Much of the chalk used for building has been quarried from more compact beds in the lower part of the White Chalk Subgroup.

## Historic Use

| | |
|---|---|
| Roman | Used in walls and floors of numerous Roman buildings |
| Norman | Lewes Castle walls, Lewes Priory. |
| Late-Medieval | Aldingbourne - roof vaulting, Arundel - Dominican Priory (1253AD), Chichester Cathedral - cloister wall. |
| Modern | New Shoreham Church, replacement roof vaulting. |

Converted barn with Chalk ashlar walls and brick dressings. Hamsey, north of Lewes.

Vaulting constructed of roughly-cut Chalk blocks. Aldingbourne Church.

A Chalk rubble building. The remains of Heene Chapel, Worthing.

Chalk window architrave. Rodmell Church.

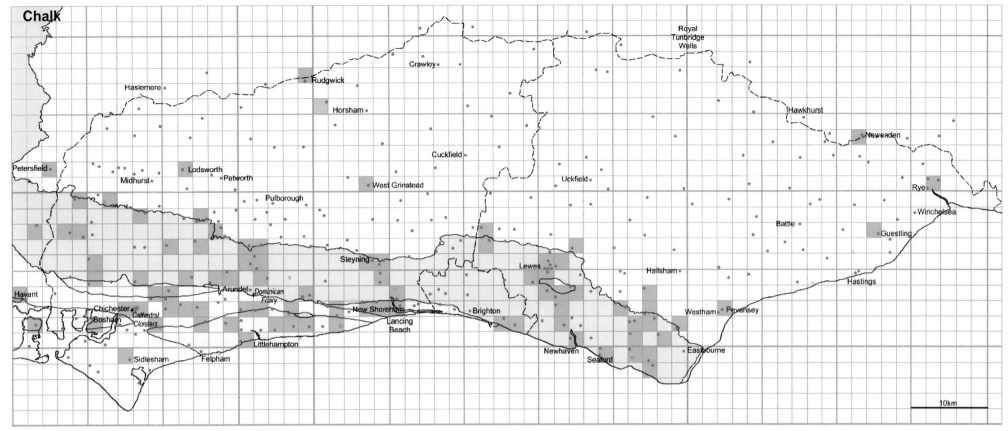

**Chalk**

**Key**

Chalk

Chalk Group Outcrop along the South Downs

Chalk Group sub-outcrop beneath Quaternary cover on the West Sussex Coastal Plain

## Distribution of Chalk

The use of Chalk as a building stone in Medieval churches strongly correlates with the chalk outcrop of the South Downs and sub-outcrop beneath the West Sussex coastal plain. There is a further concentration along the lower courses of all the Sussex Rivers, indicating transport along these waterways. Considerable use of Chalk rubble-stone is recorded across the West Sussex Coastal Plain, where it often contains borings by the marine bivalve, *Pholas* and the serpulid *Polydora*, indicating that it was quarried from the foreshore exposures between Felpham and Lancing Beach.

Chalk was only occasionally used north of its outcrop on the South Downs, as better quality building stone such as Hythe Sandstone, which is more resistant to weathering, was easier to obtain. Small amounts of Chalk rubble seen in churches in the Rye area were probably imported from the coastal chalk outcrop at Dover.

Remains of the Dominican Priory alongside the River Arun at Arundel. The ruins expose the core of the walls built of chalk blocks. Flint facing is present along the upper part of the wall.

Superficial Deposits

Bracklesham Group

Thames Group

Lambeth Group

White Chalk Subgroup

Grey Chalk Subgroup

Selborne Group

Lower Greensand Group

Weald Clay Group

Hastings Group

Purbeck Group

| Age | Upper Cretaceous |
|---|---|
| **Lithostratigraphy** | Portsdown Chalk Formation |
| | White Chalk Subgroup |
| | Chalk Group |

## Geology

Towards the end of the Cretaceous the chalk in South East England rose above sea level and was subject to denudation for a period of at least 15Ma before the first Palaeocene strata were deposited. This resulted in the formation of an etched, karstic chalk surface, displayed on the foreshore at Felpham, and also at Hope Gap on the west side of Cuckmere Haven.

In some places, for a depth of up to 50cm below the top surface, the chalk has become hardened to a tough limestone by the growth of crystalline calcite within the rock. This process has produced a bedrock calcrete as opposed to pedogenic calcretes formed in the upper layers of the soil.

Apart from flint nodules, harder rock within the chalk includes crystalline calcite and brecciated, chalk fissure infill.

## Building Stone

## Varieties and Alternative Names

| | |
|---|---|
| Chalk Calcrete, Top Chalk - | Hard limestone from the top surface of the chalk. |
| Crystalline Calcite - | From fissure deposits in the chalk. |
| Chalk Breccia, Coombe Rock - | From fissures and solifluction deposits. |

Chalk Calcrete is a white to iron-stained, hard limestone which has been used as a rubble building stone close to its coastal exposures in south-west West Sussex. Much of this stone shows recent surface borings by marine organisms indicating that it was quarried from foreshore exposures, e.g. at Felpham, and Dell Quay alongside Chichester Harbour.

## Historic Use

| Roman | Fishbourne Roman Palace and Angmering Roman Villa (hard chalk/limestone reported). |
|---|---|
| Medieval | Felpham, Bosham and West Wittering churches. |
| 19th century | Garden walls in Bognor Regis and Felpham. |

Vertical view of the Top Chalk surface at Felpham showing a zone of NNE-trending fractures which have cut the hard chalk into slabs.

Crystalline Calcite rubble, East Lavington Church. This rock was probably collected from fields on the top of the chalk downs to the south.

Hard Chalk Calcrete rubble in a 19th century wall at Bognor Regis. The surface of the chalk shows borings by marine organisms.

Rubble block of Chalk Breccia, Newhaven Church.

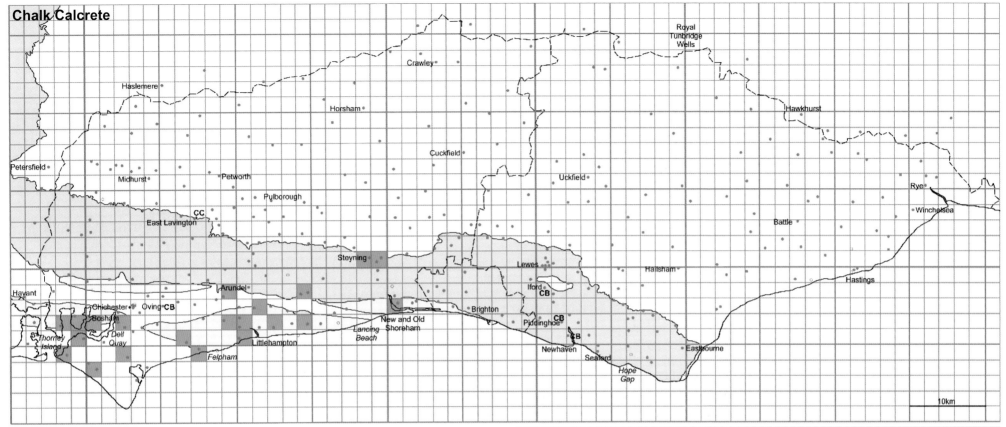

Chalk Calcrete

## Distribution of Chalk Calcrete

Chalk Calcrete used in the walls of Medieval churches is concentrated around four areas in the south of West Sussex: Chichester Harbour, Felpham, Littlehampton and Steyning. This distribution correlates with exposures of this rock along the coast, at Dell Quay, Thorney Island, Felpham foreshore and Lancing Beach shown in italics on the map.

Rubble blocks of Chalk Breccia have been used as a building stone in the Lower Ouse Valley (CB on the map), between Newhaven and Lewes. This building stone was probably obtained from beach rubble eroded from fissures and joints in the chalk cliff below Castle Hill at Newhaven. Boulders of crystalline calcite occasionally occur lying on the surface of the highest parts of the chalk downs. This rock type has only been identified at East Lavington Church (CC on the map).

| Key | | Chalk Group outcrop | | Chalk Calcrete |
|---|---|---|---|---|
| | | Chalk Group sub-outcrop beneath Quaternary cover | | |
| CB | | Chalk Breccia (fissure infill and solifluction deposits) | | |
| CC | | Crystalline Calcite (fissure infill. East Lavington Church) | | |

**Left**
Calcrete boulders on the beach at Hope Gap, west of Cuckmere Haven.

**Right**
Karst features on the Top Chalk surface at Felpham Beach.

Superficial Deposits

Bracklesham Group

Thames Group

Lambeth Group

White Chalk Subgroup

Grey Chalk Subgroup

Selborne Group

Lower Greensand Group

Weald Clay Group

Hastings Group

Purbeck Group

| Age | Campanian | Upper Cretaceous |
|---|---|---|
| **Lithostratigraphy** | Newhaven Chalk Formation White Chalk Subgroup Chalk Group | |

## Geology

Lavant Stone is a phosphatic calcarenite, a gritty, fossiliferous limestone with particles composed of broken shell debris and calcium phosphate grains. The rock contains abundant, minute, siliceous sponge spicules, and scattered grains of glauconite. Lavant Stone is notable for its well-preserved fossils which include echinoids, belemnites, bivalves, serpulids and shark's teeth. This rock formerly cropped out over a limited area on the chalk downs near Mid Lavant, 6km north north-west of Chichester. Quarrying of Lavant Stone reached a peak in the 13th century and then declined rapidly; the quarry was backfilled in the 1960s and returned to farmland.

Phosphatic chalk, such as Lavant Stone is rare in Sussex with one other known occurrence in the Lewes area. It is thought to have been formed on the chalk seabed when submarine currents flowing down, fault-controlled channels on a gentle slope, caused winnowing of the fine chalk sediment and deposited calcium phosphate grains and pellets. The shell debris remaining formed a lithified deposit known as a hardground, which was colonised by serpulids and oysters.

## Building Stone

The main variety of Lavant Stone commonly used in Medieval churches in the Chichester area is a massive, white calcarenite. The surface of the stone is rough to the touch, and often reveals shiny, buff-coloured, fossil sharks' teeth. Blocks of Lavant Stone have commonly been used for ashlar and quoins but most occur as scattered rubble-stone, some of which may be reused stone from former Roman buildings in Chichester.

A large amount of Lavant Stone was used in the construction of Boxgrove Church and Priory, where it displays two further, less-cohesive varieties:
1. Massive, grey, bioturbated, phosphatic limestone, with scattered glauconite grains.
2. Pale-brown, rough-textured limestone containing numerous brown calcium phosphate pellets.

## Historic Use

Lavant Stone was used in Roman times and later in the early-12th to 14th centuries with some probable reuse of the original Roman stone.

| | |
|---|---|
| Roman | Chichester (Noviomagus), Chilgrove Roman Villa. |
| Norman | Chichester Cathedral, East Lavant Church, Boxgrove Priory and Church. |
| Late Medieval | Oving Church, Chichester walls near the Cathedral. |

**Left**
Late 12th century door entrance in Lavant Stone. Boxgrove Priory.

**Right**
Lavant Stone quoins. Oving Church.

Ashlar showing gritty texture with red algal growth common on Lavant Stone. Westbourne Church.

Lavant Stone with fossil shark's tooth, coral, bivalves and numerous minute sponge spicules. Earnley Church.

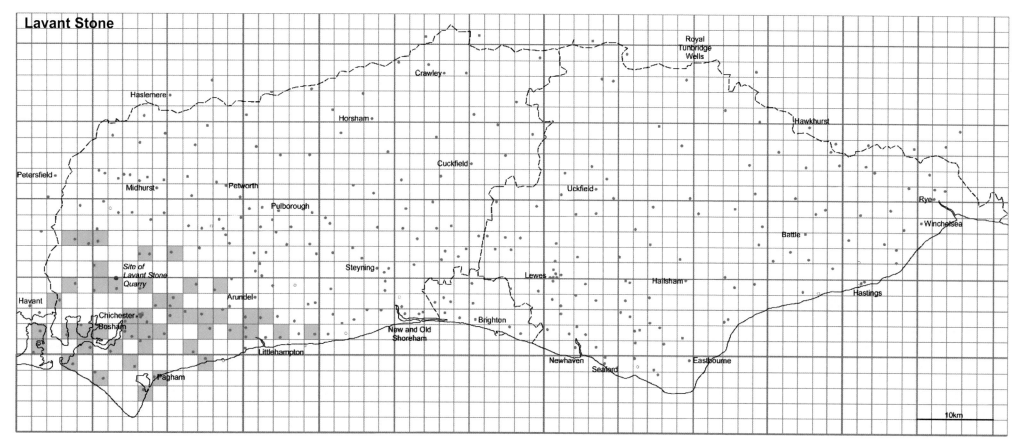

**Lavant Stone**

## Distribution of Lavant Stone

Lavant Stone shows a concentrated distribution in a well-defined area around Chichester within a radius of *c.* 14km, to the extent that almost every Medieval church in this zone includes at least some of this building stone. This distribution pattern suggests that Chichester acted as a distribution centre for this building stone in Medieval times.

Lavant Stone was obtained from a single quarry situated on the chalk downs *c.* 5km north-north-west of Chichester. Lavant Stone would have been transported from the quarry by wagon to a central store in Chichester, probably at the Cathedral, where it was used to supply building projects in the surrounding area.

**Key**

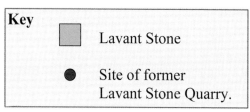

▣ Lavant Stone

● Site of former Lavant Stone Quarry.

Late 12th century fluted capital carved in highly bioturbated Lavant Stone. Softer Lavant Stone column below shows considerable weathering. Former nave of Boxgrove Priory Church.

**Superficial Deposits**

**Bracklesham Group**

**Thames Group**

**Lambeth Group**

**White Chalk Subgroup**  <

**Grey Chalk Subgroup**

**Selborne Group**

**Lower Greensand Group**

**Weald Clay Group**

**Hastings Group**

**Purbeck Group**

| | |
|---|---|
| **Age** | Upper Cretaceous |
| **Lithostratigraphy** | White Chalk Subgroup |
| | Chalk Group |

## Geology

Flint occurs as rounded, irregularly-shaped nodules, and more rarely tabular sheets, within the White Chalk Subgroup. It is a very hard rock composed of silica in the form of microscopic quartz crystal aggregates, much of which was formed in layers of nodules below the sea-bed during deposition of the chalk sediment. Flint nodules average 10 to 20cm across and often contain fossils such as echinoids, sponges and burrow structures. Because flint is very resistant to erosion and weathering it is preserved in later Tertiary and Quaternary deposits, particularly on beaches, raised beaches and river terraces. Flints are slightly porous so that after they have been eroded from the chalk and deposited in later beds, they often become bleached, or discoloured by percolating groundwater rich in iron salts.

## Building Stone
**Main Varieties** (see page 56)
    Quarry Flint (Fresh Flint), Field Flint and Beach Flint.

Flint walls are generally constructed of flint nodules of similar size, set in a soft lime mortar. Quarry and Field Flints were commonly used for building on the chalk downs while rounded, ellipsoidal-shaped Beach Flints were mainly used within a few kilometres from the beaches where they were collected. Flint was generally used as found but for higher quality and ornamental work it was cleaved, and sometimes the outward-facing surface was squared.

## Historic Use

| | |
|---|---|
| Palaeolithic (Cromerian) | Hand-axe production at Boxgrove. |
| Neolithic | Flint mining on the South Downs. |
| Roman | Chichester City walls. Pevensey Castle walls. |
| Late Saxon | Sompting Abbots and Bishopstone churches. |
| Norman | Bramber and Lewes Castles, Steyning Church. |
| Late Medieval | West Dean Church (E. Sussex). |
| Georgian | Goodwood House. West Dean House (W. Sussex). Bank building, South Street, Chichester. |
| Victorian | Hastings, R.C. Church. Brighton, St Pauls Church. |

**Left**     Botolphs Church dates from the 11th c.

**Below**    Bank building *c.* 1820. South Street, Chichester.

12th century round-plan tower built of Field Flint. Southease Church.

Beach Flint with Bath Stone quoins. St Barnabas Church (1891), Bexhill.

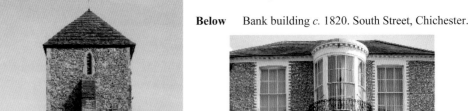

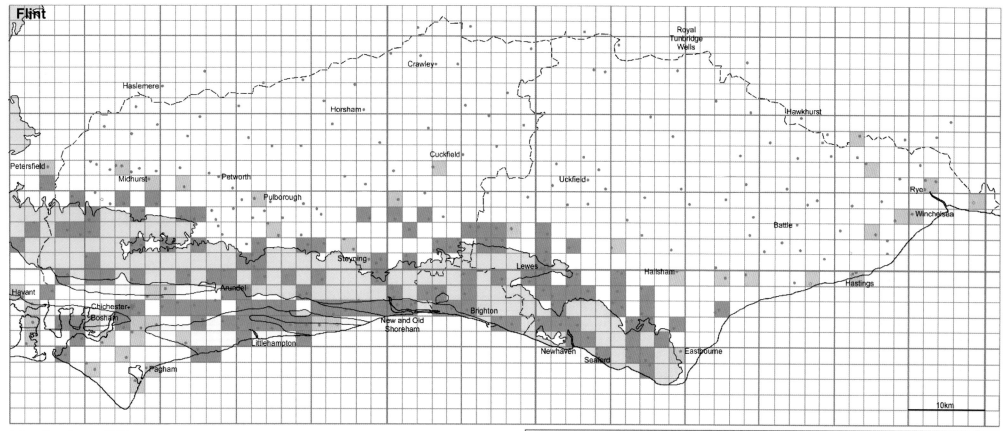

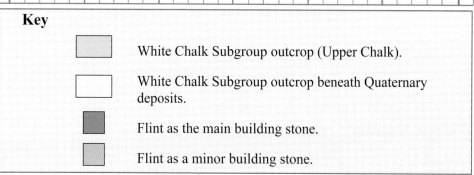

## Distribution of Flint

Flint has been recorded in more Medieval churches than any other building stone. Its distribution strongly concentrated in the south of Sussex, mainly on the chalk downs (Quarry and Field Flint), and the West Sussex Coastal Plain (Beach Flint). The main rivers, particularly the Adur and Ouse, provided transport routes for a relatively small amount of Flint for building work to the north of the South Downs.

## Flint Resources

Flint was readily available in the past from chalk quarries, fields on the chalk downs, and Quaternary deposits. Shingle beaches, which extend along much of the coastline, supplied considerable amounts of Beach Flint for building in coastal areas. Beach flint is transported by longshore drift eastwards along the coast between Selsey Bill and Rye, but modern sea defences have now impeded this natural movement.

The majority of the quarries in the chalk and Quaternary deposits have closed and extraction of beach shingle is now prohibited, so that little flint is now obtained from onshore deposits. Considerable quantities of flint for ballast in the construction industry are dredged from offshore terrace deposits of the main rivers and landed at Littlehampton, Shoreham and Newhaven.

Flint is very resistant to weathering and erosion, and has commonly been recycled and preserved in later Tertiary and Quaternary deposits. The best quality flint for working, such as cleaving and shaping, is Quarry or Fresh Flint obtained from quarries in the chalk. Flints from beach and solifluction deposits which have been subjected to freeze-thaw action during the Sub-Arctic climate of the last Ice Age, often contain micro-fractures and crumble when cleaved.

**Varieties of flint from different deposits can often be recognised by shape, colour and fracture:**

## 1. Quarry or Fresh Flints.
These are Flints quarried directly from the chalk. They are of irregular, rounded shapes, and have often formed within and around fossil burrow structures or other fossils including echinoids and sponges. They have a black interior with a white rind or cortex, and break with a conchoidal, or sometimes a prismatic fracture.

## 2. Downland Flints.
Downland Flints are those which have been collected from the soil overlying the chalk downs. They often show some surface wear and fracturing due to frost action and plough strikes, the latter leaving a brown mark on the flint surface. Downland Flint when freshly exhumed from the underlying chalk is similar to Quarry Flint.

## 3. Beach Flints.
Flints become rounded by persistent attrition and concussion when subjected to a high-energy marine environment on beaches. The pebbles evolve towards a typical ellipsoidal shape with time, the surface being covered in small curved fractures known as chatter marks. The raised beaches of West Sussex, formed at times of higher sea level during Interglacial Stages, have also in the past been a source of Beach Flint.

## 4. Field Flints and flints from Superficial Deposits.
Flints incorporated within Quaternary sediments, including soils, solifluction (head and coombe rock) and brickearth deposits, develop a brown colour over time due to staining by ferruginous water. These flints are often fractured with a patina on the cleaved surfaces. When subjected to the heat of a fire brown-stained flints develop a bright red colour.

## 5. River Terrace and Fan-Gravel Flints.
River terraces alongside the lower reaches of the main rivers, including the Arun, Adur, and Ouse, which traverse the chalk outcrop, are rich in flint gravel. These terraces were formed during Quaternary Glacial Stages when sea level was much lower than today, hence they extend southwards well beyond the coast, across the sea floor of the English Channel.

Fan-gravel flint deposits are formed when river flow is impeded on reaching a lake or flat land where gravel fans or deltas are deposited. Chichester is built on a Quaternary fan-gravel deposit, where the River Lavant reaches the West Sussex Coastal Plain. Flints from fan-gravels vary in colour from white to grey and brown depending on the nature of the sediment in which they were deposited. They generally show some rounding and may contain old, weathered or patinated fracture surfaces.

## 6. Black, Ellipsoidal Flint Pebbles.
Black, ellipsoidal flint pebbles (Tertiary Flint Pebbles), occur in thin beds of generally dispersed pebbles within Palaeocene and Eocene (Early Palaeogene) strata. These pebbles were originally flints which were eroded from the chalk in Early Palaeogene times and suffered rounding in a high-energy shoreline environment. They were often further recycled into Quaternary deposits and are found as isolated examples in modern flint beaches. The black colour of the pebbles is due to impregnation with iron salts when they were enclosed within the Palaeogene strata. Although Black Elipsoidal Pebbles have considerable potential for decorative purposes they have rarely been specifically used for this purpose.

Sheet or tabular Flint in a wall of Yapton Church.

Although most flint was formed as nodules within the chalk, thin sheets of flint also occur. Broken pieces of tabular flint have occasionally been used as building stone.

(1) A layer of flint nodules embedded in chalk. Many of the nodules are fractured to reveal a black, glassy interior. Chalk cliffs at Seaford.

(1) A cleaved, Quarry Flint nodule showing the glassy black interior and surrounding white cortex. Eartham Church.

(2) Field flints on the chalk downs collected to the side of a field. Springhead Hill, Storrington.

(3) Worthing beach showing moderately-rounded Beach Flint pebbles. Much of the Sussex coastline is flanked by flint-pebble beaches.

Numbers relate to the classification of flint deposit varieties on facing page.

(3) Well-rounded flint pebbles beneath Brickearth. Selsey Raised Beach dating from the last Interglacial Stage (c. 125Ka).

(4) Exposure of a solifluction deposit of Flints in a clay matrix, along the southern margin of the chalk downs. Former flint quarry, Boxgrove.

(5) Chichester Fan Gravel flint deposits. Drayton Quarry, near Chichester (2006). This former quarry is now a Nature Reserve.

(6) Vertical view of a black ellipsoidal flint pebble bed in the London Clay at Snow Hill, adjacent to East Head, Chichester Harbour.

# TYPES OF FLINT-WORK

Construction with Flints present a considerable challenge due to their variety of shapes and sizes. However these properties and their various colours make them ideal for numerous types of ornamental work. Because of their irregular shapes Flints need to be set in large amounts of soft lime mortar, which has to harden before overlying courses are constructed, so that only a few layers can be built at a time.

## 1. Coursed or Layered Work with Quarry or Field Flint Nodules.
Most flint walling is constructed in horizontal layers, with the flints chosen to be of a similar size and shape to aid construction. Quarry flints display a white outer skin or cortex but can be cleaved to display a dark-coloured interior.

## 2. Coursed or Layered Work with Beach Flint Pebbles and Cobbles.
Ellipsoidal-shaped Beach Flints were formerly quarried along much of the Sussex coast and were mainly used for building within a few kilometres of the shoreline. They are generally set with their long axis at an angle in an imbricate pattern.

## 3. Tabular Flint-work.
Tabular flint-work is relatively rare reflecting the difficulty in sourcing this variety of flint. Isolated examples are present in flint buildings on the chalk downs. Flint slabs are occasionally set flat on a wall surface to give a mosaic effect.

## 4. Flush-work, Knapped, Faced or Cleaved Flint-work.
This is a type of Flint-work where the outer face of the flints is knapped to give a cleaved surface. Quarry flints are best for flush-work as they break with a smooth, often conchoidal fracture. Higher-quality work involves selecting concave and convex profiles of the flints to interlock, one above the other.

## 5. Block-work or Squared Flint-work.
This is higher-quality flint-work where the outer surface of the flints is carefully cleaved to a square shape to give the impression that the wall is made of squared flint blocks.

## 6. Chequer Work.
This is a relatively common type of wall decoration constructed with a chequer-board pattern of flints, which are often cleaved, and ashlar blocks.

## 7. Ornamental Flint-work.
Complex-shaped Quarry Flints set in or on walling to give a decorative effect.

## 8. Flint Mosaic-work.
Use of cleaved and shaped flints to form a mosaic within an ashlar surround.

## 9. Flint Flake Galleting.
A common type of decorative flint-work where flint flakes are set in the wall between the flints: galleting also strengthens the wall and saves on mortar. Large numbers of flint flakes would have been produced when preparing flush-work and block-work.

**Right**
(8) Flint mosaic or inlay-work in the shape of a dove. Southwick Church.

**Below**
(7) Ornamental flint-work using complex-shape Quarry Flints. Great Ballards, Eartham.

**Below**  (5) Flint block-work with brick ornamentation. Note randomly-placed flints in the surrounding wall. Angmering, Old School.

(1) Field Flints laid in a chevron pattern.
The Gatehouse, Bramber Castle.

(2) Courtyard paved with Beach Flint Pebbles.
Ashburnham House.

(2) Beach Flint wall. Shoreham-by-Sea.

(4) Flint Flushwork where the flints have been
laid with concave side above convex.
Lancing College, school building.

Numbers refer to Flint-work Types on facing page.

(5) Roughly-squared Field Flint and Fan Gravel Flint, used for
facing the Roman Walls of Chichester.

(5) High-quality Flint Blockwork. Cottage
wall, South Bersted, Bognor Regis.

(6) Flint and Caen Stone Chequer Work.
The flints have been roughly squared.
Marlipins, Shoreham-by-Sea.

(9) Field Flint with Flint Galleting.
Oving Church.

Superficial Deposits

Bracklesham Group

Thames Group

Lambeth Group

White Chalk Subgroup

Grey Chalk Subgroup

Selborne Group

Lower Greensand Group

Weald Clay Group

Hastings Group

Purbeck Group

| | |
|---|---|
| **Age** | Palaeocene |
| | Palaeogene (Early Tertiary) |
| **Lithostratigraphy** | Upnor Formation |
| | Lambeth Group |

## Geology

At Castle Hill, Newhaven *c.* 5m of flint gravel and sand belonging to the Upnor Formation lies directly on the chalk, in an outlier of Palaeogene strata. Evidence that this Formation was more extensive in the past is suggested by the occurrence of Upnor Conglomerate in church walls on the downs between Brighton and Eastbourne. In some areas silica-rich groundwater cemented patches of the sand to form silcrete (sarsen boulders), while in other areas sand and flint gravel were cemented with iron oxides to form ferruginous sandstone and conglomerate. Boulders of these more resistant rocks have often been transported down-slope during cold periods of the Quaternary, becoming incorporated within solifluction deposits in the valleys.

Upnor Conglomerate is composed of sub-rounded flints which were subsequently fractured by the effects of freeze-thaw weathering during the last Ice Age. Some of the flints have a green, glauconite-rich coating indicating the Upnor Conglomerate was deposited in a marine environment.

## Building Stone

### Varieties and Alternative Names

Upnor Conglomerate - Upnor Breccia, Upnor Ferricrete.
Upnor Ferruginous Sandstone - Upnor Ironstone.
Ferruginous Siltstone - Upnor Ironstone.

Building stone from the Upnor Formation includes flint conglomerate, sandstone and ironstone, all variably cemented with iron-oxides. The enclosed flint pebbles in the conglomerate are generally fractured so that this rock may be more correctly called a 'brecciated conglomerate'. Iron-oxide-cemented conglomerate and sandstone are softly cemented when quarried but the matrix hardens on exposure. Upnor Conglomerate is the commonest variety of this building stone present in Medieval church walls.

## Historic Use

| | |
|---|---|
| Roman | Newhaven and Bishopstone (former buildings). |
| Norman | Lewes Priory. |
| Medieval | Seaford, Newhaven and Telscombe churches. |
| 18-19th century | Falmer Church. |

Fractured flints, some with a green coating, in an iron-oxide cemented sandstone. Kingston-near-Lewes Church.

Ferruginous Sandstone quoins. Telscombe Church.

Ferruginous Siltstone (Ferricrete) with an open flaky texture. Falmer Church.

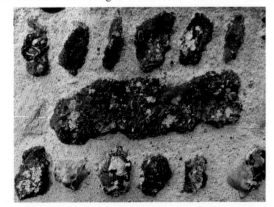

Ferruginous Sandstone and brecciated conglomerate rubble-stone containing fractured flints. Telscombe Church.

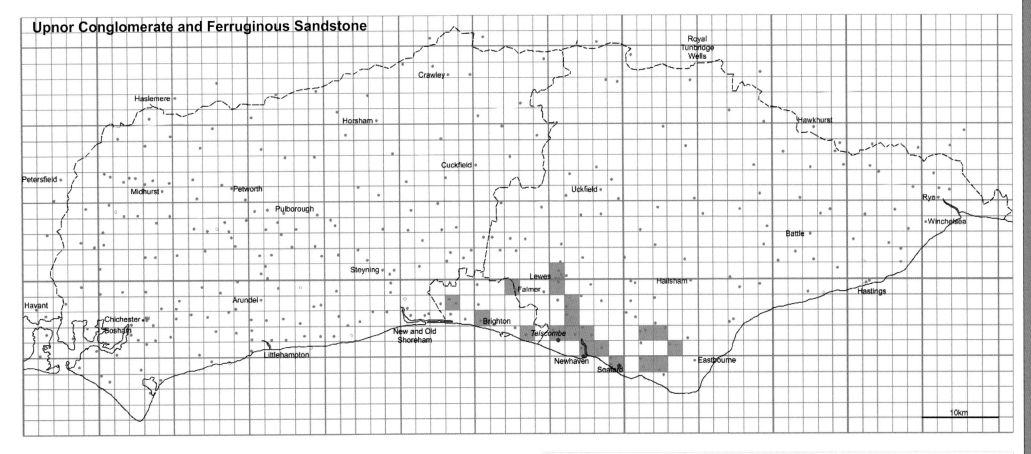

**Upnor Conglomerate and Ferruginous Sandstone**

## Distribution of Upnor Conglomerate and Ferruginous Sandstone

The concentrated distribution of this rubble building stone in the south of East Sussex relates to former sporadic outcrops of Upnor Conglomerate on the chalk downs in the Brighton-to-Eastbourne area. Upnor Conglomerate and Ferruginous Sandstone shows a concentration of use in Medieval churches along the lower Ouse valley from Seaford to Lewes, indicating that the river acted as a transport route for this building stone as far north as South Malling.

Upnor Conglomerate, Sandstone and Ironstone was notably utilized in Norman times in the construction of Lewes Priory. This building stone was used much later at Falmer Church, rebuilt 1815 and 1840, where it was obtained from residual boulders collected from nearby fields.

### Key

 Upnor Conglomerate and Ferruginous Sandstone (Ironstone).

● Outcrops of Upnor Conglomerate on the chalk downs near Seaford, Newhaven and Telscombe.

Upnor Conglomerate composed of fractured flints in a sandy, iron-oxide-cemented matrix. Some of the flints have a green coating, possibly of the mineral glauconite. Although originally formed as a conglomerate later fracturing of the flints means that this rock could be classified as a breccia. Seaford Church.

| | | |
|---|---|---|
| **Age** | Palaeocene | |
| | Palaeogene (Early Tertiary) | |
| **Lithostratigraphy** | Upnor Formation | |
| | Lambeth Group | |

Superficial Deposits

Bracklesham Group

Thames Group

Lambeth Group

White Chalk Subgroup

Grey Chalk Subgroup

Selborne Group

Lower Greensand Group

Weald Clay Group

Hastings Group

Purbeck Group

## Geology

Sarsen Stone is a quartzite which is believed to have been formed during the Neogene by silicification of near-surface Palaeogene sands. Although the age of the original sand from which the Sarsens were formed is uncertain, sand in the Upnor Formation at the base of the Palaeogene strata in East Sussex appears to be the most likely source.

Sarsen Stone occurs as boulders, cobbles and pebbles in 3 main locations:
1. On and close to the chalk downs in the Brighton-to-Eastbourne area. Numerous boulders were transported to the north and south down the cuesta slopes by floods during severe weather in the last Ice Age.
2. As boulders and cobbles within the lower raised beaches around Chichester Harbour and as far east as the River Arun.
3. As a minor rock type within the mainly-flint beach shingle along the Sussex coast. Sarsen pebbles are more abundant in the west where they have been eroded from raised beach deposits. Longshore drift has transported beach pebbles eastward along the coast.

## Building Stone

### Alternative Names and Varieties
Sarsen Stone - Greywethers, Druid Stones, Silcrete.
Puddingstone (rare in Sussex).

Boulders of Sarsen Stone are found in the Chichester Harbour and Brighton areas but were not specifically selected as a building stone as in the London Basin. Sarsen cobbles and pebbles were however commonly incorporated into Beach Flint walls in coastal areas between Hayling Island and Seaford.

**Pudding-stone,** is a variety rich in rounded-flint pebbles found in the north part of the London Basin, particularly Hertfordshire. Occasional boulders of Sarsen Stone containing slightly rounded flints occur in the Falmer area.

## Historic use of Sarsen Stone

| Roman | Chichester and Fishbourne Roman Palace. |
|---|---|
| | Newhaven Roman building. |
| Norman | Arlington and West Wittering churches. |
| Later Medieval | Earnley Church, South Bersted Church. |
| 18-19th century | Scattered cobbles within flint walls in towns and villages along the West Sussex coast. |

**Right**
Column base placed on a Sarsen Stone.
Arlington Church.

Water rounded and cleaved Sarsen Stone cobble in the wall of Iford Church, near Lewes.

A collection of Sarsen Stones adjacent to the village pond at Falmer.

Sarsen Stone in the churchyard wall at Ditchling.

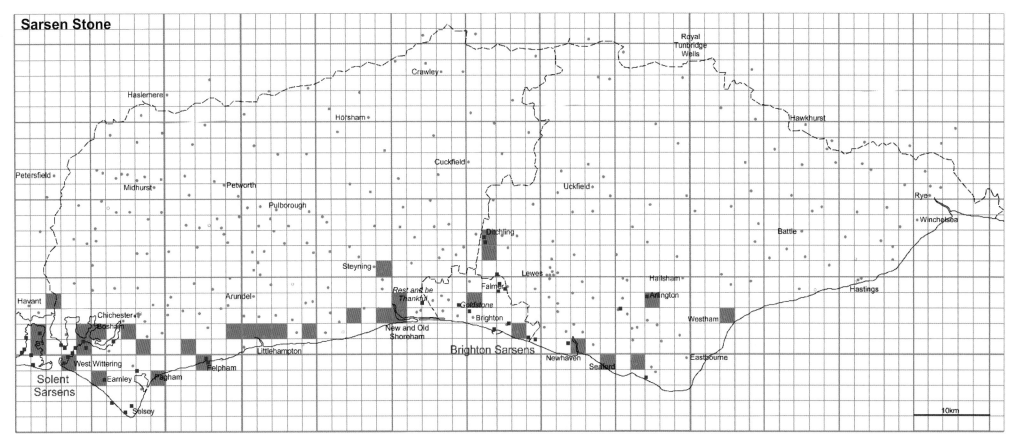

Sarsen Stone

## Distribution of Sarsen Stone

Pebbles and cobbles of Sarsen Stone are a minor constituent within Flint walls of Medieval churches, and garden walls, within *c*. 4km of the coast between Hayling Island and Seaford. There is a notable concentration of Sarsen Stone use in the Chichester Harbour-to-Felpham area where Sarsen Stone boulders and pebbles are more abundant in the raised-beach and modern beach deposits. Notable use of Sarsen stone pebbles and cobbles in Medieval churches along the lower Adur valley show that they have been shipped upriver with Beach Flint, probably from Shoreham Beach.

**Sarsen Stone boulders,** used at Ditchling, Westmeston and Arlington, have been derived from the the crest of the chalk downs, having been transported down the chalk escarpment by either human or natural processes. At North Hayling (Hampshire) and Arlington churches large Sarsen Stones have been used for the foundation of columns.

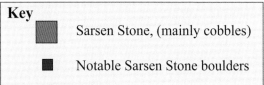

**Key**

Sarsen Stone, (mainly cobbles)

Notable Sarsen Stone boulders

The largest known Sarsen Stone in West Sussex is a 3m-long boulder on the foreshore of Chichester Harbour, near West Wittering, (photograph right).

Two Sarsen boulders have been named; 'The Goldstone' at Hove, and 'Rest and be Thankful' lying on the South Downs north of Southwick.

**Below**

Sarsen boulder showing typical tabular form, located on the foreshore of Chichester Harbour at Ella Nore, West Wittering.

| | |
|---|---|
| **Age** | Palaeocene |
| | Palaeogene (Early Tertiary) |
| **Lithostratigraphy** | Reading and Woolwich Formations |
| | Lambeth Group |

**Superficial Deposits**

**Bracklesham Group**

**Thames Group**

**Lambeth Group**

**White Chalk Subgroup**

**Grey Chalk Subgroup**

**Selborne Group**

**Lower Greensand Group**

**Weald Clay Group**

**Hastings Group**

**Purbeck Group**

## Geology

Palaeocene strata, which crop out in the south of Sussex, comprise a sequence of progressively-overlapping Formations deposited as a marine transgression spread from the east. The oldest Palaeocene strata are marine sand and flint gravel of the Upnor Formation, which lie directly above the chalk at Castle Hill, Newhaven. They are in turn overlain by estuarine strata of the Woolwich Formation. West of Worthing the Woolwich Formation grades into continental deposits of the Reading Formation.

The Woolwich Formation consists mainly of shelly, estuarine clays with thin beds of lignite, sandstone with fossil oysters, and ferruginous siltstone concretions.

The Reading Formation is composed of pedogenic and alluvial clay with thin beds of ferruginous sandstone and siltstone, which was deposited across a wide floodplain. Fluviatile and back-swamp deposits with a lignite bed and fossil tree stumps, trunks and leaves occur near the middle of the Formation.

## Building Stone

### Alternative Names and Varieties

Woolwich and Reading Ironstone, Ferruginous Sandstone, Ferruginous Siltstone.
Ostrea (Oyster) Sandstone.

Woolwich and Reading Ironstone is a minor rubble building stone which occurs as scattered, rubble-stone in flint walls. Some of this building stone may have been quarried from exposures along the coast, especially around Chichester Harbour, but most probably came from Quaternary solifluction deposits found along the southern margin of the South Downs. The ironstone is massive, fine-grained and very resistant to weathering.

Ostrea Sandstone from the Woolwich Formation in the Shoreham area is a soft, buff-weathering, silty sandstone containing fossil oyster shells.

### Historic Use

| | |
|---|---|
| Roman | Fishbourne Roman Palace (possibly Carstone). |
| Medieval | Bosham, North Mundham and Angmering Churches (isolated, single rubble blocks). |

**Right**
Reading Ironstone cobble in flint solifluction deposits. Former Boxgrove Quarry.
**Below**
Reading Ironstone cobble.
North Mundham Church.

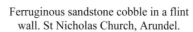

Woolwich Sandstone with fossil oyster shells. Old Shoreham Church.

Ferruginous sandstone cobble in a flint wall. St Nicholas Church, Arundel.

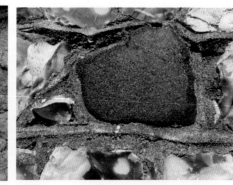

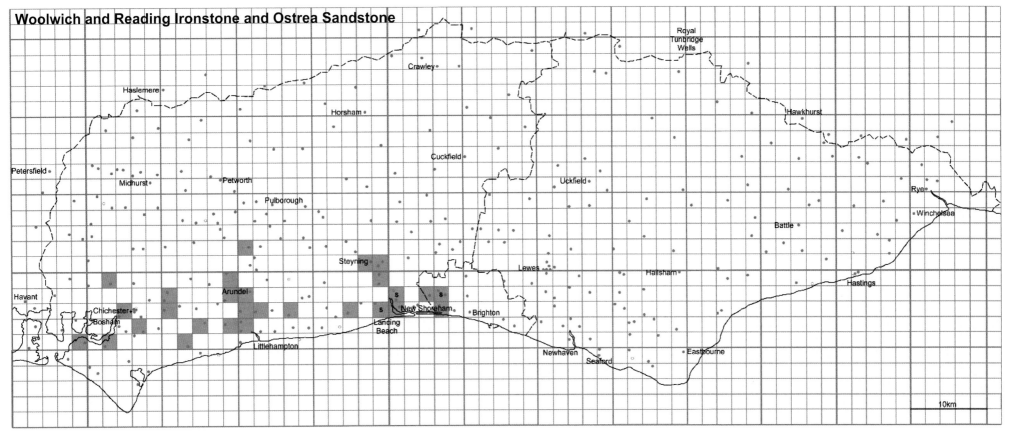

Woolwich and Reading Ironstone and Ostrea Sandstone

## Distribution of Woolwich and Reading Ironstone and Ostrea Sandstone

Ferruginous Sandstone has been used as scattered rubble-stone in Medieval churches across the West Sussex Coastal Plain, particularly in those situated within the lower Arun and Adur valleys. Establishing the geological age of ferruginous sandstones and ironstones used in Medieval buildings is challenging, as similar rock types occur in strata ranging from Lower Cretaceous to Palaeogene in age. Ironstone rubble in Medieval churches in the Chichester Harbour area may have been derived from foreshore exposures of the Reading Formation. Carstone of Roman context reported at Fishbourne Roman Palace and Chichester suggests that recycled Roman stone may have been used in later buildings in the surrounding area.

Ostrea Sandstone is present in only three churches: North Lancing, Old Shoreham and Hangleton. It was most likely quarried from foreshore exposures of the Woolwich Formation at Lancing Beach.

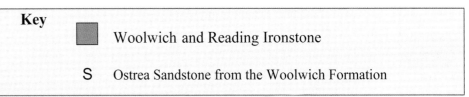

Key

■ Woolwich and Reading Ironstone

S Ostrea Sandstone from the Woolwich Formation

## Ferruginous Sandstone and Ironstone

Ferruginous sandstone or ironstone is common in the Lower Cretaceous, Folkestone and Sandgate Formations and in the Palaeogene, Woolwich and Reading Formations. Identification of these building stones is often problematic. It is based on petrology and on the location of the buildings in which these rocks have been used in relation to distance and ease of transport from the rock outcrop. Cretaceous Ironstones tend to be gritty with small yellow-stained quartz and black chert pebbles, while the Palaeogene Ironstones are mainly fine-grain ferruginous sandstones and siltstones.

| Age | Eocene<br>Palaeogene (Early Tertiary) |
|---|---|
| **Lithostratigraphy** | Bognor Sand Member<br>  (Top of Division A3)<br>London Clay Formation<br>Thames Group |

## Geology

The London Clay Formation contains numerous layers of calcareous concretions, the most notable of which occur within a sand-rich bed, the Bognor Sand Member, at the top of Stratigraphic Division A3. Around low tide, hard calcite-cemented concretions of glauconitic sandstone up to 3m across form an east-south-east trending reef across the foreshore at Bognor Regis. The fossil bivalve *Glycymeris brevirostris* and the coiled serpulid *Rotularia bognoriensis,* which occur in abundance in some of the concretions, serve as a useful guide to the identification of this building stone in old walls.

Concretions of Bognor Rock also occur within the London Clay in the Chichester area, but are absent from exposures of the Bognor Sand Member around Chichester Harbour. Bognor Rock 'erratics' on the foreshore of Chichester Harbour may have been transported there from the London Clay outcrop to the north by floods during the Quaternary.

## Building Stone

Building stone from the Bognor Rocks is traditionally known as Bognor Rock rather than Bognor Stone, and was formerly obtained by collecting rocks during low tide from the wide foreshore at Bognor Regis. Much of the building stone is a rather soft green-grey, glauconitic sandstone, which is prone to weathering, and so was mainly used as rubble-stone. In exposed walls it develops a rusty-brown colour due to the oxidation of iron-rich glauconite. Much of the building stone is massive and highly bioturbated; fossil shells and burrow structures are common. Some of the Bognor Rock is cemented by calcite and therefore very hard, although this variety has been little used for building.

The Barn Rocks, a similar reef exposed on the beach at Aldwick at low-water spring tide, have supplied a similar concretionary sandstone, although in much smaller amounts.

## Historic Use

| Roman | Fishbourne Roman Palace. |
|---|---|
| Medieval | South Bersted, Chidham and Oving churches. |
| 18-20th century | Garden and house walls, Bognor Regis.<br>Manor Farm, Merston. |

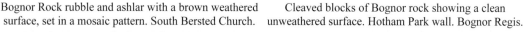

Bognor Rock rubble and ashlar with a brown weathered surface, set in a mosaic pattern. South Bersted Church.

Cleaved blocks of Bognor rock showing a clean unweathered surface. Hotham Park wall. Bognor Regis.

Bognor Rock rubble with fossil bivalve *Glycymeris*. Bognor Regis, garden wall.

Bognor Rock and possibly Barn Rock rubble in cottage wall. Pagham.

1cm scale

Superficial Deposits

Bracklesham Group

Thames Group

Lambeth Group

White Chalk Subgroup

Grey Chalk Subgroup

Selborne Group

Lower Greensand Group

Weald Clay Group

Hastings Group

Purbeck Group

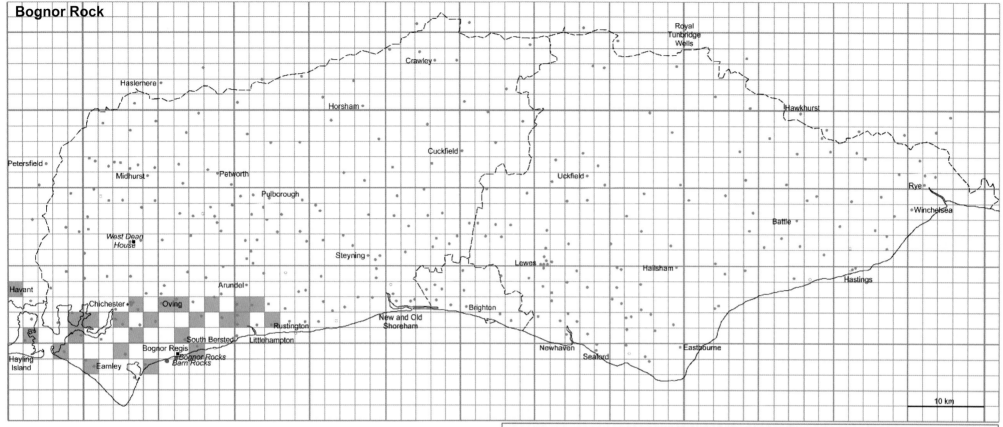

Bognor Rock

## Distribution of Bognor Rock

Bognor Rock was mainly quarried from beach exposures at Bognor Regis, with a much smaller amount obtained from the outcrop in the Chichester Syncline around Chichester. The use of Bognor Rock in Medieval churches shows a concentrated distribution pattern in the area between Hayling Island and Littlehampton, extending for about 8km inland from the coast. Generally it was only a minor rubble building stone with its greatest use seen in the walls of the 13th century church at South Bersted.

An important use of this building stone was for the gatehouse and wall around Hotham Park, Bognor Regis (1809). It was utilized extensively in 19th to early-20th centuries for garden and house walls in Bognor Regis. Inland from the coast Bognor Rock was used in the walls of Georgian farmhouses and cottages at Merston, Colworth and Westergate.

**Key**

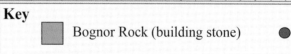

Bognor Rock (building stone)

Bognor Rocks and Barn Rocks (sites of former foreshore quarries)

Bognor Rock rubble, Oving Church with sections of the fossil serpulid *Rotularia bognoriensis*.

Irregularly-shaped concretions of Bognor Rock used to decorate the parapet of an ornamental bridge. West Dean House Gardens.

| Age | Eocene |
|---|---|
| | Palaeogene (Early Tertiary) |
| **Lithostratigraphy** | London Clay Formation |
| | Thames Group |

*(Stratigraphic column on left margin, top to bottom):*
Quaternary
Bracklesham Group
Thames Group
Lambeth Group
White Chalk Subgroup
Grey Chalk Subgroup
Selborne Group
Lower Greensand Group
Weald Clay Group
Hastings Group
Purbeck Group

## Geology

London Clay crops out in two east-west trending belts beneath Quaternary cover, across the West Sussex coastal plain between Havant and Worthing, along the axis of the Chichester Syncline, and between Hayling Island and Bognor Regis along the northern margin of the Hampshire Basin. In the latter area the beds dip very gently to the south to give extensive foreshore exposures. In East Sussex the basal beds of the London Clay crop out in an outlier at Castle Hill, Newhaven. The strata consist of *c.* 100m of grey marine clay and silt, with sand towards the top. Within the London Clay cementstone concretions, up to 60cm across, occur at numerous horizons.

The Harwich Formation, at the base of the London Clay, was formerly known as the London Clay Bottom Bed. It is up to 4m thick in the Chichester Harbour area where it contains layers of fossiliferous, calcareous concretions, notably with masses of small, straight tubes of the fossil serpulid *Ditrupa*.

## Building Stone
### Varieties and Alternative Names

London Clay Cementstone (Concretions) - Septaria, Septarian Concretions, Turritella Concretions.

Harwich Stone - Ditrupa Siltstone (from the Harwich Formation).

London Clay Cementstone is a minor rubble building stone which was used in the vicinity of exposures of London Clay around Chichester Harbour and at Bognor Regis. Septarian Concretions contain cracks filled with honey-coloured calcite, while Turritella Concretions contain large numbers of fossil turret shells. Cementstone concretions from Bognor Regis beach were formerly calcined for the production of cement, which was particularly used for stucco applied to protect the walls of seaside villas from the elements.

## Historic Use

| | |
|---|---|
| Roman | Fishbourne Roman Palace, Sidlesham Roman Villa. |
| Medieval | West Wittering Church. |
| 18-19th century | Bognor Regis and Felpham garden walls. |

An exposure of London Clay showing a layer of Cementstone Concretions. Bognor Regis foreshore.

London Clay Septarian Concretion divided by calcite-filled fractures. 19th century wall, Bognor Regis.

Turritella Concretion rubble showing aligned shells of fossil *Turritella,* West Wittering Church. These concretions were quarried from the Turritella Bed on the foreshore of Chichester Harbour at Ella Nore

Freshly-split Septarian Concretion on the beach at Bognor Regis. Honey-coloured calcite lines the sides of the septa along which the rock has split into segments.

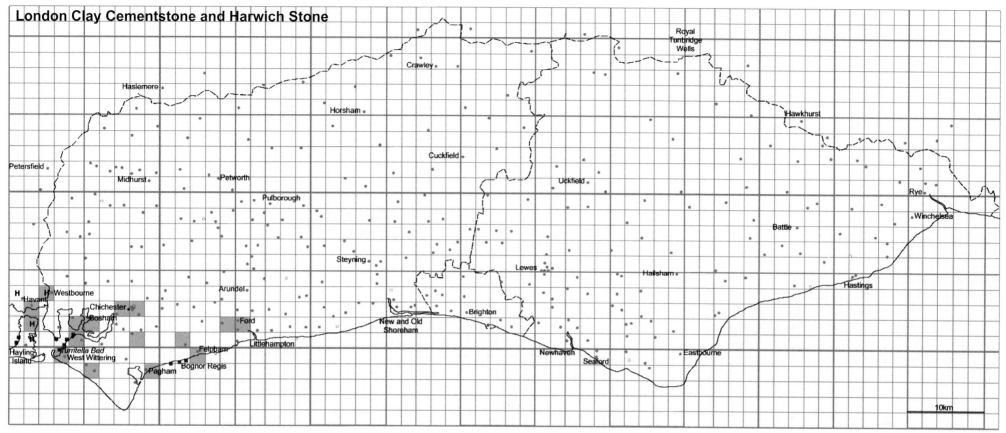

London Clay Cementstone and Harwich Stone

10km

## HARWICH STONE

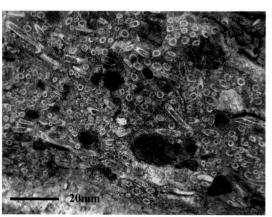

20mm

**Left**
Close-up of Harwich Stone at Havant Church, Hampshire.

**Harwich Stone** was formerly obtained from fossiliferous, calcareous, and sometimes ferruginous concretions in the Harwich Formation, immediately below the London Clay. This building stone typically contains masses of small straight tubes of the fossil serpulid *Ditrupa*. Small rounded pebbles of limonite are common in some of the rock. Exposures occur at Copperas Point south of Dell Quay and on the west coast of Hayling Island. It has been used as a minor rubble building stone in the walls of Westbourne Church.

### Distribution of London Clay Cementstone

This is a minor, rubble building stone which is restricted to the south-west part of West Sussex and bordering parts of Hampshire. It was used close to where it was quarried on the foreshores of Langstone and Chichester Harbours, and Bognor Regis.

**Turritella Concretions** were formerly collected from the foreshore of Chichester Harbour at Ella Nore north of West Wittering, and used for rubble building stone at West Wittering and Bosham Churches.

69

Quaternary

< Bracklesham Group

Thames Group

Lambeth Group

White Chalk Subgroup

Grey Chalk Subgroup

Selborne Group

Lower Greensand Group

Weald Clay Group

Hastings Group

Purbeck Group

| | |
|---|---|
| **Age** | Eocene<br>Palaeogene (Early Tertiary) |
| **Lithostratigraphy** | Beds S10 and S11<br>Selsey Formation<br>Bracklesham Group |

## Geology

Mixon (Mixen) Stone is a foraminiferal limestone which contains minor amounts of quartz and glauconite grains. It was formerly quarried from the Mixon (Mixen) Rocks located 1.5km offshore, southeast of Selsey Bill. During the first millenium this area would have been part of the 'Selsey Island' (map p.73), but sea level rise and coastal erosion averaging *c.* 3m per year has left these rocks as an offshore reef, now only visible at low tide.

The Mixon Stone Bed lies in the upper part of the Selsey Formation, but the offshore geology south of Selsey Bill is poorly known. When the rocky outcrop of The Mixon is traced across the seabed to the west it is displaced by a fold and/or fault and appears to come ashore as 'The Clibs', close to Selsey Coastguard Station. Followed further west across Bracklesham Bay the strata outcrop again on the sea-bed as The Hounds or Houndgate Rocks.

## Building Stone
**Alternative names and varieties -**
   Mixon (Mixen) Stone - Mixon Limestone, Mixon Rock.
   Hounds or Houndgate Stone.
   Wittering Sandstone (from Wittering Formation) - Bracklesham Stone.

**Mixon Stone** is a good-quality, limestone building stone much of which naturally breaks into large brick-size blocks. The rock varies from massive ochre limestone, to grey, finely-bedded, sandy limestone, weathering brown. It readily identified from numerous fossil shells of benthic foraminifera: minute spherical *Milliolids,* and larger, scattered spindle-shaped *Alveolina.*

**Hounds or Houndgate Stone** is a soft, massive, grey, slightly- glauconitic sandstone, used as a rubble-stone, was obtained from the Hounds or Houndgate Rocks, an offshore reef in Bracklesham Bay, near Earnley.

## Historic Use

| | |
|---|---|
| Roman | Fishbourne Roman Palace, Chichester.<br>Sidlesham Roman Villa. |
| Norman | Aldingbourne Motte. |
| Late-Medieval | Pagham and North Mundham churches. |
| 17-19th century | Selsey Village cottages and walls. |

Sea-eroded blocks of Mixon Stone in the Norman tower of Pagham Church.

Mixon Stone rubble was used for sea walls around Chichester and Langstone Harbours. Bosham Harbour wall.

Mixon Stone in early19th century buildings. South Street, Chichester.

Shaped, brick-size blocks of Mixon Stone used with brick dressings. Cottages in Selsey High Street.

Mixon Stone and Hounds Stone

## Distribution of Mixon Stone

The use of Mixon Stone in Medieval churches is strongly concentrated in the Selsey-to-Chichester area, to the extent that every Medieval church within an 8km radius of Birdham, south-west of Chichester, includes at least some of this building stone.

It was first utilized in Roman times, especially at Fishbourne Roman Palace. During the Medieval Period it was used for church walls and other stone buildings e.g. Aldingbourne Motte, and later, in the 18-19th centuries, for houses and cottages in Selsey and Chichester, and sea walls around Chichester Harbour. Some of the Mixon Stone rubble present in old walls and the city walls of Chichester may be reused Roman building stone.

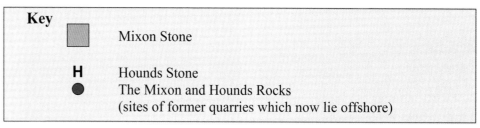

Key

- ▨ Mixon Stone
- **H** Hounds Stone
- ● The Mixon and Hounds Rocks (sites of former quarries which now lie offshore)

## Hounds Stone

This soft rubble-stone from the Hounds Rocks in Bracklesham Bay was mainly used in the walls of West Wittering Church, with smaller amounts at Bosham and Earnley churches.

Close-up view of a polished surface of honey-coloured Mixon Stone from Selsey beach, showing masses of spherical *Milliolid* foraminifera, together with the larger spindle-shaped *Alveolina*. This variety would make a good ornamental stone.

Grey Mixon Stone with a shell of the modern burrowing bivalve *Pholas,* indicating that the stone was quarried from the foreshore. Sidlesham Church.

Close-up of Mixon Stone in Bosham Church wall. The spherical hollows have been left by the moulds of *Milliolid* foraminifera shells. Note the small glassy, quartz grain, centre left.

Sea-rounded blocks of Mixon Stone in Selsey Church wall. Much of this stone was recycled from the former nave of Church Norton Church for the new church at Selsey, built 1864.

Ochre-coloured Mixon Stone in double courses interlaid with single layers of grey weathered Hounds Stone. Boathouse, Sidlesham Quay.

Cleaved blocks of grey Mixon Stone interlaid with beach flints. Cottage wall in Selsey.

## MIXON STONE IN BUILDINGS

Hounds Stone, a soft, green-grey, glauconitic sandstone randomly laid with flints. Wall at the entrance to West Wittering churchyard.

# INDIGENOUS BUILDING STONES IN THE SOUTH WEST OF WEST SUSSEX
Geology shown on the land surface extending to the interpreted coastline during the first millennium

## Coastal Building Stone Resources between Hayling Island and Felpham

The southwest coastal area of West Sussex is underlain by Upper Cretaceous (Chalk), Palaeogene (Early Tertiary) and Quaternary strata that include few resources of higher-quality building stone apart from flint. Chichester and its hinterland was an important population centre in Roman times, and then again from Late-Saxon and Norman times. Large amounts of building stone were required particularly during the Norman period for religious and military buildings. A few beds of more resistant rock, shown on the map, were quarried along the foreshore, mainly for rubble building stone.

Towards the end of the last Glacial Stage (Devensian) sea level began to rise, inundating the English Channel floor; by about 4,000 years ago the sea had risen to *c.* 2m below its present level. During the first millennium the Sussex coastline extended several kilometres further south, flanked by wide shingle bars and a number of broad estuaries. A considerable amount of coastal erosion has taken place around the low-lying Selsey-Manhood Peninsula in the last millennium so that the sites of former quarries at The Mixon and Hounds (Houndgate Rocks), now lie offshore.

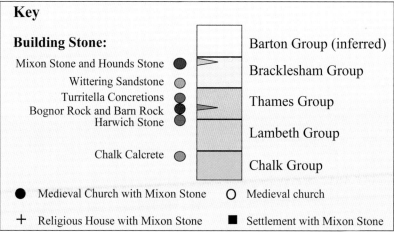

## Key

**Building Stone:**

Mixon Stone and Hounds Stone ●
Wittering Sandstone ●
Turritella Concretions ●
Bognor Rock and Barn Rock ●
Harwich Stone ●

Chalk Calcrete ●

☐ Barton Group (inferred)

Bracklesham Group

Thames Group

Lambeth Group

Chalk Group

● Medieval Church with Mixon Stone    ○ Medieval church

+ Religious House with Mixon Stone    ■ Settlement with Mixon Stone

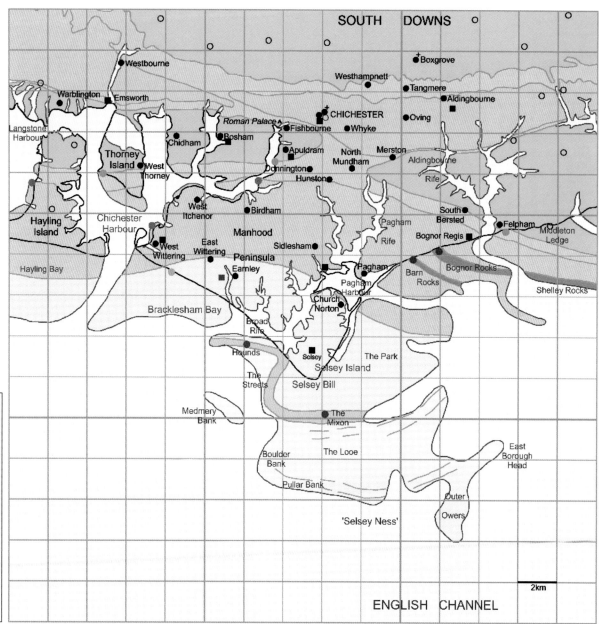

Quaternary  <

Bracklesham Group

Thames Group

Lambeth Group

White Chalk Subgroup

Grey Chalk Subgroup

Selborne Group

Lower Greensand Group

Weald Clay Group

Hastings Group

Purbeck Group

| | |
|---|---|
| **Age** | Pleistocene and Holocene (Recent) Quaternary |
| **Lithostratigraphy** | River Terrace deposits Raised Beach deposits (very minor) |

## Geology

Ferricrete is an iron-rich duricrust produced by iron-oxide and hydroxide cementation of superficial and soil deposits. Quaternary Ferricrete has formed within gravel layers at the base of the lower terraces of Sussex rivers by seasonal percolation of ferruginous water, which on evaporating deposits iron salts, leaving softly-cemented rock. Upnor Conglomerate, a similar rock type, is described on page 60.

Ferricrete occurs as discontinuous layers up to 50cm thick within river terrace gravels of the Arun, Adur, Ouse, and rivers draining into Pevensey and Rye Harbours. Within the Low Weald, Ferricrete deposits contain Hastings Sandstone, Hythe Sandstone and Hythe Chert pebbles, while further south where the rivers cross the chalk outcrop the pebbles are of flint. Ferricrete is occasionally exposed along river banks where the river has recently eroded into former terraces.

## Building Stone
**Alternative Names -**

Iron Pan, Ironstone, Iron-bound Conglomerate, Ragstone, Crowstone, Chevick.

Ferricrete from river terrace deposits is a variably-consolidated, ferruginous conglomerate, breccia or sandstone. It has been used as a rubble building stone along the main river valleys where little other stone was easily available. River terrace, flint-rich Ferricrete is very similar to Upnor Flint Conglomerate from the basal Palaeogene strata of East Sussex, but does not contain green-coated flints.

## Historic Use

| | |
|---|---|
| Roman | Bishopstone building, Pevensey Castle walls. |
| Late Saxon | Reported in Surrey. |
| Medieval | Northiam and Billingshurst churches. |
| 17-18th century | Ferricrete is reported to have been used as low-grade iron ore in the upper Arun valley. |

The tower of Northiam Church is constructed of blocks of Ferricrete quarried from a terrace of the nearby River Rother.

Ferricrete rubble with Weald Clay Sandstone clasts. Billingshurst Church.

Roughly-cut Ferricrete blocks. Pevensey Castle walls.

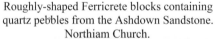
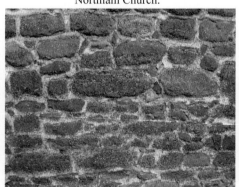

Roughly-shaped Ferricrete blocks containing quartz pebbles from the Ashdown Sandstone. Northiam Church.

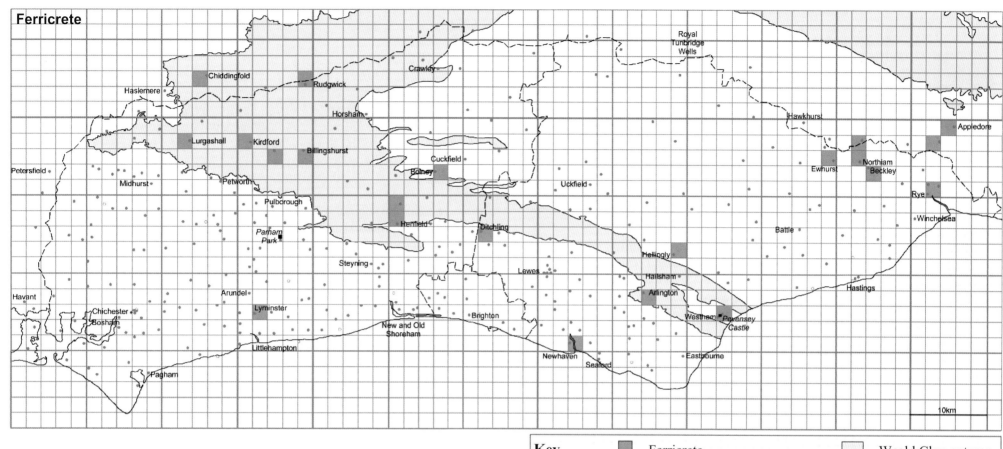

Ferricrete

## Distribution of Ferricrete

Ferricrete use in Medieval Sussex churches shows a widely-dispersed pattern related to 2 physical features:

1. Its distribution is strongly correlated with the Weald Clay outcrop in a *c.* 10km-wide zone extending from Haslemere to Eastbourne. Ferricrete was obtained from the lower river terrace of the main rivers which cross the clay belt of the Low Weald, where there is very little other building stone available locally.

2. Its distribution also relates to the rivers draining into the Rye Levels where it was obtained from the adjacent river terraces. Ferricrete used as a building stone in this area is generally of a more consolidated variety with clasts of fine sandstone and quartz pebbles derived from the Hastings Group. Northiam Church walls contain an abundance of roughly-cut blocks of Ferricrete.

**Key**   ▨ Ferricrete   ▢ Weald Clay outcrop

Ferricrete rubble in Parham Park wall. This building stone was quarried from the lower river terrace of the River Arun. It contains fractured flints and Hythe Sandstone pebbles.

Ferricrete rubble, Beckley Church. The rock includes pebbles of quartz derived from the Hastings Group.

| Quaternary |
|---|
| Bracklesham Group |
| Thames Group |
| Lambeth Group |
| White Chalk Subgroup |
| Grey Chalk Subgroup |
| Selborne Group |
| Lower Greensand Group |
| Weald Clay Group |
| Hastings Group |
| Purbeck Group |

| Age | Quaternary to Precambrian |
|---|---|
| Lithostratigraphy | Not established. Found within: Brighton-Norton Raised Beach Pagham Raised Beach Modern Beaches |

## Geology

Erratics are rocks which have been transported by natural processes from well beyond the area in which they naturally occur. Pebbles and cobbles of a wide range of all classes of rocks are a minor but notable constituent of the predominantly flint gravel beaches which flank the Sussex coastline. Erratic boulders occur along the foreshore and within the Quaternary deposits in the south-west of West Sussex, to the west of Littlehampton, especially around Bracklesham Bay and Chichester Harbour.

Although there is no direct evidence for the origin or mode of transport of Erratics into Sussex, it has often been suggested that they were transported into the area within icebergs during cold Stages of the Pleistocene. Some of the Erratics such as granites and metamorphic rocks appear to match rocks from the Channel Islands and the Cotentin Peninsula in Normandy, while others such as Bunter pebbles, appear to have originated in South West England. Upper Greensand chert from the Isle of Wight has probably been moved eastwards along the coast by longshore drift.

## Building Stone

**Varieties** (most abundant)
Igneous -    Granite, Diorite, Syenite, Dolerite, Gabbro, Vein Quartz.
Metamorphic -  Metasiltstone, Schist, Hornfels, Gneiss, Quartzite.
Sedimentary -  Bunter Sandstone Pebbles, Chert and Cherty Sandstone (Isle of Wight Upper Greensand), Sandstone, Grit, Conglomerate, Sarsen Stone (Chichester Harbour area).

Pebbles and cobbles of Erratics stand out as minor building stones within flint walls in the coastal area of West Sussex. They have mainly been quarried from local beaches but do not appear to have been preferentially selected even though they could have been used to add decoration. Erratic boulders of granite, diorite and schist in the Bracklesham Bay and Chichester Harbour area occur sporadically along the shoreline and have occasionally been used for building in house and garden walls in Selsey village.

## Historic Use

| | |
|---|---|
| Roman | Reported from a number of Roman sites in coastal areas including Fishbourne Roman Palace and Southwick Villa. |
| Medieval | Earnley and West Wittering churches. |
| 18-20th century | House, garden and Victorian church walls located on the West Sussex Coastal Plain, notably in Selsey, Bognor Regis, Worthing and Chichester. |

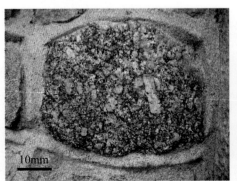
Granite cobble. Hunston Church.

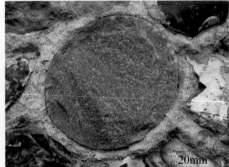
Cleaved Bunter Sandstone pebble. Chichester.

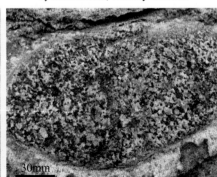
Syenite cobble, Earnley Church.

1m-wide boulder of igneous rock. Selsey High Street.

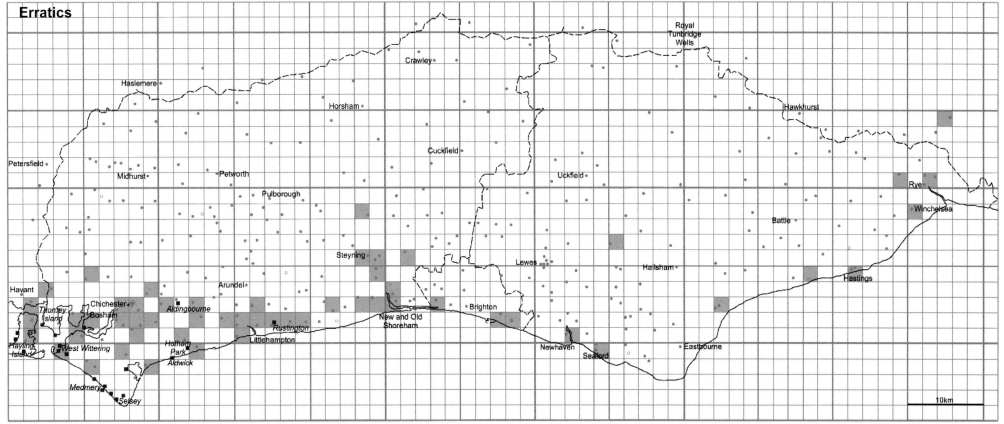

**Erratics**

## Distribution of Erratics

The distribution of Erratic cobbles and pebbles is strongly associated with that of beach flint. Their occurrence in Medieval church walls is concentrated across the West Sussex Coastal Plain particularly in the Chichester Harbour area where they are most abundant in the flint-rich, raised beach and modern beach-gravel. The concentration of Erratics along the lower Adur valley is most likely due to their inclusion in flint gravel brought upriver from beach bar deposits at Lancing and Shoreham Beach. Erratics used as building stones at Rye and the surrounding area were probably quarried with flints from the extensive beach-gravel deposits around Rye Harbour.

East of Selsey Bill beach shingle is transported eastwards along the Sussex coast by the process of longshore drift. This means that erratic pebbles and cobbles are transported along the coastline so they occur, although in lesser numbers, along the East Sussex coast.

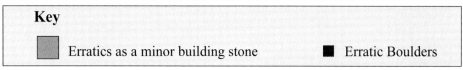

**Key**

Erratics as a minor building stone

■ Erratic Boulders

Erratic boulder of schist with quartz veins displayed in the centre of Rustington.

1m Erratic boulder of porphyritic granite on the foreshore of Chichester Harbour at Snow Hill, West Wittering.

| Quaternary < | | |
|---|---|---|
| **Bracklesham Group** | | |
| **Thames Group** | | |
| **Lambeth Group** | | |
| **White Chalk Subgroup** | | |
| **Grey Chalk Subgroup** | | |
| **Selborne Group** | | |
| **Lower Greensand Group** | | |
| **Weald Clay Group** | | |
| **Hastings Group** | | |
| **Purbeck Group** | | |

| **Age** | Pleistocene and Holocene (Recent) Quaternary |
|---|---|
| **Lithostratigraphy** | Not defined |

## Geology

Travertine or Calcareous Tufa is a very porous, low-density, light-grey limestone deposited from calcareous springs. The term Travertine is sometimes restricted to banded limestone precipitated from hot springs. Deposits of Travertine are of variable thickness and limited in extent, being confined to the immediate area around a spring but they may cover a greater area when the spring issues into a pond. Travertine is forming at the present day in Sussex, at Duncton Mill where springs feeding the millpond issue from the Upper Greensand. Calcium carbonate is more soluble in cold water so that greater amounts of Travertine would have been precipitated around calcareous springs during Cold Stages of the Quaternary.

In Sussex most Travertine has been and is still being deposited by springs emerging from the Upper Greensand, where it forms a bench-like feature, parallel to and just north of the Chalk Escarpment. Travertine deposits have also been recorded around springs issuing from the Horsham Stone south of Horsham and from Sussex Purbeck Limestone in the Burwash area of East Sussex.

## Building Stone
### Alternative Names
Travertine, Calcareous Tufa, Tufa.

Travertine was a much sought-after building stone in Roman and Medieval times due to its light weight and the ease with which it could be carved into ashlar blocks when freshly quarried. When excavated the soft stone slowly hardens upon exposure to the air so it has to be left to mature for up to a year before it can be used. Travertine deposits are confined to the area around calcareous springs therefore supplies were limited and quickly exhausted.

Polished slabs of banded Travertine from the Mediterranean area have been used since Victorian times for ornamental and facing stonework.

## Historic Use

| Roman | Fishbourne Roman Palace, Pulborough and Newhaven Roman buildings. Broomershill Mausoleum near Pulborough. |
|---|---|
| Medieval | Steyning, Burton (near Duncton) and Wilmington churches. Chichester (old walls). |

Travertine ashlar in Steyning Church tower. Photograph right shows chequerwork of Travertine with cleaved flint, Hythe Sandstone and Caen Stone.

Rubble block of travertine at Burton Church, south of Petworth, showing stalactitic structure.

1cm scale

Roughly-squared block of Travertine with included chalk pebble. Steyning Church .

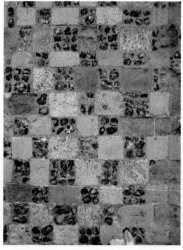

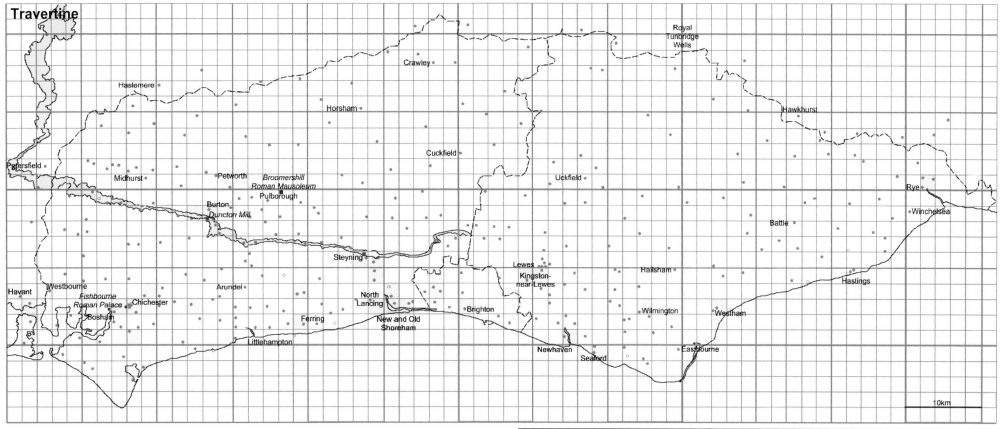

Travertine

## Distribution of Travertine

Travertine is a minor building stone which displays a generally-dispersed distribution across the southern part of Sussex, with concentrations of use particularly in the Chichester area, and the lower Adur valley from Steyning to Shoreham-by Sea.

The large spring emerging from the Malmstone at Duncton Mill is actively depositing Travertine at the present time, and was probably the source of the stone at Burton, Barlavington and East Lavington Churches. It may also have been the source of Travertine of Roman context recorded at Chichester and Fishbourne Roman Palace. The main use of Travertine was in the lower Adur valley, where a considerable amount is visible in Steyning Church tower. The source of this building stone was probably in the adjacent valley immediately to the north of the church. Travertine from this Steyning source was shipped down the River Arun as far as the coast, where it was used in New Shoreham Church.

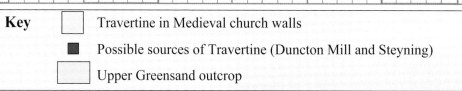

**Key**

☐ Travertine in Medieval church walls

■ Possible sources of Travertine (Duncton Mill and Steyning)

☐ Upper Greensand outcrop

View of the calcareous spring at Duncton Mill, south of Petworth, showing luxuriant growth of hydrophilic plants in the stream bed. The spring-fed stream is strewn with algal-covered blocks of very soft, open-textured Travertine.

| Quaternary |
|---|
| Neogene |
| Palaeogene |
| 66Ma |
| Cretaceous |
| Jurassic |
| Triassic |
| 252Ma |
| Permian |
| Carboniferous |
| Devonian |
| 420Ma |
| Silurian |
| Ordovician |
| Cambrian |
| 541Ma |
| Precambrian |

| | |
|---|---|
| **Age** | Pragian to Emsian |
| | Lower Devonian |
| **Lithostratigraphy** | Meadfoot Group |

## Geology

During the Devonian Period South Devon lay to the south of the Old Red Sandstone continent, which extended north from the Bristol Channel to the Orkney Islands. A warm tropical sea, the Rheic Ocean, covered southern England and central Germany. Faulting across the sea bed created a series of shoals upon which coral reefs developed, with adjacent deeper basins filled with muddy sediments. At the end of the Devonian (*c.* 360Ma), an episode of mountain building known as the Variscan Orogeny, caused by southern Europe moving northwards, metamorphosed the deeply buried sediments. Mudstones belonging to the Meadfoot Group, which extend in an east- to-west belt across the South Hams in the Kingsbridge area were lightly metamorphosed to phyllites, chlorite schists and slates. These rocks have been extensively quarried in the past for roofing slates.

Part of the west elevation of New Shoreham Church (12th century), which was partly rebuilt when the nave, which extended to the west, was removed. The wall shows a section of a former roof-line displaying Devon Slates.

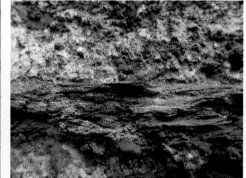

Close-up shows a section of reused Devon Slate in the north wall of New Shoreham Church.

## Building Stone Varieties

Devon Slate - South Devon Slate, Blue Slate, Green Slate.

Devon Slate has been recorded from numerous archaeological excavations of Medieval sites in Sussex, especially near the coast and adjacent to navigable rivers. It has also been recorded from Fishbourne Roman Palace and a number of Roman Villas in West Sussex.

Blue-grey to green-grey roofing slate from South Devon is known as 'Blue Slate'. A small amount of green and lilac-coloured slate described from archaeological excavations in Sussex may be a variety of Devon Slate or possibly Fumay Slate from Belgium, or slate from the Cotentin Peninsula in Normandy. Roofing slate from South Devon is rather soft and prone to weathering, which means the slates need to be relatively thick (in the order of 20mm), to provide long-term wear. With the advent of the railways in the 1840s large quantities of superior, grey roofing-slate from North Wales began to be imported.

## Historic Use

| Roman | Fishbourne Roman Palace, |
|---|---|
| | Bignor and Southwick Roman Villas, and |
| | Chichester buildings. |
| Medieval | New Shoreham Church. |

Considerable quantities of roofing slate were obtained in Medieval times from quarries in the Meadfoot Group strata near Kingsbridge and Torcross, in the South Hams District of South Devon. The Pipe Rolls of 1180 record 800,000 slates sent from Totnes to Winchester Castle and 100,000 to Porchester Castle. Slate from South Devon was shipped westward along the English Channel, and carried as far as London.

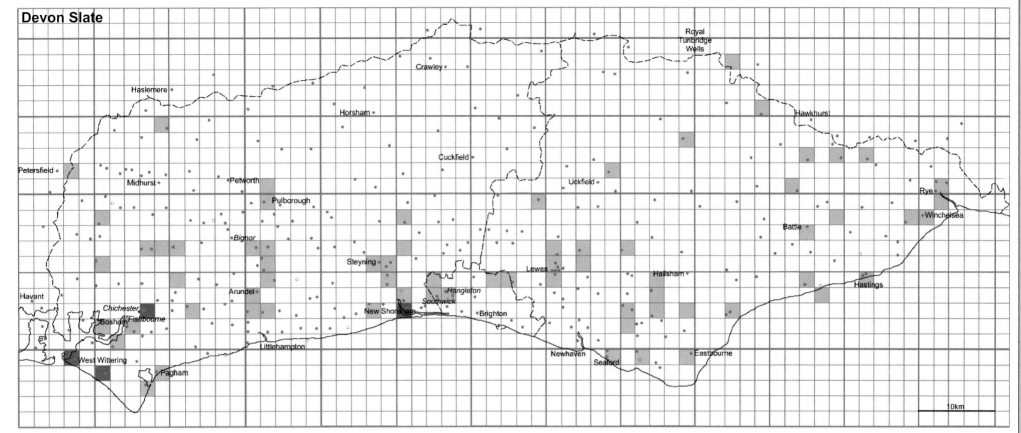

**Devon Slate**

## Distribution of Devon Slate

The map shows the distribution of imported Medieval roofing slate identified as Devon Slate, recorded by Holden (1989) from archaeological excavations, together with records from the Atlas survey of Medieval churches. Roman sites where imported roofing slate has been recorded from archaeological excavations include Chichester, Fishbourne Roman Palace, Southwick Roman Villa and Hangleton.

The concentration of use along the main river valleys indicates that Devon Slate was shipped into ports and estuaries along the Sussex coast, including Chichester Harbour, the Rivers Arun, Adur and Ouse, and the Pevensey and Rother Levels, and then conveyed upriver. There was little utilization of Devon Slate in Medieval times in the High Weald, where Horsham Stone-slate roofing slate was more readily available.

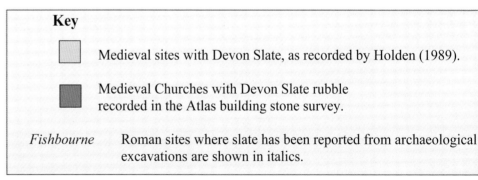

**Key**

Medieval sites with Devon Slate, as recorded by Holden (1989).

Medieval Churches with Devon Slate rubble recorded in the Atlas building stone survey.

*Fishbourne* — Roman sites where slate has been reported from archaeological excavations are shown in italics.

### References

Murray, J. W. 1965. The Origin of some Medieval Roofing Slates from Sussex. *Sussex Archaeological Collections*. **103**. 79-82.
Holden, E. W. 1989. Slate Roofing in Medieval Sussex - an Appraisal. *Sussex Archaeological Collections*. **127**. 73-88.

| Quaternary | 2.6Ma |
|---|---|
| Neogene | |
| | 23Ma |
| Palaeogene | |
| | 66Ma |
| Cretaceous | |
| | 145Ma |
| Jurassic Upper | |
| Middle | |
| Lower | |
| | 201Ma |

| **Age** | Tithonian |
|---|---|
| | Upper Jurassic |
| **Lithostratigraphy** | Base Bed, Whit Bed and Roach |
| | Portland Stone Formation |
| | Portland Group |

## Geology

The Portland Group consist of massive limestones, sandstones and marl deposited in a warm shallow marine environment at the end of the Jurassic about 150 million years ago. In its outcrop in Dorset and South Wiltshire the Portland Group has been divided into 2 Formations, the Portland Stone Formation and the underlying Portland Sandstone Formation, both of which are up to 38m thick in the Isle of Portland.

In its type area of the Isle of Portland the Portland Stone Formation underlies a gently southward-dipping plateau surface. It also crops out along the south coast of the Isle of Purbeck where it was quarried in the area between Worth Matravers and Durlston Head. The Portland Stone Formation can be traced north into Wiltshire where the limestone beds become progressively thinner.

## Building Stone
### Varieties
Dorset, Isle of Portland - Base Bed, Whit Bed and Roach
Wiltshire -             Chilmark Stone, Wardour Stone, Tisbury Stone

Portland Stone is a massive, white to light-grey, often oolitic, limestone calcarenite. It is a high-quality building stone extensively used across the United Kingdom from the late-17th century, and also widely exported. The best building stone comes from the Whit and Base Beds.

**Chilmark Stone**, a variety of Portland Stone from quarries near Chilmark in Wiltshire is a slightly arenaceous limestone containing small amounts of glauconite. It typically shows sections of the large bivalve *Trigonia*.

## Historic Use

| Roman | Fishbourne Roman Palace (very small-scale use). |
|---|---|
| Medieval | Seaford Church (minor rubble). Rare in Sussex. |
| Late-17 to 18th centuries | Petworth and Goodwood Houses. |
| 19 -20th centuries | Lewes Law Courts, Worthing Town Hall. |

Portland Stone campanile, St Johns Chapel, Chichester, built 1812. The church is 'almost unique in its unaltered extreme Low Church plan.'

John Edes House, Chichester. A fine town house, built 1696, with Portland Stone dressings.

Petworth House, west facade, built by the 6th Duke of Somerset in the 1690s. The house is constructed mainly of Hythe Sandstone, with a central section (on the left) of Portland Stone.

Detail of finely-moulded Portland Stone carving, Petworth House, dating from the 1690s. The window frames are also of Portland Stone.

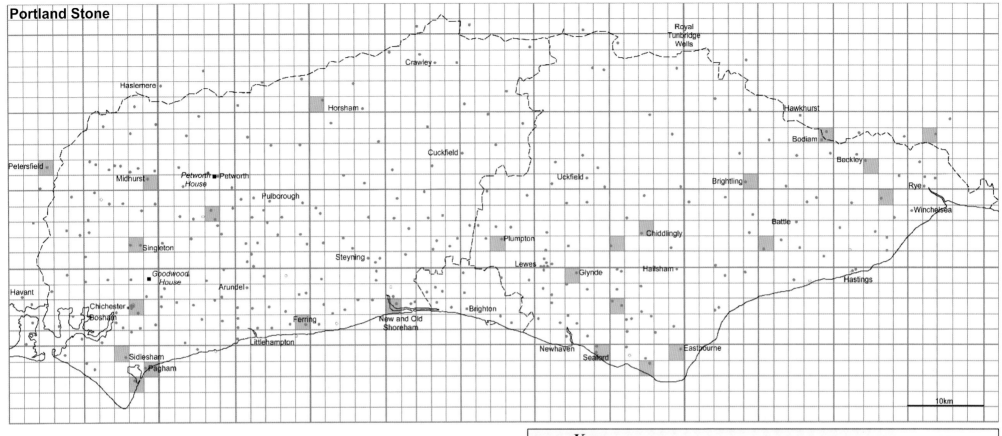

**Portland Stone**

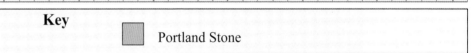

**Key**

Portland Stone

## Distribution of Portland Stone

Portland Stone is one of the finest-quality building stones from the South of England but it appears to have been little used, if at all, as a building stone in Sussex during Medieval times. The map shows a dispersed distribution for this building stone, much of it being used for 19th and 20th century repairs to decayed stonework. It is possible that occasional rubble blocks, in old walls in the Chichester area, could date from Medieval times or even be reused Roman building stone.

## Portland Stone in Sussex

Quarrying of Portland Stone during Roman and Medieval times was on a small scale compared to the Purbeck Stone industry. In Sussex small amounts of Portland Stone from a Roman context have been recorded at Chichester, Fishbourne Roman Palace and Bignor Roman Villa. This stone was however widely used for querns and mortars.

Large-scale use of Portland Stone began in the late-1660s after the Great Fire of London with the construction of many prestigious buildings such as St. Paul's Cathedral built under the direction of Sir Christopher Wren. Portland Stone began to be imported into Sussex in the late-17th century for specialist work e.g. columns and mouldings in grand houses, including those at Petworth House and Goodwood House.

Portland Stone was imported into Sussex on a much larger scale after the coming of the railways in the mid-19th c., as seen in many imposing buildings, such as Banks. This use has continued to the present day, mainly as cladding for large buildings in many towns and cities including Banks and Post Offices e.g., the facade of the Law Courts in Lewes (1936) and Worthing Main Post Office.

| | |
|---|---|
| **Age** | Berriasian and Tithonian<br>Lower Cretaceous / Upper Jurassic |
| **Lithostratigraphy** | Durlston and Lulworth Formations<br>Purbeck Group |

## Geology

The Purbeck Group of Dorset consists of beds of limestone and shale deposited in a shallow sea and lagoons adjacent to a low-lying coast. The climate of Southern England, at this time, was hot and dry, similar to that around the present-day Persian Gulf. These strata were deposited at the end of the Jurassic / beginning of the Cretaceous Period about 145 million years ago. Precise dating of these beds is difficult due to the lack of marine fossils, with the Jurassic-Cretaceous boundary now placed in the lower part of the Durlston Formation. The main building stones occur within the upper and middle parts of the Durlston Formation, named after the classic exposure in Durlston Bay, south of Swanage.

## Building Stone

Over 20 varieties each with its own provincial name and often specific use were recognised by quarrymen in the past. Uses include roughly-cut wall stone, paving stone, kerb-stones, memorials, ledgers, decorative stone and roofing stone.

Purbeck Limestone building stone is typically a finely-bedded to massive light-grey rock, often packed with the small freshwater bivalve *Neomiodon*. It was used from Roman times in Dorset, but little was exported before the 16th century, with the major exception of a number of ornamental stones which take a high polish, such as Purbeck Marble, Unio Marble and Thornback (see page 86).

## Historic Use

| | |
|---|---|
| Roman | Fishbourne, Roman building (reported). |
| Medieval | Not recorded. |
| 17th-20th century | Lewes, Chichester, Arundel Castle and town.<br>West Wittering and Fishbourne churches (walling). |

Purbeck Limestone paving.
The Pallant, Chichester.

**Right**
Purbeck Limestone paving, kerbstones and gutter stones, Arundel.
**Below**
Isolated block of Purbeck Limestone rubble showing bedding surface packed with fossil bivalve shells.
Pagham Church.

Roughly-cut blocks of Purbeck Limestone used for stone replacement. West Wittering Church.

Quaternary — 2.6Ma
Neogene — 23Ma
Palaeogene — 66Ma
Cretaceous — 145Ma
Jurassic Upper / Middle / Lower — 201Ma

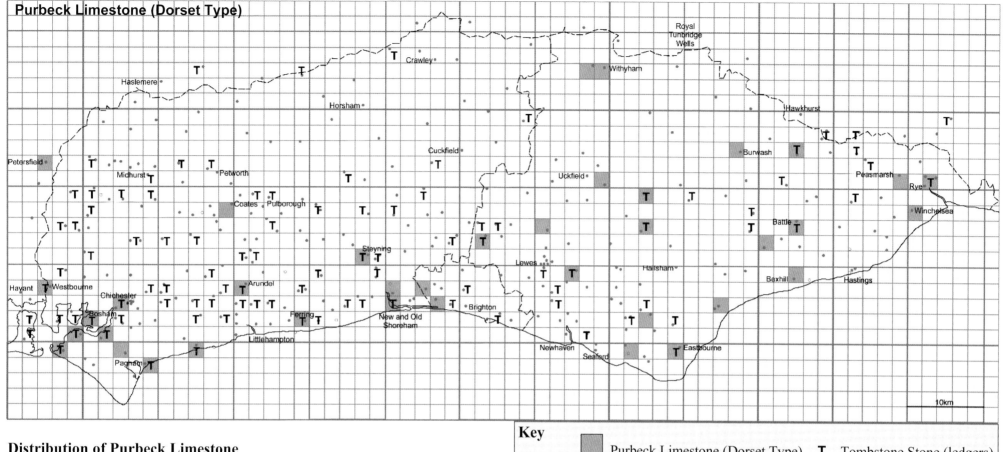

Purbeck Limestone (Dorset Type)

*(map labels, reading across the region)*

Royal Tunbridge Wells · Haslemere · Crawley · Withyham · Horsham · Hawkhurst · Cuckfield · Burwash · Petersfield · Midhurst · Petworth · Uckfield · Peasmarsh · Rye · Winchelsea · Coates · Pulborough · Battle · Steyning · Lewes · Hailsham · Bexhill · Hastings · Havant · Westbourne · Chichester · Arundel · Bosham · Ferring · New and Old Shoreham · Brighton · Littlehampton · Newhaven · Seaford · Eastbourne · Pagham

10km

## Distribution of Purbeck Limestone

Purbeck Limestone from Dorset shows a scattered distribution mainly across the southern part of Sussex, with much of it imported during the 19th and 20th centuries for paving slabs, kerbstones and stone replacement. Although this building stone was shipped as far as London in Medieval times, little if any appears to have been used in Sussex during this period.

Tombstone Stone (**T** on the map), a light-ochre limestone which takes a fine polish, was obtainable in large slabs. It was widely imported for ledgers set into the floor of many churches in Southern Sussex during the 17th and 18th centuries.

**Key**

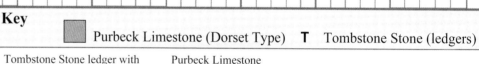

Purbeck Limestone (Dorset Type)   **T** Tombstone Stone (ledgers)

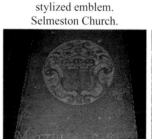

Tombstone Stone ledger with stylized emblem. Selmeston Church.

Purbeck Limestone memorial slab dated 1698. Arundel Church path.

Blocks of freshly-quarried Purbeck Limestone. Lander's Quarry, Langton Matravers, Dorset.

| | |
|---|---|
| **Age** | Berriasian |
| | Lower Cretaceous |
| **Lithostratigraphy** | Durlston Formation |
| | Purbeck Group |

### Geology

Purbeck Marble is a dark-coloured, shelly, freshwater limestone from the Isle of Purbeck in Dorset. Three separate beds of Purbeck Marble, each up to 50cm thick, occur near the top of the Durlston Formation at Peveril Point, Swanage. The rock is closely packed with masses of a small (10mm size) species of the freshwater gastropod *Viviparus,* formerly known as *Paludina,* a smaller-size species than that in Sussex Marble. Purbeck Marble was deposited in extensive, shallow freshwater lakes in which pond snails thrived in large numbers.

Beds of Unio Marble containing the large freshwater bivalve *Unio*, and Thornback, with dark-coloured fossil oyster shells, underlie the Purbeck Marble beds.

### Building Stone
### Alternative Names and Varieties

Purbeck Marble - Small Paludina Limestone, Paludina Limestone. Other ornamental limestones include - Unio Marble and Thornback.

Purbeck Marble and the similar Unio Marble and Thornback are all shelly limestones which are popularly referred to as 'Marbles' as they all take a high polish. These limestones were used for ornamental work in Roman times and then on a large scale from the late-12th to 16th centuries. They are only suitable for interior work as they are prone to weathering when exposed to the elements. In Medieval times Purbeck Marble was a very desirable ornamental stone which was used for polished flooring, columns, shafts, bases, capitals, altars, tomb stones, ledgers and ornately-carved canopy tombs. It is present in cathedrals and churches as far north as Durham.

### Historic Use

| | |
|---|---|
| Roman | Fishbourne Roman Palace. |
| Medieval | Chichester Cathedral, Battle Abbey. |
| Modern | Chichester Cathedal, Slaugham Church. |

Drum-section column with capital and base. West Wittering Church.

Early 13th century crocket capital. Chichester Cathedral.

Octagonal font of a traditional Norman design. Bosham Church.

Chest tomb of Sir Roger Lewkenor, d. 1478. The sides of the tomb are made of 2m-long slabs of Purbeck Marble. Trotton Church.

Left column geological timescale:

Quaternary — 2.6Ma
Neogene — 23Ma
Palaeogene — 66Ma
Cretaceous — 145Ma
Jurassic Upper / Middle / Lower — 201Ma

# Purbeck Marble

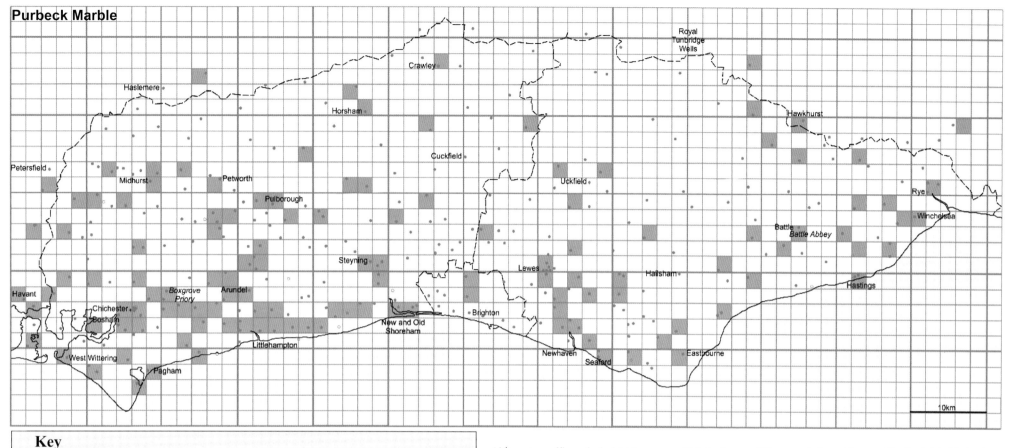

## Key

| | |
|---|---|
| ▨ | Purbeck Marble including Unio Marble and Thornback |

## Distribution of Purbeck Marble

Purbeck Marble is widely distributed throughout the Medieval churches of Sussex to the extent that most churches would at one time have displayed memorials of this stone. Ready-cut and highly-polished stonework was prepared at the Marblers' Workshop at Corfe Castle in the Isle of Purbeck, and was shipped to ports along the Sussex coast for distribution further inland. Many Purbeck Marble memorials and altar slabs were destroyed during the Dissolution and the Civil War; the shattered stone was often later reused in church walls. In churches near the coast including West Wittering and Chichester Cathedral, larger blocks of Purbeck Marble for bases, columns and capitals, were manufactured during the 13th century.

13th century effigy of a knight in armour. This basic design was either ordered from the Marblers' workshop in London, or more probably, from the workshop at Corfe in Dorset.

Pillars, capitals and bases of Purbeck Marble in the magnificently-vaulted undercroft which was the Novices Common Room, Battle Abbey.

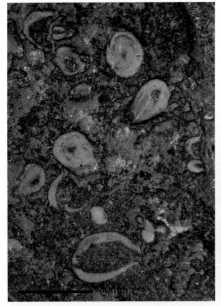

Polished slab of Purbeck Marble displaying sections of well-preserved *Viviparus*. Haysom's Quarry, Langton Matravers, Dorset.

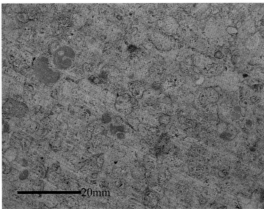

Cut slab of Purbeck Marble with iron-stained infill in some of the fossil *Viviparus* shells. Haysom's Quarry, Langton Matravers, Dorset.

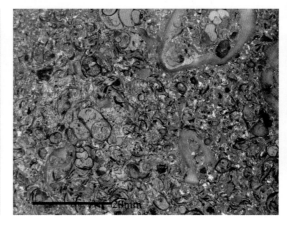

Polished slab of Unio Marble showing sections of the freshwater bivalve *Unio,* together with *Viviparus* and masses of minute Ostracods. Haysom's Quarry, Langton Matravers, Dorset.

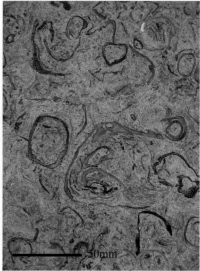

Polished slab of Thornback Marble displaying sections of black-stained fossil oyster shells. Haysom's Quarry, Langton Matravers, Dorset.

Unio Marble showing sections of the thick-shelled bivalve, *Unio.* Chichester Cathedral.

Purbeck Marble floor tiling showing the decorative use of different colour varieties. Nave floor Chichester Cathedral.

Purbeck Marble rubble in exterior wall showing considerable surface weathering. The rubble stone seen in church walls has mainly been derived from destroyed memorials and altar slabs. Rye Church.

Purbeck Marble calcarenite composed of shattered *Viviparus* shells. Surface of a shaft, Chichester Cathedral.

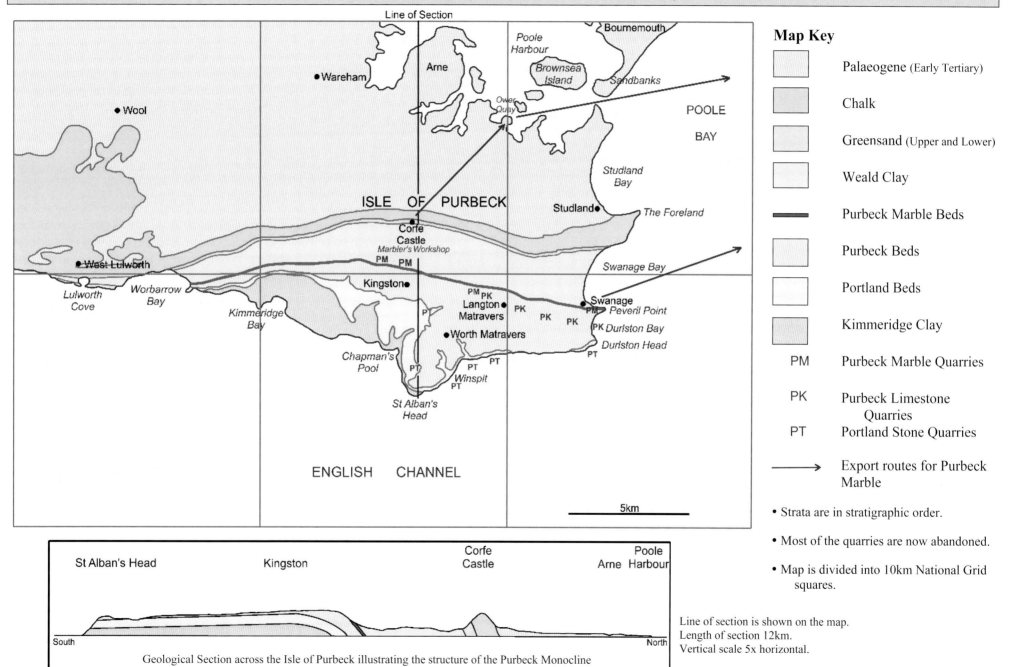

## ISLE OF PURBECK - GEOLOGY AND STONE QUARRIES

Line of Section

Bournemouth

Poole Harbour

Brownsea Island

Sandbanks

Arne

• Wareham

Ower Quay

POOLE

BAY

• Wool

Studland Bay

ISLE OF PURBECK

Studland•

The Foreland

Corfe Castle

Marbler's Workshop

PM   PM

• West Lulworth

Swanage Bay

Kingston•

Worbarrow Bay

Lulworth Cove

PM PK

Langton• Matravers

PK

Swanage

Peveril Point

Kimmeridge Bay

PK   PK

PK Durlston Bay

P

•Worth Matravers

Durlston Head

Chapman's Pool

PT

PT   PT

Winspit

PT

PT

St Alban's Head

ENGLISH   CHANNEL

5km

**Map Key**

Palaeogene (Early Tertiary)

Chalk

Greensand (Upper and Lower)

Weald Clay

Purbeck Marble Beds

Purbeck Beds

Portland Beds

Kimmeridge Clay

PM   Purbeck Marble Quarries

PK   Purbeck Limestone Quarries

PT   Portland Stone Quarries

→   Export routes for Purbeck Marble

• Strata are in stratigraphic order.

• Most of the quarries are now abandoned.

• Map is divided into 10km National Grid squares.

St Alban's Head

Kingston

Corfe Castle

Poole Arne Harbour

South

North

Geological Section across the Isle of Purbeck illustrating the structure of the Purbeck Monocline

Line of section is shown on the map.
Length of section 12km.
Vertical scale 5x horizontal.

| Age | Aptian |
| --- | --- |
| | Lower Cretaceous |
| **Lithostratigraphy** | Hythe Formation |
| | Lower Greensand Group |

Quaternary

Bracklesham Group

Thames Group

Lambeth Group

White Chalk Subgroup

Grey Chalk Subgroup

Selborne Group

Lower Greensand Group

Weald Clay Group

Hastings Group

Purbeck Group

## Geology

In West Sussex the Hythe Formation is composed mainly of sandstone, but along its outcrop in Kent, from Maidstone to the Channel coast at Hythe, much of this Formation is composed of beds of hard grey limestone (Rag or Ragstone), alternating with beds of soft sand and sandstone (Hassock). The Hythe Formation of Kent varies from 10 to 20m in thickness, becoming thicker towards the west where very gently-dipping strata form an 8km-wide plateau south of Maidstone. Kentish Ragstone was quarried on a large scale in Medieval times in the Maidstone area where beds of Ragstone range from 20 to 60cm in thickness. The limestone includes beds of chert and cherty sandstone, fossils are relatively rare but sections of the large fossil oyster, *Exogyra latissima,* are visible in some blocks of building stone.

## Building Stone

During Medieval times Kentish Ragstone was one of the most important building stones in Kent and London. It was only used on a very small scale in the east of East Sussex. It is a tough, grey to blue-grey, sandy limestone containing *c.* 85% calcite present as small crystals, together with quartz and scattered glauconite grains. Veins and beds of chert occur within some of the rock.

Kentish Ragstone was often prepared as roughly-cut and cleaved blocks with a rock-faced surface. Its dense texture makes it a noticeably heavy rock with a specific gravity of 2.7. The better quality stone develops a hard protective crust, but the partly-weathered stone from the upper part of a quarry is liable to exfoliate where exposed to the elements. The harder stone was commonly used as a crushed aggregate for road-stone. Hermitage Quarry near Maidstone is now the only full-time working quarry.

## Historic Use
Quarrying began in Roman times in the Maidstone area of Kent, from whence the stone was shipped down the River Medway and round to London.

| Roman | London city walls. |
| --- | --- |
| Medieval | Seaford and Iden churches. Dover Castle keep (Kent). |
| Victorian and | Eastbourne (Methodist, 1907), Bexhill (RC. 1907), |
| Edwardian | Polegate (St John's, 1874), Worthing (Tabernacle, 1896) and Littlehampton (St Catherine's R.C. 1862-1904). |

Castellated tower of St Mary's R.C. Church (1907), Bexhill. The walls show a tessellated pattern of various sizes of ashlar blocks.

Cleaved chert nodule, Seaford Church. This is an unusual rock type in the Seaford area and may be from Kentish Ragstone, or an Erratic.

Kentish Ragstone rubble. Seaford Church.

Kentish Ragstone quoin, Stone-in-Oxney Church, Kent, close to the East Sussex county border.

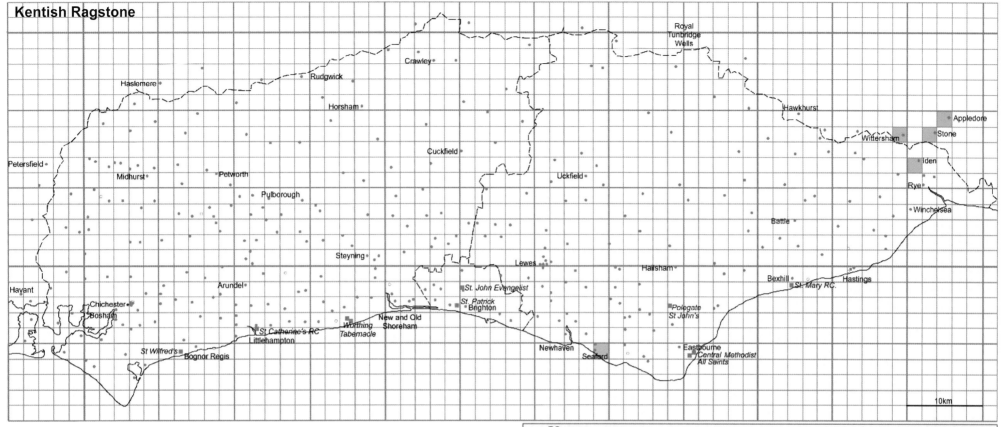

**Kentish Ragstone**

**Key**

Kentish Ragstone — A selection of Victorian and Edwardian churches constructed of Kentish Ragstone are named in italics.

## Distribution of Kentish Ragstone

Kentish Ragstone is a very common Medieval building stone in Kent but was little used in Sussex during this period. This was due to easier access to Hastings Sandstone within the High Weald, as well as the difficulty of transporting stone south across the intervening Low Weald. Its use in Medieval churches is confined to the far east of East Sussex in the Rye area, where it is recorded at Iden Church. Kentish Ragstone used here and in churches at Wittersham, Stone in Oxney and Appledore adjacent to the East Sussex border in Kent, may have been brought around the coast by ship, as there are records of its use at Dover Castle. It may also have been transported overland from quarries in the Ashford area *c.* 20km to the north-east.

Kentish Ragstone was used in the late-19th to early-20th centuries in the construction of churches at Bognor Regis, Littlehampton, Worthing, Brighton, Eastbourne and Bexhill.

Quoins to a buttress at Iden Church are provisionally identified as a Variety of green Kentish Ragstone from the Hythe area.

Eastbourne Central Methodist Church (1907), constructed of Kentish Ragstone ashlar blocks of various sizes, with Portland Stone dressings.

**Superficial Deposits**

**Bracklesham Group**

**Thames Group**

**Lambeth Group**

**White Chalk Subgroup**

**Grey Chalk Subgroup**

**Selborne Group** <

**Lower Greensand Group**

**Weald Clay Group**

**Hastings Group**

**Purbeck Group**

| Age | Albian<br>Lower Cretaceous |
|---|---|
| **Lithostratigraphy** | Freestones Beds<br>Upper Greensand Formation<br>Selborne Group |

## Geology

During the Albian Stage of the Lower Cretaceous (113-100Ma) the sea which covered South East England was separated into 2 basins by a land ridge which extended across the south of Sussex. Upper Greensand strata in the northern basin are of Malmstone facies (see page 42), while glauconitic sandstone with beds of chert is the major rock type in the southern basin, which includes the Isle of Wight, and the Eastbourne area of East Sussex.

The Upper Greensand is *c.* 35m thick in the Ventnor area of the Isle of Wight where sandstones include the 1-2m thick Freestone Beds, which lie below the Chert Beds in the upper part of the Formation. Fossils are common including long straight serpulid tubes and bivalve shells. Small, brown phosphatic nodules lie scattered within the rock.

## Building Stone
### Alternative Names and Varieties
Ventnor Stone - Green Ventnor Stone
Bonchurch Stone

**Ventnor Stone** is a massive, glauconitic sandstone. Because it is loosely cemented it is prone to weathering in exposed positions; over time the surface exfoliates and falls away in thin layers. Because the rock is soft it was easy to carve and shape into window mouldings and large blocks. Quarrying of this stone ceased in the mid-20th century. Ventnor Stone is similar to Eastbourne Stone, for which it can easily be mistaken.

**Bonchurch Stone** was quarried from the Freestone Beds in the Bonchurch area to the north of Ventnor. It is a tough grey sandstone, much more resistant to weathering than Ventnor Stone, and was commonly used as a coping-stone on walls.

## Historic Use

| | |
|---|---|
| Roman | Fishbourne Roman Palace. |
| Norman | Bosham and West Wittering churches. |
| Later Medieval | Chichester Cathedral Bell Tower, Coombes Ch. |
| 18-20th century | Westbourne and Chichester (Bonchurch Stone eg. Canon Lane). |

Ventnor Stone ashlar used in the walls of the late-14th c. Bell Tower of Chichester Cathedral

Bonchurch Stone used for triangular capstones along a wall at Westbourne Church.

Surface of a block of Ventnor Stone showing brown phosphatic nodules and fossil shell. West Wittering Church.

**Right**

16th c. window, with tracery of Ventnor Stone. Coombes Church, Lower Adur Valley.

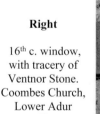

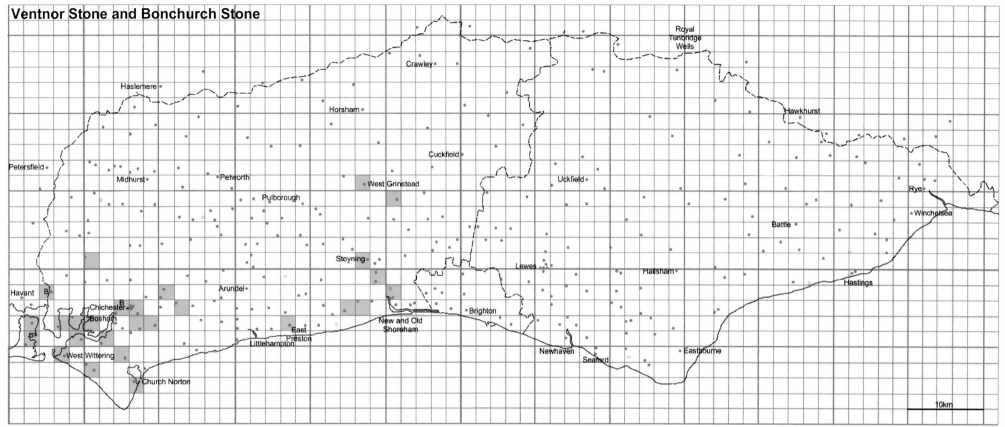

**Ventnor Stone and Bonchurch Stone**

## Distribution of Ventnor Stone

During Medieval times Ventnor Stone was shipped from coastal quarries at Ventnor on the south-east coast of the Isle of Wight into Chichester Harbour and the River Adur estuary. Its use is strongly concentrated within *c*. 10km of Dell Quay, the port for Chichester. One of the most important building projects in Ventnor Stone in Sussex was the construction of the late-14th century Bell Tower of Chichester Cathedral. Its greatest penetration inland was some 18km up the River Adur where it was used at West Grinstead and Shermanbury churches. Soft glauconitic sandstone used as a building stone east of the River Adur in the Brighton and Hove area has been mapped as Eastbourne Stone but could be Ventnor Stone.

An isolated use of Ventnor Stone was for the former spire of East Preston Church which was dismantled in 1961, with some stone reused in a nearby cottage wall.

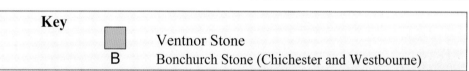

**Key**

Ventnor Stone

B  Bonchurch Stone (Chichester and Westbourne)

Ventnor Stone Ashlar showing the effects of weathering which has caused flaking of the stone surface. Singleton Church.

| Quaternary |
| Bracklesham Group |
| Thames Group |
| Lambeth Group |
| White Chalk Subgroup |
| Grey Chalk Subgroup |
| Selborne Group |
| Lower Greensand Group |
| Weald Clay Group |
| Hastings Group |
| Purbeck Group |

| **Age** | Albian |
| | Lower Cretaceous |
| | |
| **Lithostratigraphy** | Upper Greensand Formation |
| | Selborne Group |

## Geology

The Upper Greensand of the Reigate area in Surrey consists of up to 20m of sand and silt with harder siliceous beds of Firestone, and softer beds of Hearthstone in the middle and upper part of the Formation. Beds of Reigate Stone within these strata provided an important building stone in the past in Surrey and the London area. The building stone beds extend for about 10km along the Upper Greensand outcrop between Brockham, Reigate and Godstone; east of Godstone the Upper Greensand becomes thinner and dies out completely east of Limpsfield.

Reigate Stone is a soft, grey to blue-grey, silty sandstone with small amounts of calcite, amorphous silica and scattered glauconite grains. Reigate Stone can be distinguished from similar Upper Greensand sandstones by the presence of small flakes of muscovite mica. Macrofossils are rare apart from burrow structures, but minute sponge spicules are abundant in some of the building stone.

## Building Stone
### Varieties and Alternative Names

Reigate Stone, Freestone of Reigate, Merstham Stone.
Firestone (for furnace linings), Hearthstone (for whitening hearths).

Reigate Stone is one of a number of similar building stones from the Upper Greensand Formation in southeast England, including Malmstone, Eastbourne Stone and Ventnor Stone. Reigate Stone is easily carved and could be obtained in large blocks, making it an ideal stone for intricate window tracery, and even statues. Because it has a soft, open texture with little calcite cement it is prone to weathering in exposed positions.

## Historic Use

| Roman | Not recorded from Sussex. Used in London. |
| Late-Saxon | Not recorded from Sussex. Used in Surrey and London e. g.Westminster Abbey (1050s). |
| Medieval | Crawley, Iden, Peasmarsh and Playden churches. |

Reigate Stone was a very important building stone in Medieval times in Surrey and Kent, but only used to a very minor extent in Sussex. It was transported to London in wagons from quarries and mines located between Reigate and Godstone. This building stone was shipped from London along the north Kent coast as far east as Canterbury and possibly to the Rye area in the far east of East Sussex.

**Right**

A simple window architrave in Reigate Stone. This building stone is easily carved and was commonly used for window and door surrounds. Crawley Church.

Weathered ashlar block of Reigate Stone showing typical exfoliation of the surface. Crawley Church.

Reigate Stone rubble at Charlwood Church, close to the West Sussex border in Surrey.

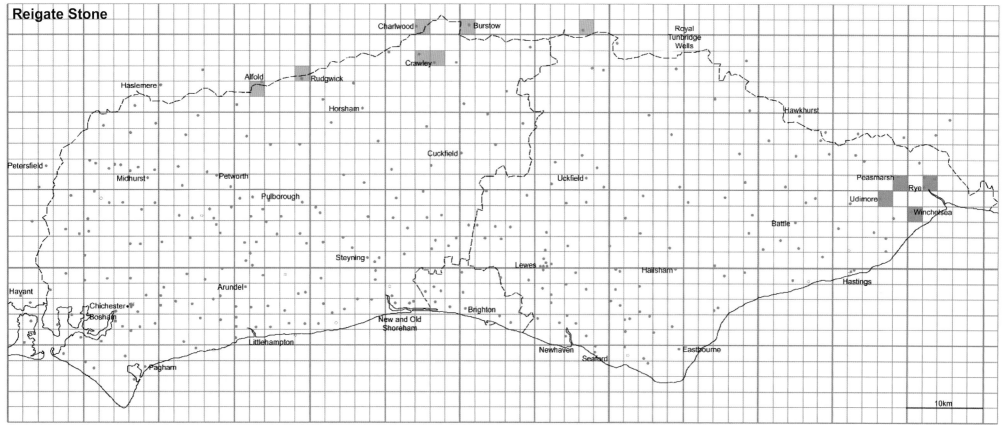

**Reigate Stone**

## Distribution of Reigate Stone

Reigate Stone is found in a few churches in the north of West Sussex located close to the Surrey border, and also possibly in the Rye area. It was quarried and mined along the outcrop of the Upper Greensand in the Reigate-to-Godstone area, about 10km north of the West Sussex border. Transport of this stone by wagon south across the Low Weald from Reigate was arduous in Medieval times which accounts for the absence of Reigate Stone south of Crawley in West Sussex. Reigate Stone has previously been reported at Alfold and Rudgwick churches (shown on the map), but was not recorded during the present survey.

A calcareous, glauconitic sandstone recorded during the Atlas survey in the Rye area in the far east of East Sussex has been recorded as Reigate Stone, but could be a variety of Kentish Ragstone. Reigate Stone is present in Medieval buildings in Canterbury and may have been shipped westwards along the Channel coast as far as the Cinque Ports of Rye and Winchelsea.

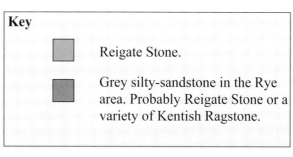

**Key**

| | |
|---|---|
| | Reigate Stone. |
| | Grey silty-sandstone in the Rye area. Probably Reigate Stone or a variety of Kentish Ragstone. |

16th century window tracery in Reigate Stone at Burstow Church, Surrey, close to the West Sussex border. Although this stone lends itself to intricate carved detail it is prone to weathering in exposed positions so that much original exterior work in Medieval churches has had to be replaced.

Superficial Deposits

Bracklesham Group

Thames Group

Lambeth Group

White Chalk Subgroup <

Grey Chalk Subgroup

Selborne Group

Lower Greensand Group

Weald Clay Group

Hastings Group

Purbeck Group

| Age | Turonian |
|---|---|
| | Upper Cretaceous |
| **Lithostratigraphy** | Holywell Nodular Chalk Formation |
| | White Chalk Subgroup |
| | Chalk Group |

## Geology

The chalk of East Devon is a much thinner, condensed sequence than that in Sussex. It is composed of hardgrounds, bioclastic limestones and sands, deposited in a shallow sea close to the former land area of Cornubia to the west.

Beer Stone comes from a 4 to 5m thick bed of massive calcarenite within the lower part of the White Chalk Subgroup, where it crops out over a small area near Beer in East Devon. Like Lavant Stone (page 52), it was formed as a hardground over a relatively restricted area of shallow sea floor where the sea bed was subject to currents which carried away the finer chalky sediment, to leave a gritty limestone composed of comminuted shell debris.

## Building Stone

### Varieties and Alternative Names

Sutton Stone, Sutton Freestone (from quarries 12km north of Beer).

Beer Stone is a massive, gritty, cream-to-grey-coloured calcarenite, which was easily cut when freshly quarried and could be obtained in large blocks. It was often used for interior work as the stone is prone to weathering. Although Beer Stone has a similar texture to other gritty chalk building stones such as Lavant Stone, with which it can be mistaken, Beer Stone often contains small rounded quartz grains.

## Historic Use

| Medieval | Chichester Cathedral (reported), |
|---|---|
| | Amberley Castle, Porchester Castle (Hants.), |
| | New Shoreham, Steyning, Rye and Udimore churches. |

Beer Stone was first quarried and mined near Beer in East Devon in Roman times. During Medieval times it was widely used in southern England, including ashlar at Winchester Cathedral; the first records of its use in London date from the 14th century. Production ceased *c.* 1910 due to the difficulty and expense of extracting the stone from adits driven into the hillside.

13th c. Beer Stone arch above Sussex Marble pillars. Amberley Castle (Hotel).

Weathered Norman Beer Stone ashlar. Udimore Church.

Close-up showing the gritty texture of Beer Stone. New Shoreham (St Mary de Haura) Church.

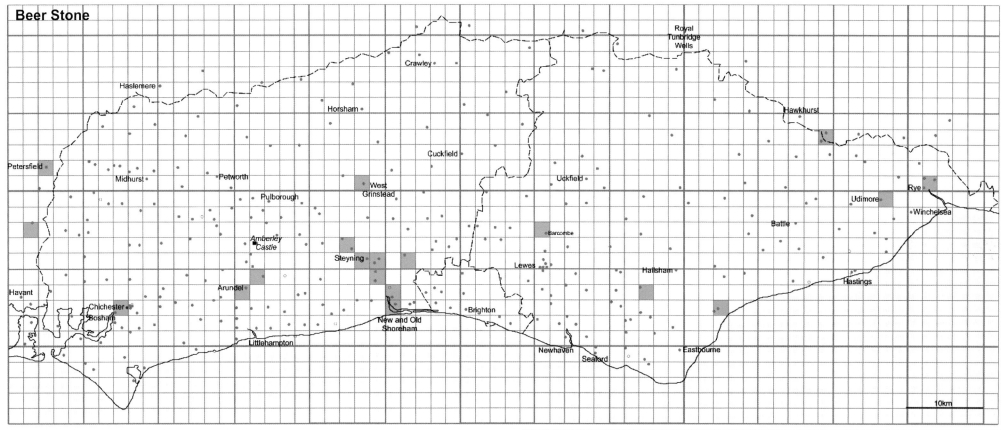

**Beer Stone**

## Distribution of Beer Stone

Beer Stone is a minor building stone, and where present in Medieval church walls occurs as isolated rubble blocks. Its distribution is probably more extensive than shown as this building stone may not always have been recognised. Beer Stone is mainly found in Medieval churches along the lower courses of the river valleys. The stone was shipped from East Devon into Sussex ports, particularly those along the lower Adur valley.

## Beer Stone and Lavant Stone

Beer Stone and Lavant Stone are both gritty varieties of Chalk: Lavant Stone contains numerous minute sponge spicules and scattered phosphate grains, while Beer Stone is not phosphatic and often includes small scattered quartz grains.

**Key**

Beer Stone

Beer Stone in the south wall of Branscombe Church, East Devon, 3km west of Beer. This building stone includes small rounded quartz grains.

Plaque of Beer Stone at the entrance to the Beer Stone Caves shows that it can be sharply carved. Mining of Beer Stone dates from Roman times.

# 34 QUARR STONE

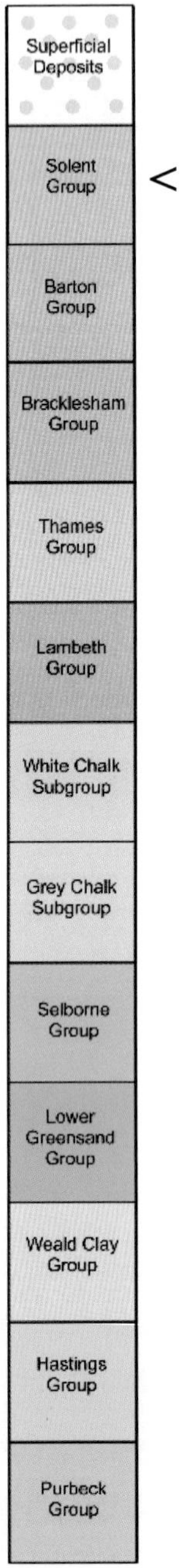
Superficial Deposits
Solent Group
<
Barton Group
Bracklesham Group
Thames Group
Lambeth Group
White Chalk Subgroup
Grey Chalk Subgroup
Selborne Group
Lower Greensand Group
Weald Clay Group
Hastings Group
Purbeck Group

| | |
|---|---|
| **Age** | Eocene<br>Palaeogene (Early Tertiary) |
| **Lithostratigraphy** | Bembridge Limestone Formation or<br>Ryde Formation<br>Solent Group |

The stratigraphic position of Quarr Stone is problematic as the ancient quarries from which the stone was obtained have been backfilled and built-over. Quarr Stone has been referred to a variety of Bembridge Limestone but it may have been obtained from the underlying St Helens Member, the uppermost division of the strata formerly known as the Osborne Beds.

## Geology

Quarr Stone is a void-rich, freshwater, limestone calcarenite composed of coarsely-layered broken fossil shell debris, which formerly cropped out over a limited area within the Binstead Valley *c.* 2km west of Ryde, in the Isle of Wight. It was deposited towards the end of the Eocene (*c.* 34Ma). Its lithology suggests it was formed in a high-energy environment within a wide channel cut into underlying strata. Blocks of Binstead Stone (see page 100), in Victorian buildings in Ryde and Newport contain thin layers of Quarr Stone, indicating that both rocks are intimately associated.

The crushed-shell matrix of Quarr Stone is mainly composed of 10-20cm size fragments of fossil shells of the freshwater snail *Viviparus.* Other fossils include rich-brown, rolled fragments of turtle bone. Sections of the crushed shells along the bedding plane have the appearance of feathers, hence the alternative name Featherbed Stone.

## Building Stone

**Alternative name**

Quarr Stone, Featherbed Stone.

Quarr Stone is a pale-grey to buff-coloured, coarse-textured, freshwater calcarenite with cm-size shell fragments. It provided high quality ashlar for early Norman buildings close to the south coast, in London, and as far north as Norwich. Quarr Stone is a relatively low density limestone due to the high percentage of cavities between the shell fragments. The surface of the rock weathers light-grey and contrasts with pale-cream Caen Stone with which it has often been intermixed, as in the walls of Chichester Cathedral.

**Binstead Stone** (page 100), obtained from the same quarries as Quarr Stone, is a more compact grey, freshwater limestone with layers of small shell fragments.

## Historic Use

| | |
|---|---|
| Roman | Porchester, Southampton (Hants). Chichester (unconfirmed). |
| Late-Saxon | Sompting Abbots and Bosham churches. |
| Norman | Chichester Cathedral. Lewes Priory, Tangmere and Steyning churches. |
| Medieval | Chichester walls, Buncton Church (reuse of Norman stone). |

**Far Left**

Grey-coloured Quarr Stone and lighter Caen Stone ashlar, laid in random fashion. Chichester Cathedral.

**Left**

Intermixed Quarr Stone and Caen Stone moulding around a door arch. Chichester Cathedral.

Fluted capital in Quarr Stone. East Wittering Church.

Late-Saxon Quarr Stone and Bembridge Limestone pilaster. Sompting Abbots Church.

**Quarr Stone**

## Distribution of Quarr Stone

The distribution of Quarr Stone is strongly concentrated in the Chichester area where almost all Medieval churches within a 15km radius of the city contain this building stone. It seems probable that Chichester was the distribution centre for this stone. A further concentration of Quarr Stone occurs in the Shoreham to Lewes to Seaford area.

## Quarr Stone Use in the Past

The main use of Quarr Stone was in the early Norman period although it was first utilized to a small extent in Roman and then late-Saxon times. Little use was made of this stone after *c.* 1120 AD when it is probable that the quarries were worked-out. Reuse of Quarr Stone rubble is common in many Medieval parish churches on the West Sussex coastal plain. Some Quarr Stone rubble in old walls in Chichester, especially around the Cathedral precinct, may be reused Roman building stone.

Quarr Stone was rarely used on the Isle of Wight; Quarr Abbey, founded 1132 AD, located 1km west of the quarries, was constructed of the more massive Binstead Stone (page 100).

**Key**

Quarr Stone

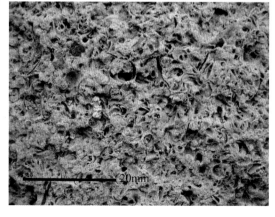

Close-up of the surface of Quarr Stone ashlar showing the open texture of the calcarenite, which consists of up to 30% by volume of voids. Enough remains of the comminuted fossil shells to identify them as the freshwater snail, *Viviparus*. Tangmere Church.

Superficial Deposits

Solent Group

Barton Group

Bracklesham Group

Thames Group

Lambeth Group

White Chalk Subgroup

Grey Chalk Subgroup

Selborne Group

Lower Greensand Group

Weald Clay Group

Hastings Group

Purbeck Group

| Age | Eocene |
| --- | --- |
| | Palaeogene (Early Tertiary) |

**Lithostratigraphy** (recently proposed for the north-east part of the Isle of Wight)

St. Helens Member
Osborne Member
Fishbourne Member
Laceys Farm Member
Nettlestone Member
Fort Albert Member
Ryde Formation (upper part of Headon Hill Formation)

## Geology

The Ryde Formation, the name proposed for the upper part of the Headon Hill Formation in the north-east of the Isle of Wight, comprises the former Osborne Beds. These strata date from *c.* 35Ma, in the latter part of the Eocene Epoch. They consist of *c.* 30m of clay, limestone, siltstone, sandstone and conglomerate which were deposited in a variety of estuarine, lacustrine, fluvial and terrestrial environments. Freshwater and estuarine fossils are abundant including bivalves, gastropods, minute seeds of the freshwater alga *Chara*, and fish and turtle bone. Limestone and siltstone beds within the St. Helens and Nettlestone Members have been quarried in the past for building stone.

## Building Stone

Ryde Stone includes a number of freshwater limestones and siltstones from the Ryde Formation, where this Formation is exposed along the north-east coast of the Isle of Wight between Wootton, Ryde and Seaview.

## Varieties

**Quarr Stone** (described separately in previous Chapter)
A coarse-grain, freshwater, open-texture calcarenite probably obtained from a lens of strata of limited extent within the Binstead Stone, near the top of the St. Helens Member at Binstead, west of Ryde.

**Binstead Stone**
A massive to coarsely-bedded calcarenite from the top of the St Helens Member at Binstead. Used in 13th c. walls of Quarr Abbey, in Binstead Church, and many 19th c. buildings and walls in Ryde. Not recorded in the Sussex survey.

**Nettlestone Stone**
A finely cross-bedded siltstone from the base of the St. Helens Member at Binstead, and within the Nettlestone Member at Seaview, east of Ryde.

## Historic Use

| | |
| --- | --- |
| Roman | Porchester Castle, Hants (Nettlestone Stone string courses). |
| Medieval | West Wittering and Bosham churches (Nettlestone Stone). |
| | Binstead Church and Quarr Abbey (Isle of Wight). |
| 18th-20th C | House, garden and church walls in Ryde and Newport. |

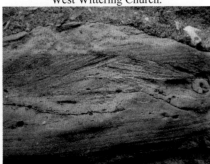
Cross-bedded Ryde Stone (Nettlestone Stone variety), showing a section of a fossil bivalve *Galba*. West Wittering Church.

Tabular blocks of Ryde Stone (Nettlestone Stone) exposed on the Solent foreshore at Binstead, west of Ryde, Isle of Wight.

Freshwater limestone with large fossil *Viviparus*, possibly a variety of Ryde Stone. Wall at the Oxmarket, Chichester.

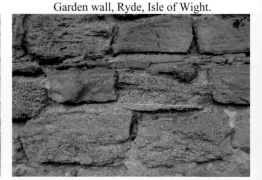
Roughly-cleaved blocks of Binstead Stone packed with crushed freshwater shells, with massive to finely bedded Nettlestone. Garden wall, Ryde, Isle of Wight.

# Ryde Stone

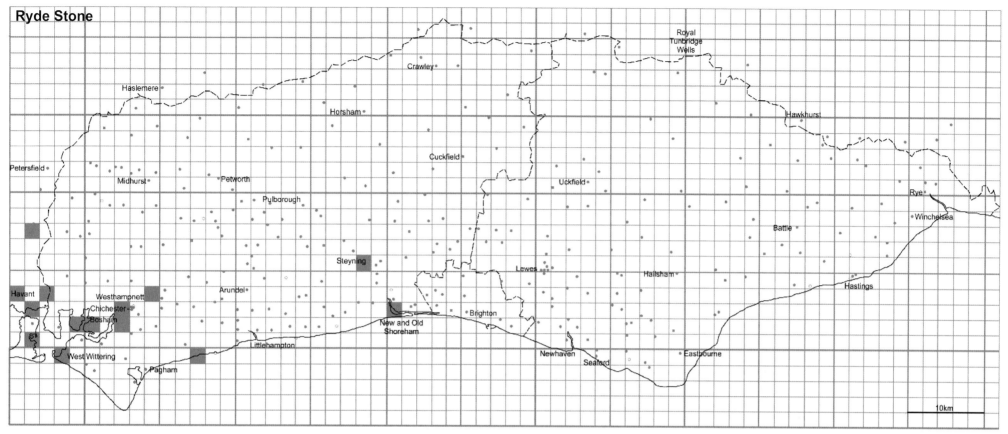

## Distribution of Ryde Stone

Ryde Stone was used in small amounts as a rubble building stone in Medieval churches in the south-west corner of West Sussex. Its distribution indicates it was mainly shipped into Chichester Harbour. A much smaller amount was imported through the ports of Shoreham and Steyning.

**Key**

Ryde Stone

**Right**
Seaview Limestone, at the top of the Nettlestone Member has been used in the local area as a building stone. This stone may be present at Bosham Church and in the nearby sea wall. Nettlestone Point, Seaview, Isle of Wight.

10mm

**Left**
Close-up view of the surface of a large block of probable Ryde Stone showing spherical, millimetre-size seeds of the freshwater alga *Chara*. Bosham sea wall.

**Right**
Stone carving in Portland Stone commemorating the Binstead and Quarr Stone Quarries. Binstead, Isle of Wight.

Superficial Deposits

Solent Group <

Barton Group

Bracklesham Group

Thames Group

Lambeth Group

White Chalk Subgroup

Grey Chalk Subgroup

Selborne Group

Lower Greensand Group

Weald Clay Group

Hastings Group

Purbeck Group

| Age | Eocene/Oligocene boundary Palaeogene (Early Tertiary) |
|---|---|
| **Lithostratigraphy** | Bembridge Limestone Formation Solent Group |

## Geology

Bembridge Limestone was deposited in shallow lakes which extended across the southern part of the Hampshire Basin at the end of the Eocene / beginning of the Oligocene about 34 million years ago.

Bembridge Limestone is a massive freshwater limestone, one of the most important building stones from the Isle of Wight. It crops out along the north coast of the Island from Headon Hill in the west to Bembridge in the east, where it occurs in up to three separate beds which reach a total thickness of 8m. Thickly-bedded, massive limestone is typical, although beds of soft chalky, nodular, and tufaceous varieties also occur. Bembridge Limestone displays numerous, scattered centimetre-scale cavities, the external moulds of the fossil pond snail, *Galba*. Millimetre-size, ornamented spheres, the fossil seeds of the freshwater alga *Chara* (Stonewort), are common in some beds of the rock.

## Building Stones

**Bembridge Limestone** - This building stone is a massive, cream to light-grey limestone building stone which could be cut into large blocks for ashlar. The building stone used in Sussex most likely came from the Bembridge area where it forms a series of extensive ledges around the shoreline of Bembridge Foreland, at the eastern extremity of the Isle of Wight.

**Binstead Stone** - This name has been applied to what was thought to be a variety of Bembridge Limestone from the Binstead area. However this freshwater calcarenite, as with Quarr Stone, may have been quarried from the St. Helens Member, immediately beneath the Bembridge Limestone and as such is a variety of Ryde Stone (page 100).

## Historic Use

| | |
|---|---|
| Roman | Fishbourne Roman building. Southampton (Clausentum) and Porchester Castle (Hants.). |
| Late-Saxon | Sompting Abbots Church. |
| Norman | Old Shoreham and Steyning Churches. |
| Medieval | Wilmington Church and Priory, West Wittering Church. |
| 18th-20th c. | Bosham sea wall (possibly recycled stone). |

Close-up of the surface of Bembridge Limestone showing external moulds of fossil shells of the freshwater snail *Galba*. Bosham sea wall.

Bembridge Limestone quoin at Wilmington Church. This is the farthest east that Bembridge Limestone was used in Sussex.

Bembridge Limestone quoin displaying sharply cut sides. The surface of this stone shows the typical centimetre-size spherical voids left by dissolved-out fossil freshwater snails. Bosham Church.

Carved Bembridge Limestone capital alongside the west door of Shipley Church.

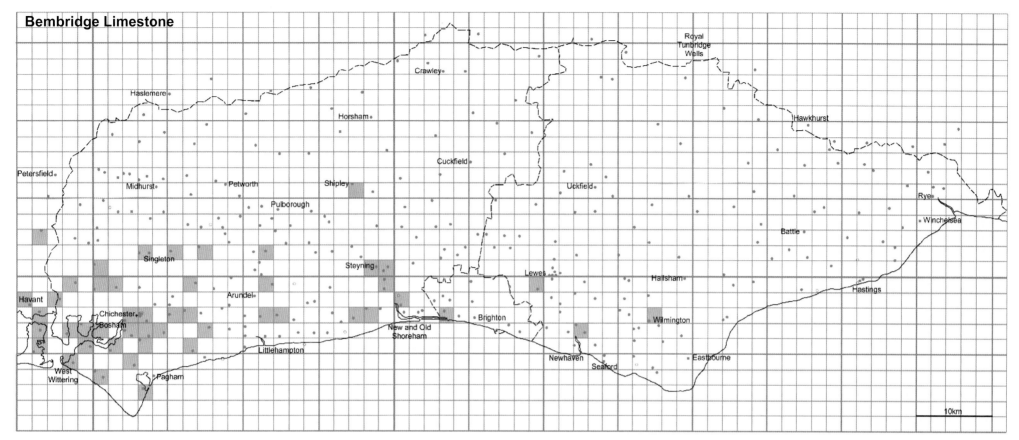

**Bembridge Limestone**

## Distribution of Bembridge Limestone

The distribution pattern of Bembridge Limestone in Medieval Sussex churches is similar to that of Quarr Stone but it was utilized on a much smaller scale. Bembridge Limestone building stone shows a concentration within a *c*. 15km radius around Chichester, and also along the Adur and Arun valleys. An isolated occurrence at Shipley Church was probably the furthest north up the River Adur accessible by shallow-draught vessels in Norman times.

In East Sussex Bembridge Limestone was used in minor amounts at Kingston-near-Lewes and Tarring Neville churches, both situated in the Lower Ouse Valley. The furthest east it was recorded is in the walls of Wilmington Church and Priory.

Exports to the mainland from quarries on the foreshore at Bembridge continued during the 17th to 19th centuries, particularly for sea defences at Portsmouth.

| Key | |
| --- | --- |
| 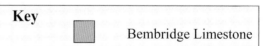 | Bembridge Limestone |

Bembridge Limestone wall
and coping stones.
Westbourne Church.

| Building Stone | Age | Epoch |
|---|---|---|
| Mosan Marble | Visean | Lower Carboniferous |
| Tournai Marble | Tournaisian | Lower Carboniferous |
| Belgian Black | Frasnian / Givetian | Upper Devonian / Middle Devonian |

## Geology

During Devonian and Lower Carboniferous times the Rheic Sea extended across what is now central and southern Belgium in a swathe that stretched from south Devon into central Germany. Sedimentation was controlled by a series of fault blocks where clay was deposited in the deeper water and limestone on the upfaulted areas. During late Carboniferous times these rocks were folded and metamorphosed in the Variscan Orogeny, caused by the northward movement of a number of small crustal plates that constituted southern Europe at that time. The Rheic Ocean crust was subducted beneath northern Europe and a series of generally east-west oriented folds, including the Namur and Dinant Synclinoriums, were formed in what is now Belgium.

Some of the limestone beds are black, indicating that they were formed in reducing conditions where little oxygen was present in the sea. These rocks have long been quarried to provide ornamental stone, particularly for memorials.

## Building Stone

**General Name -** Belgian Black (Noire Belge).
**Varieties -** Mosan, Tournai and Belgian Black Marble.

Black limestones occurs at a number of different geological horizons within Middle Devonian-to-Lower Carboniferous strata of Belgium. They take a high polish, and were greatly prized in the past for memorials, fonts, ledgers and carved columns and capitals. Tournai Marble was first used by the Romans, and then, in Medieval times, was exported to England for fonts and tomb slabs. This black, finely-laminated limestone was quarried close to the River Schelde where it could be transported by barge downstream to Ghent for trans-shipment. Belgian Black Marble from the Dinant and Namur areas is a more massive black limestone which was commonly used for ledgers in the 17th-19th centuries.

## Historic Use

**Tournai Marble**
12th century    Gundrada's tomb slab, Southover Church, Lewes.
Carved shafts, capitals and bases from Lewes Priory.

**Belgian Black**
17-19th centuries    Used throughout Sussex for church ledgers.

**Left**
Belgian Black ledgers dating from the early 18th century. Glynde Church.

**Centre and far right**
Detail and view of the Tournai Marble tomb slab of Gundrada (d. 1085), wife of William de Warrene. The high-quality carving was probably made at Lewes Priory workshop in the second half of the 12th century. Southover Church, Lewes.

Geological time column (left margin):
Quaternary / Neogene
Palaeogene
66Ma
Cretaceous
Jurassic
Triassic
252Ma
Permian
Carboniferous
Devonian
420Ma
Silurian
Ordovician
Cambrian
541Ma
Precambrian

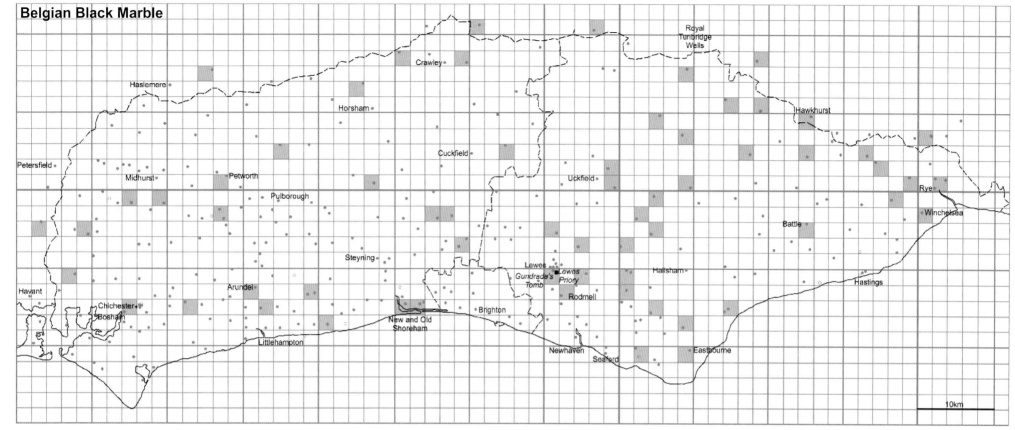

**Belgian Black Marble**

## Distribution of Belgian Black Marble

Belgian Black Marble shows a very widely-scattered distribution pattern which reflects the fashion for this austere, black stone for ledgers for the social elite in the 17th-19th centuries. The higher percentage of churches with Belgian Black Marble recorded in East Sussex is probably due to greater access to churches in that county, and also fewer church floors having been cleared of ledgers.

## Tournai Marble

Pieces of carved Tournai Marble shafts, capitals and bases obtained from the ruins of Lewes Priory are preserved at Anne of Cleves House Museum, Southover, Lewes. At the Dissolution of the Priory (1538) much of the building stone was appropriated for rebuilding in the town and surrounding area. Parts of a 12th century shaft and base of Tournai Marble are preserved in Rodmell Church, south of Lewes.

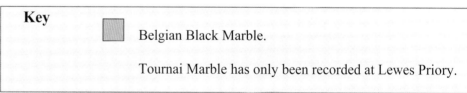

**Key**

Belgian Black Marble.

Tournai Marble has only been recorded at Lewes Priory.

## Gundrada's Tomb Slab

Lewes Priory, one of the largest monastic houses in England, was founded by William de Warenne, 1st Earl of Surrey, and his wife Gundrada c. 1081, following their visit to the Priory of Cluny in Burgundy in 1077. Gundrada died in childbirth in Norfolk in 1085 and her remains were brought back to Lewes Priory. Her finely-carved Tournai Marble tomb slab, made in the late-12th century, was removed from the Priory and taken to Isfield Church soon after the Dissolution. In 1775 it was moved to Southover Church near the site of the Priory by Sir Richard Burrell.

| Quaternary | 2.6Ma |
| Neogene | |
| | 23Ma |
| Palaeogene | |
| | 66Ma |
| Cretaceous | |
| | 145Ma |
| Jurassic Upper | |
| Middle | |
| Lower | |
| | 201Ma |

| **Age** | Bathonian |
| | Middle Jurassic |
| **Lithostratigraphy** | Calcaire de Caen Formation |

## Geology

The Middle Jurassic, Bathonian strata of Normandy consist of up to 150m of limestone beds with mudstones at the base. Caen Stone, the premier building stone from these strata, is found over a limited area around the city of Caen. It was deposited during the middle part of the Bathonian Stage (*c.* 167Ma), and is the same age as Bath Stone. Caen Stone is a very fine-grained limestone composed of a mixture of comminuted shell debris, mainly from echinoids and echinoderms, and minute calcium carbonate pellets. The rock was laid down in a warm, tropical, shelf sea flanking the ancient landmass of Armorica to the west.

## Building Stone

Caen Stone - Pierre de Caen.
Ashlar blocks of Caen stone were formerly known as gobbets.

Caen Stone was quarried and mined from a 7m thick sequence of limestone in and around the city of Caen. The uppermost limestone bed, the 1.1m thick 'Gros Banc', provided the highest quality building stone, with lower beds supplying stone for sculpture and rubblestone. The proportion of comminuted shell debris to microscopic calcium carbonate pellets determines the degree to which the stone resists weathering: the best quality stone is rich in shell debris and has a calcite cement. This is a cream-coloured limestone, while the softer, more readily-weathered, pellet-rich stone is ochre. Norman walling reveals that it was often supplied ready-cut into *c.* 20cm side cubes.

## Historic Building with Caen Stone

| Roman | Fishbourne Roman Palace. |
| Late Saxon | Sompting Abbots Church. West Wittering Cross. |
| Norman | Chichester Cathedral, Lewes Priory, Steyning Church. |
| Late Medieval | Chichester Market Cross (dating from 1501 AD.). |

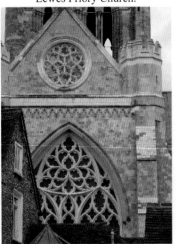

Chichester Cathedral, south transept. Caen Stone ashlar, the whiter stone, was randomly mixed, during early rebuilding work, with Quarr Stone. More Caen Stone was used in the Cathedral than any other building in Sussex, except perhaps Lewes Priory Church.

Marlipins Museum, Shoreham-by-Sea dates from the 12th century and may have been a custom house. Fine chequer-work of Caen Stone and roughly-cleaved flint.

South transept doorway dating from the 12th century, Old Shoreham Church. Caen Stone with chevron moulding around the arch.

Lower High Street, Lewes. An 18th century building constructed of Caen Stone ashlar recycled from Lewes Priory ruins.

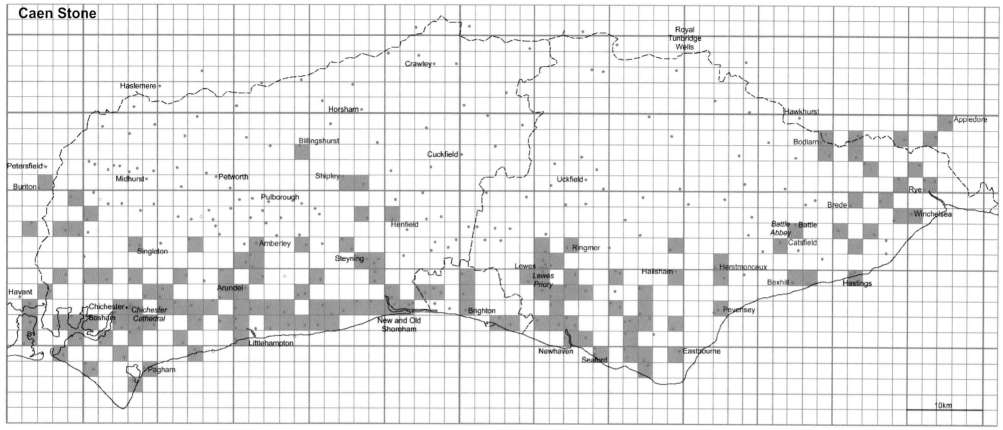

## Distribution of Caen Stone

The map shows the distribution of Caen Stone used as a building stone in Sussex Medieval churches; it does not record its use in memorial sculptures common in later Medieval times until the 17th century. It was a prestigious stone commanding a high price, and therefore often reserved for the most important stonework including dressings, arches, columns, bases and capitals.

Caen Stone is present in almost every Medieval church in Sussex within c. 12km of the coast. Churches within this zone where it is now absent, such as Aldrington and Hove, were completely remodelled in the Victorian era. The stone was landed at Chichester (Dell Quay), Arundel, Bramber, Shoreham, Seaford and the Cinque Ports of Hastings, Winchelsea and Rye where it could be loaded on to barges or wagons for transport to building sites. Navigable waterways acted as transport routes leading into the Weald as far north as Billingshurst, Shipley and Bodiam.

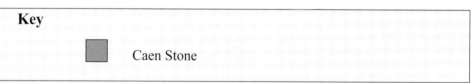

**Key**

Caen Stone

Soon after the Norman Conquest large quantities of Caen Stone began to be shipped across the Channel for numerous building projects including cathedrals, churches and castles in settlements extending around the coast of England from Exeter to Durham. Caen stone continued to be imported to a lesser extent during later Medieval times until the Dissolution of the Monasteries in 1537. The greatest use of this building stone was in the walls of Chichester Cathedral and Lewes Priory.

# CAEN STONE STONEWORK

Caen Stone ashlar with a weathered surface. Note the percussion mark possibly from a bullet or musket ball in the upper centre. Rye Church.

Recycled Caen Stone shaft section in wall of Rye Church. Note the hole into which the nib of the adjacent section would have been fitted when in place.

Lighter-shade Caen Stone with darker Quarr Stone in random pattern. Chichester Cathedral, south wall.

East wall of Buncton Church built with cubes of Caen Stone ashlar and field flint towards the top. The wall displays evidence that it has been rebuilt with recycled stone; the upper parts are poorly constructed.

Caen Stone quoin constructed of long and short work possibly dating back to late-Saxon times. Bishopstone Church.

Caen Stone recycled from Lewes Priory in a wall of Southover Grange, Lewes. The ashlar has been carefully assembled.

Caen Stone with inset cleaved-flint cross, Seaford Church. The stonework is poorly laid except for the lower two courses, indicating reconstruction with this stone by unskilled workers.

Caen Stone pier with lateral roll moulding. High-quality 12th c. stonework at Steyning Church.

# CAEN STONE ORNAMENTAL WORK and SCULPTURE

Chichester Market Cross dates from 1501 when it was erected to give shelter to poor market traders.

Ornately-carved 16th c. canopied tomb of the 10th, 11th and 12th Earls of Arundel. Fitzalan Chapel, Arundel Church.

Late-Saxon porticus, now the entrance doorway on the south side of Bishopstone Church.

Richly-ornamented capital and arches dating from the late 12th century. *'..virile and inventive; certainly the best in Sussex and among the best in the whole country.'* (Pevsner). Steyning Church.

Late-Saxon tower arch to the nave displays crudely-carved capitals. Sompting Abbots Church.

New Shoreham Church displays finely-carved capitals and arches of Transitional to Early English styles of the late-12th century.

Moulding of a serpent on a column base. Bosham Church.

Finely-carved Caen Stone font dating to the mid-12th century. St. Nicholas Church, Brighton.

Tomb and effigy; probably Gervase de Alard (d. 1310), First Admiral of the Cinque Ports. Winchelsea Church.

Geologic column (left margin):
Quaternary — 2.6Ma
Neogene — 23Ma
Palaeogene — 66Ma
Cretaceous — 145Ma
Jurassic: Upper, Middle <, Lower — 201Ma

**Marquise Stone**

| | |
|---|---|
| **Age** | Bajocian |
| | Middle Jurassic |
| **Lithostratigraphy** | Oolithe de Marquise |

## Geology

The Middle Jurassic strata (174-163Ma) of northern France, as in southern England, are dominated by thick beds of limestone, many of which have been used for building stone. These strata underlie two areas adjacent to the English Channel:

1. The Normandy coast north of Bayeux, where Jurassic strata crop out along the western margin of the Paris Basin.

2. The Nord-Pas-de-Calais near Boulogne, where Middle Jurassic limestone crops out near the Channel coast, along the axis of the Weald-Artois Anticline.

## Building Stone

**Middle Jurassic Limestone** - A Middle Jurassic calcarenite present in a number of Medieval churches situated near the coast of Sussex is believed to be of French origin, possibly from the area north of Bayeux adjacent to the Normandy coast. This limestone is a relatively-soft, generally-oolitic, ochre-to-rich brown, highly-fossiliferous calcarenite. A white Middle Jurassic limestone, present at Climping Church, may also be of French origin.

**Marquise Stone** - A white, oolitic calcarenite, with small calcite pebbles, from the Marquise area some 10km north of Boulogne has been quarried since Roman times, when it was first imported into East Kent for use at Canterbury and Reculver. Small quantities of this building stone were imported, mainly into Kent and the Rye area of East Sussex, from the late-11th to 13th centuries.

## Historic Use

| | |
|---|---|
| Roman | Chichester (possible use of Middle Jurassic Limestone). |
| Medieval | Rye and Winchelsea (Marquise Stone). |
| | Climping, Bramber and Seaford churches (Jurassic Lst). |
| | Arundel Priory (Marquise Stone possibly present). |

Light-brown, highly-fossiliferous calcarenite. Seaford Church.
The church walls contain a number of rubble blocks of this and similar rock types.

Roman column base, Little London, Chichester. Massive, white fossiliferous limestone, possibly a variety of Marquise Stone.

Ashlar block of Middle Jurassic Limestone. Upper Beeding Church.

Marquise Stone, south wall of Rye Church. This white calcarenite contains small pebbles of calcite.

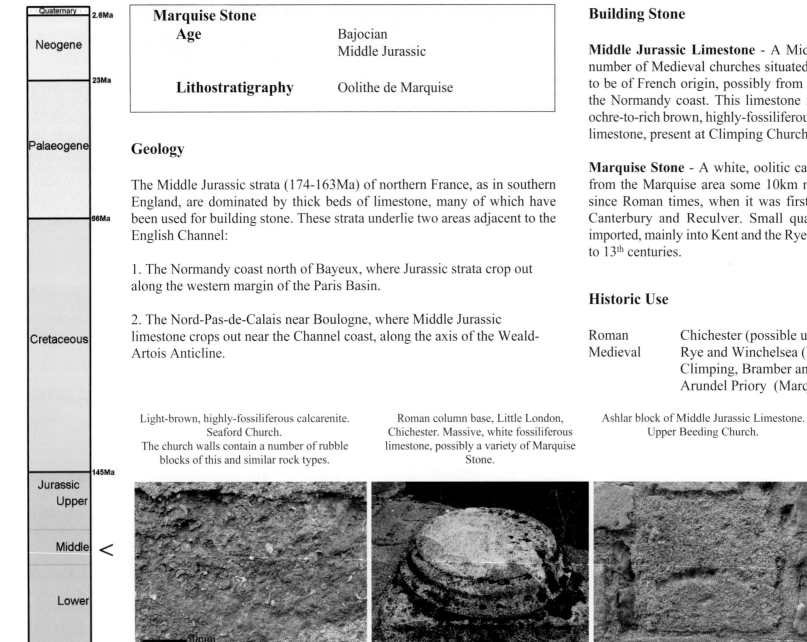

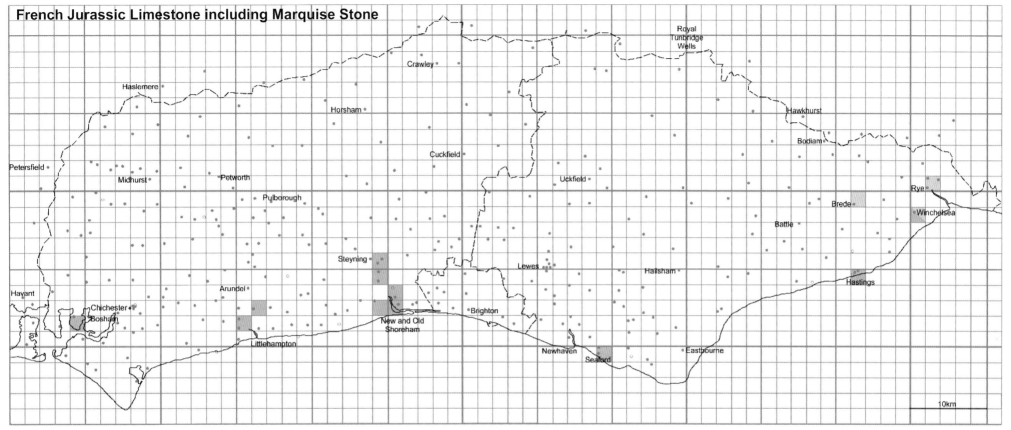

**French Jurassic Limestone including Marquise Stone**

## Distribution of French Jurassic Limestone including Marquise Stone

Middle Jurassic Limestone from the Normandy coast is present in small amounts in Medieval churches in coastal areas and along the lower courses of navigable rivers such as the Arun, Adur, Brede and Eastern Rother. This building stone was notably used in churches along the Lower Adur valley from Steyning to Shoreham, particularly at Upper Beeding. Several varieties of this building stone are present at Seaford Church, which in Medieval times was situated near the mouth of the River Ouse.

The main use of Marquise Stone in South East England was in East Kent where it was used in Roman times at Canterbury and Reculver. It has only been recorded in 3 churches in the far east of East Sussex, at Rye, Winchelsea and Brede.

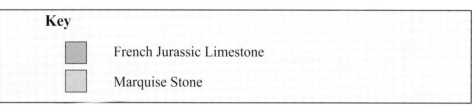

**Key**

French Jurassic Limestone

Marquise Stone

Possible French Jurassic Limestones:

**Left**
Oolitic limestone, Bodiam Church.

**Right**
Bryozoan limestone, Climping Church.

Quaternary | 2.6Ma

Neogene

23Ma

Palaeogene <

66Ma

Cretaceous

145Ma

Jurassic
Upper

Middle

Lower

201Ma

| **Age** | Lutetian (Age/Stage) |
| | Eocene |
| | Palaeogene |
| | |
| **Lithostratigraphy** | Calcaire Grossier |

## Geology

For 15 million years towards the end of the Cretaceous / beginning of the Palaeogene, Northern France and Southern England were above sea level. As the Palaeogene progressed a shallow, warm sea transgressed across the land flooding areas south from London to Paris. This sea reached its maximum extent in northern France during the Lutetian Stage c. 45Ma, when up to 15m of limestone, known as the Calcaire Grossier, was deposited. Later earth movements have preserved these marine sediments and associated estuarine and freshwater deposits in a series of basins, one of which covers a large area centred on Paris known as the Paris Basin.

Calcaire Grossier was quarried for building stone in Roman times on the south bank of the River Seine near the confluence with the River Bievre, and later from the 12th century mined extensively beneath Paris.

## Building Stone
## Alternative Names

Calcaire Grossier, Ditrupa Limestone, Lutetian Limestone, Paris Stone.

Numerous varieties of building stone occur in beds each up to c. 1m in thickness. The commonest building stone exported to Sussex was massive, white, Ditrupa Limestone.

**Calcaire Grossier Building Stone**

| Stratigraphy | Key Fossil |
|---|---|
| Banc de Roche - Courville Stone | *Milliolids* |
| Banc Franc (Liais) - St Maximin / Oise Stone | |
| Banc Vert (freshwater limestone) | *Cerithids* |
| Banc Royal | |
| Banc Verrins | |
| Banc de St. Leu - **Ditrupa Limestone** | *Ditrupa* |
| Banc a Mollusques | |
| Pierre a Liards - Nummulitic Limestone | *Nummulites* |
| Calcaire Grossier a Glauconie | |
| Sables Glauconieux | |

## Historic Use

| | |
|---|---|
| Roman | Fishbourne Roman Palace. |
| Late-Saxon | Stone-cross fragments, Selsey and Pagham. |
| Medieval | West Wittering and New Shoreham churches. |

Calcaire Grossier rubble in the north wall of Bosham Church showing sections of the small tubes of the calcareous serpulid *Ditrupa*.

Calcaire Grossier rubble; probably reused Roman building stone in the Chichester city wall.

Close-up of rubble blocks in the west wall of New Shoreham Church. These are unidentified limestones which may be varieties of Calcaire Grossier. Photograph left shows 5mm fish tooth (centre) and photograph right shows 15mm disc-shaped fossils.

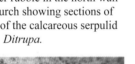

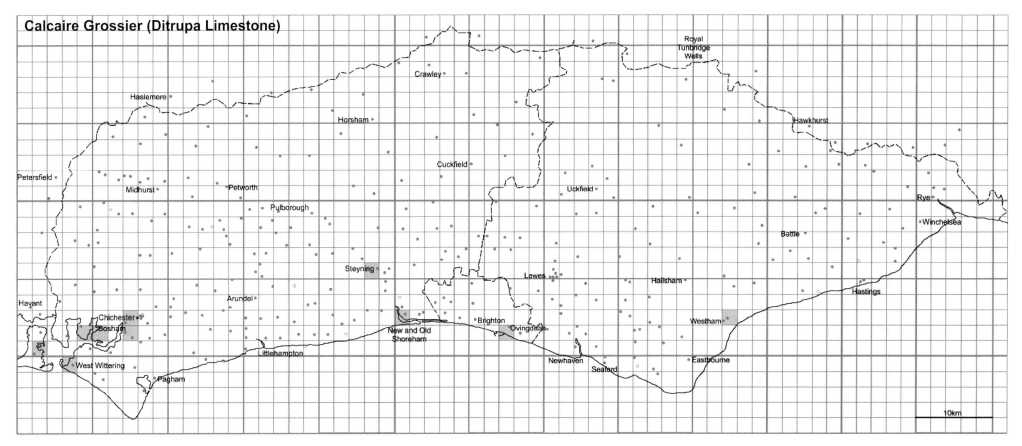

**Calcaire Grossier (Ditrupa Limestone)**

10km

## Distribution of Calcaire Grossier

Calcaire Grossier is confined to a few coastal localities, mainly in West Sussex, with a concentration around Chichester Harbour where it was imported by the Romans for use in the city of Chichester (Noviomagus) and at Fishbourne Roman Palace. Its presence at Bosham and West Wittering churches may reflect reuse of Roman stone from Chichester. A Late-Saxon fragment of a Cross preserved at Pagham Church may also have been carved from reused Roman stone.

A small amount of Calcaire Grossier was probably imported during Medieval times, when it was used in New Shoreham and Steyning Churches, in the Adur Valley

Milliolid limestone at Ovingdean Church (see photograph) and calcarenite rubblestone of debatable origin at Westham Church may be from the Calcaire Grossier.

**Key**

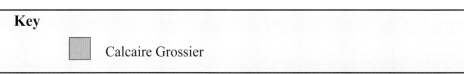
Calcaire Grossier

Foraminiferal limestone rich in fossil milliolids at Ovingdean Church. This stone which is similar to Mixon Stone could be from the Banc Franc in the upper part of the Calcaire Grossier.

Some of the Roman forces involved in the Claudian invasion of Britain in 43AD. may have entered through Chichester Harbour, as there is evidence for an early Roman military base at Fishbourne. Cross-Channel trade was well developed between Sussex coastal communities and Roman Gaul before the Invasion so there was probably little resistance by the local populace. The main area of Roman settlement and development was in a wide belt across the southern part of Sussex from the Hampshire border to Eastbourne and Pevensey in the east. Fishbourne Roman Palace and the city of Chichester (Noviomagus) were established during the first century AD. as well as a number of important Roman Villas across the West Sussex Coastal Plain, such as those at Angmering and Southwick, and in East Sussex at Eastbourne and Newhaven. To the north of the chalk downs settlements were established along the belt of rich farmland overlying the Upper Greensand, from Bignor Roman Villa east to Barcombe Roman Villa in the Ouse Valley.

The Romans introduced building with stone and kiln-fired bricks on a considerable scale. Stone and brick salvaged from derelict Roman buildings provided a ready supply of building material in Norman times in areas where suitable building stone was scarce. Reused Roman building stone is difficult to identify, but Roman brick and tiles are distinctive, and have been reused as walling stone in a number of Medieval churches in the south of Sussex, particularly in Chichester and the surrounding area.

Roman brick and tile set into the walls of Medieval churches are difficult to differentiate: sections of the bricks are thin (*c.* 40mm) and the tiles are of a similar thickness, so that they are often just referred to as 'ceramic building material' (CBM). The Romans gained the knowledge for the manufacture of kiln-fired bricks from the Greeks at the end of the 1st century BC. Previously bricks were sun dried, making them rather soft and prone to water damage.

In Sussex the Romans particularly used bricks as layers of bonding tiles or string courses to strengthen flint walls, as at Pevensey Roman Fort (Anderitum).

Roman bricks set in mortar of ground-up Roman brick and chalk. Rudgwick Church.

**Right**

Roman bricks set around a window arch dating from the Late-Saxon period. Arlington Church.

Section of Roman brick with inscribed lettering. Westhampnett Church.

Herringbone-work constructed of Roman bricks. Eastergate Church.

Poorly-fired Roman brick with a coarse texture. Willingdon Church.

Hypocaust floor tile set into the south wall of Hardham Church.

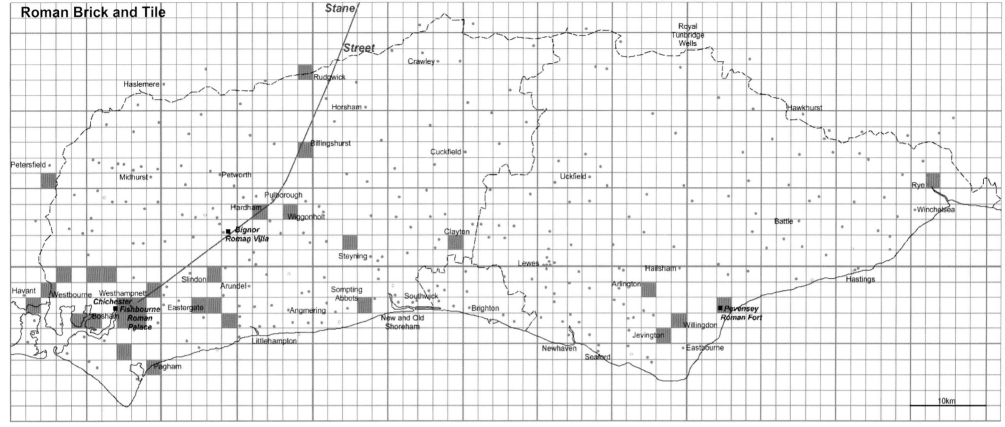

Roman Brick and Tile

## Distribution of Roman Brick and Tile

The use of Roman brick and tile in the walls of Medieval churches is concentrated in the south-west of West Sussex, reflecting the importance of Roman settlement in that area. Many churches within *c.* 12km radius of Chichester contain scattered Roman brick and tile in their walls, reclaimed from former Roman buildings in the local area or even from Chichester.

Many of the Medieval churches with Roman Brick lie on the coastal plain where supplies of good building stone were limited. A few churches are located close to Stane Street (the Roman road from Chichester to London), suggesting the occurrence of former Roman buildings close to the road.

**Key**

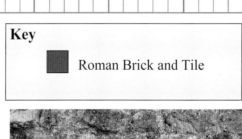 Roman Brick and Tile

### Right and Far Right

String courses (bonding tiles), used to strengthen the massive outer wall of Pevensey Roman Fort (Anderitum), built in the late-3rd century as part of the 'Saxon Shore' defences.

115

| Quaternary |  |
| --- | --- |
| Neogene |  |
| Palaeogene |  |
|  | 66Ma |
| Cretaceous |  |
| Jurassic |  |
| Triassic |  |
|  | 252Ma |
| Permian |  |
| Carboniferous |  |
| Devonian |  |
|  | 420Ma |
| Silurian |  |
| Ordovician |  |
| Cambrian |  |
|  | 541Ma |
| Precambrian |  |

| Age | Precambrian to Quaternary |
| --- | --- |

## Geology

A wide variety of non-indigenous rocks are found in buildings dating from Medieval to Victorian times in former and current Sussex seaports. Many are Erratics transported into Sussex by natural agencies, but other particularly-distinctive alien rocks are classed as Exotic Stones, having mainly been introduced into Sussex as discarded ships' ballast. Fashioned stone objects including mortars and tools, which have been reused as building stone in walls, may be regarded as Exotics but have not been recorded in the Atlas survey.

Remarkable rocks such as Rapakivi Granite and Coarse-grained Gneiss from the Baltic Shield of Scandinavia were formerly a notable feature in a quay-side wall of the historic port of Littlehampton, but unfortunately recent regeneration of the area has led to the removal of the wall displaying these unusual building stones. Exotics may still be seen in other old walls in the town, particularly in the walls of the United Church.

Exotic building stones appear to have been derived predominantly from Normandy, the Channel Islands and Scandinavia, no doubt coming from the region around the main ports with which sailing ships traded in the past.

## Building Stone

Exotic Stones include all classes of rocks and are often similar to Erratics, often making it difficult to separate them. Useful guides are:
1. Many Erratics occur as water-worn, rounded cobbles and pebbles, whereas Exotics are often coarsely cleaved from larger blocks.
2. Unlike Exotics, Erratics may usually be matched with cobbles and pebbles of similar rock types from beach gravel along the Sussex coast.

## Historical Records

Ships' ballast stones have been described as being used for building stone from Roman to Victorian times in former and present Sussex ports. Some of these may be Erratics or even misidentified local and imported building stone. Records of the discharge of ballast-stones into the harbour at Winchelsea date from the 14th century. An Act of 1549 (Edward VI), forbade the casting of ballast stone into The Camber at Winchelsea, as the rocks were causing an obstruction to shipping.

## Historic Use

| | |
| --- | --- |
| Medieval | Winchelsea, Rye, Seaford and New Shoreham churches and nearby old walls. |
| 18-19th centuries | Littlehampton United Church. Newhaven (old walls in the town). |

Rapakivi Granite from Scandinavia in a now-destroyed wall, Littlehampton Quay.

Augen Gneiss, where the quartz and feldspar crystals have been sheared into eye-shaped structures, in a wall north of the church, Winchelsea.

Coarse Grained Gneiss from Scandinavia. Littlehampton United Church.

Coarse Grit, possibly from the Channel Islands. New Shoreham Church.

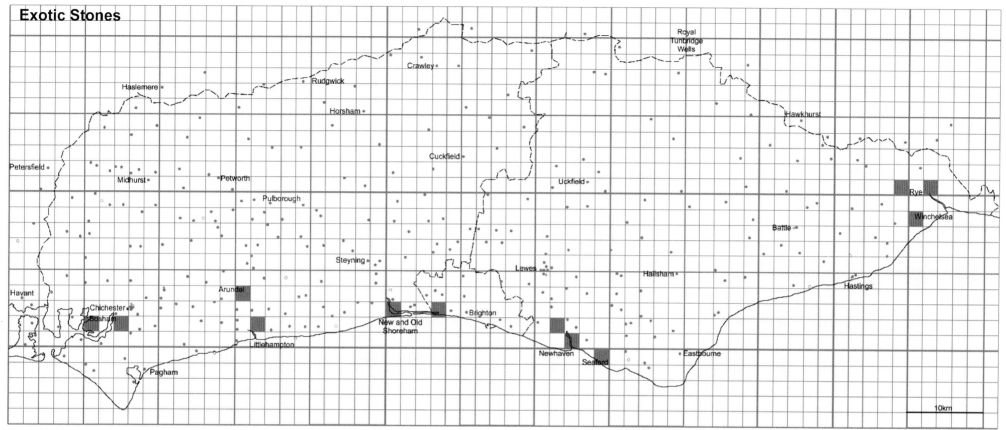

**Exotic Stones**

## Distribution of Exotic Stones

Exotic rocks have been used as building stones within a number of Medieval churches situated on or close to the Sussex coast. They comprise a minor but noticcable building-stone type in the ports, and former ports, of Bosham, Littlehampton, Arundel, New Shoreham, Newhaven, Seaford, Winchelsea and Rye, where they were discarded as surplus ships' ballast. Exotic rocks thus provide evidence of the maritime trade formerly conducted at these ports from Late-Medieval to Victorian times. Various rocks from the vicinity of ports were used to maintain the stability of shallow-draught sailing ships, as and when required, and would have been augmented and discarded as necessary.

Exotic building stones are probably underrepresented as they are often difficult to distinguish from Erratics.

**Key**

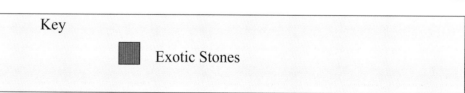 Exotic Stones

**Left** Bivalve limestone of unknown derivation. Peasemarsh Church.

**Right** 30cm long granite cobble Seaford Church.

117

## ORNAMENTAL STONE

This category of building stone includes specific types used for ornamental work, memorials, ledgers and statuary. These building stones are commonly polished to enhance their colour and texture. Ornamental building stone is often prone to weathering in exposed positions and so is mainly used for interior stonework.

## MARBLE

Marble is metamorphosed limestone, where the constituent calcite has reformed into an interlocking matrix of crystals due to the action of heat and/or pressure deep within the Earth. The best quality Marble is a massive rock which can be intricately carved and sculpted to a fine edge, and the surface polished to a high gloss. Pure white varieties, including Carrara Marble from central Italy were in great demand for statues and memorials since Classical times. Limestone often contains a small proportion of minerals beside calcite; when metamorphosed to become Marble it takes on a complex pattern of coloured streaks and bands. Coloured Marbles including Torquay Marble, were particularly popular in Victorian times.

The Romans imported Marble from France, Italy and Greece for statues, flooring slabs, *opus sectile* flooring and inlay work. Some 10 different varieties have been recorded at Fishbourne Roman Palace, the most important being Carrara Marble. Small quantities of Marble were again imported from the Mediterranean region from late Norman times. The Marble trade increased greatly in the 17th century when polished stone was required for memorials and ornamental work, many of the varieties coming from Italy, France and Belgium. Marble from Southern Europe gradually replaced Purbeck and Sussex Marble for memorials in churches in Sussex, as these marbles are far superior for carving and could also provide a wide variety of colours and patterns.

18th century
Marble font.
Beckley Church.

**Right**

Partly-painted Marble memorial tablet to Sir Nicholas Pelham (d. 1559) and his wife, which also depicts their ten children.
St. Michael's Church, Lewes.

## ALABASTER

Alabaster is a massive form of gypsum (calcium sulphate), a very soft mineral that is readily carved and takes a high polish. It was a valuable ornamental and statuary stone, mainly quarried from Triassic strata at Chellaston, near Derby. In Sussex it was utilized for interior church memorials during the 16th and 17th centuries. The streaky, white, cream and brown stone was used in a number of elaborate church memorials, including the mid-16th century memorial to Sir David Owen in Easebourne Church, and the memorial to Sir Thomas Caryll (d. 1616) and his wife at Shipley Church.

**Left**

Mid-18th century Carrara Marble memorial by Rysbrack.
West Grinstead Church.

**Below**

Ornate Marble and Alabaster memorial to first Viscount Montague (d. 1592), of Cowdray House, shown kneeling above his two wives. Easebourne Church.

Two recumbent effigies in Alabaster dating from 1596.
Fletching Church.

Victorian marble pillars supporting the pulpit, Washington Church.

Vernacular building in stone continued from the mid-16th to 19th centuries mainly for the construction of country houses, village houses, farm houses and cottages, but with far fewer building-stone types than in Medieval times. Hastings Sandstone, Hythe Sandstone and Flint continued to be the dominant building stones, but much construction was now in brick. Very few new churches were built between the time of the Reformation and the beginning of the Victorian era. Much stone was reused from former religious buildings after the Reformation, with brick becoming the main building material for houses and cottages. During Victorian times with the upsurge in religious fervour, many new churches were constructed and Medieval ones remodelled using the main indigenous building stones, together with imported stone especially Bath Stone and Clipsham Stone, brought in by rail.

**MAIN BUILDING STONES 1537 to 1840**
Listed generally in order of stratigraphic age, oldest first.

**Indigenous**
- Hastings Sandstone
- Horsham Stone-slate
- Sussex Marble
- Hythe Sandstone
- Flint
- Malmstone
- Bognor Rock
- Mixon Stone

**Imported**
- Igneous Rocks (very minor, some from the Channel Islands)
- Belgian Black (Limestone)
- Torquay Limestone and Devon Marble
- Portland Stone
- Purbeck Stone
- Purbeck Marble
- Marble (various types including Carrara Marble)

Purbeck Limestone flagstones (18th century). The Pallant, Chichester.

**Left**

Arundel Cathedral (1870). 14th c. French Gothic design built of Bath Stone.

Eades House (Westgate House) (1696), a fine Queen Anne house with a central section and dressings of Portland Stone. East Street, Chichester.

**Right**

19th century wall to Arundel Castle built of Torquay Limestone rubble.

**MAIN IMPORTED BUILDING STONES 1840 to 1900**

- Marble (numerous types including Devon Marble)
- Igneous Rock especially Granite (Scotland, S.W. England, Channel Islands)
- Torquay Limestone
- York Flagstones
- Bath Stone
- Clipsham Stone
- Portland Stone
- Chilmark Stone
- Purbeck Stone
- Kentish Ragstone
- Bargate Stone (Surrey Type)

Bath Stone. Arundel Cathedral.

Chilmark Stone with sections of fossil bivalve *Trigonia*. Chichester Cathedral bell-tower.

Portland Stone, an oolitic calcarenite. Facade of bank, Eastbourne.

Clipsham Stone. A favourite Victorian replacement stone for decayed stonework. Oving Church.

**Left**

Ancaster Stone (Streaky Bacon Stone). Polished stonework, Worthing Council Offices.

With the advent of the railways in the 1840s, and the development of sea trade, building stone could be cheaply imported from throughout the British Isles and beyond. These widely-sourced building stones progressively replaced indigenous Sussex building stones.

**Right**

Torquay Limestone rubble block showing highly-fossiliferous grey limestone with pink-coloured calcite. Bosham sea wall.

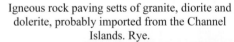

Doulting Stone base to Hastings Sandstone shafts. Lancing College.

Purbeck Limestone. 19th century entrance gatehouse to Arundel Castle. A grey austere building stone.

Black, fossil Carboniferous Limestone, probably Frosterly Marble. Hartfield Church.

Igneous rock paving setts of granite, diorite and dolerite, probably imported from the Channel Islands. Rye.

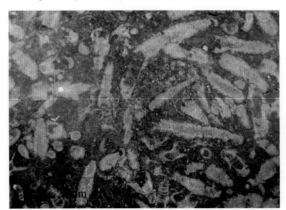

# APPENDIX

# APPENDIX

## PARISH CHURCHES SURVEYED (dating from 950 to 1550 AD)     1. WEST SUSSEX

Albourne
Aldingbourne
Amberley
Angmering
Apuldram
Ardingly
Arundel, Fitzalan Chapel
Arundel, St Nicholas
Ashington
Ashurst
Bailiffscourt (Atherington)
Balcombe
Barlavington
Barnham
Bepton
Bignor
Billingshurst
Binsted
Birdham
Bolney
Bosham
Botolphs
Boxgrove
Bramber
Broadwater
Buncton
Burpham
Burton
Bury
Chichester, All Saints
Chichester, Cathedral
Chichester, St Andrew
Chichester, St Mary (Whyke)
Chichester, St Olav
Chidham
Chithurst
Church Norton
Clapham
Clayton

Climping
Coates
Cocking
Coldwaltham
Compton
Coombes
Cowfold
Crawley
Cuckfield
Didling
Donnington
Durrington
Earnley
Eartham
Easebourne
East Dean
East Grinstead
East Lavant
East Lavington
East Marden
East Preston
East Wittering
Eastergate
Edburton
Egdean
Elsted
Felpham
Fernhurst
Ferring
Findon
Fishbourne
Fittleworth
Ford
Funtington
Goring
Graffham
Greatham
Hardham
Heene

Henfield
Heyshott
Horsham
Horsted Keynes
Houghton
Hunston
Hurstpierpoint
Ifield
Iping
Itchingfield
Keymer
Kingston Buci
Kirdford
Linchmere
Lindfield
Littlehampton
Lodsworth
Lurgashall
Lyminster
Madehurst
Merston
Midhurst
Milland
Newtimber
North Lancing
North Marden
North Mundham
North Stoke
Northchapel
Nuthurst
Oving
Pagham
Parham
Patching
Petworth
Plaistow
Poling
Poynings
Pulborough

Pyecombe
Racton
Rogate
Rudgwick
Rusper
Rustington
Selham
Shermanbury
Shipley
Shoreham New
Shoreham Old
Sidlesham
Singleton
Slaugham
Slindon
Slinfold
Sompting
South Bersted
South Harting
South Stoke
Southwick
Stedham
Steyning
Stopham
Storrington
Stoughton
Sullington
Sutton
Tangmere
Terwick
Thakeham
Tillington
Tortington
Trotton
Twineham
Up Marden
Upper Beeding
Upwaltham
Walberton

Warminghurst
Warnham
Washington
West Chiltington
West Dean
West Grinstead
West Hoathly
West Itchenor
West Stoke
West Tarring
West Thorney
West Wittering
Westbourne
Westhampnett
Wiggonholt
Wisborough Green
Wiston
Woodmancote
Woodmansgreen (near Linch)
Woolbeding
Worth
Yapton

### RUINED PARISH CHURCHES and CHAPELS
#### With visible stonework

Chichester, St Martin
Duncton
Heene
Old Erringham
Pagham, St Andrews Chapel
Treyford

### LOST CHURCHES and CHAPELS
#### With some building stone present or previously recorded

Kingston Gorse
Linch (near Bepton)
Middleton-on-Sea
Upper Barpham (Angmering)

Bosham Church as depicted in the Bayeux Tapestry (*c.* 1070) showing Harold, the future king, entering the church in 1064 before embarking for Normandy. Bosham was an important port in late-Saxon times. A monastery was established there in the 7th century.

## 2. BRIGHTON and HOVE

Aldrington
Brighton
Falmer
Hangleton
Hove
Ovingdean
Patcham
Portslade
Preston
Rottingdean
West Blatchington

## 3. EAST SUSSEX

Alciston
Alfriston
Arlington
Ashburnham
Barcombe
Battle
Beckley
Beddingham
Berwick
Bexhill
Bishopstone
Bodiam
Brede
Brightling
Burwash
Buxted
Catsfield
Chailey
Chalvington
Chiddingly
Crowborough
Crowhurst
Dallington
Denton
Ditchling
East Blatchington
Eastbourne
East Chiltington
East Dean
East Guldeford
Etchingham
Ewhurst
Fairlight
Falmer
Fletching
Folkington
Framfield
Friston
Glynde
Guestling
Hailsham

Hamsey
Hartfield
Hastings, All Saints
Hastings, St Clements
Heathfield
Hellingly
Herstmonceux
Hollington
Hooe
Icklesham
Iden
Iford
Isfield
Jevington
Kingston-near-Lewes
Laughton
Lewes, All Saints
Lewes, St Anne
Lewes, St John the Baptist
Lewes, St John Sub Castro
Lewes, St Michael
Lewes, St Thomas à Becket
Litlington
Little Horsted
Lullington
Maresfield
Mayfield
Mountfield
Newhaven
Newick
Ninfield
Northiam
Peasmarsh
Penhurst
Pett
Pevensey
Piddinghoe
Playden
Plumpton
Ringmer
Ripe

Rodmell
Rotherfield
Rye
Salehurst
Seaford
Sedlescombe
Selmeston
Southease
South Malling
Streat
Tarring Neville
Telscombe
Ticehurst
Uckfield
Udimore
Wadhurst
Waldron
Warbleton
Wartling
West Dean
Westfield
West Firle
Westham
Westmeston
Whatlington
Willingdon
Wilmington
Winchelsea
Withyham
Wivelsfield

### RUINED PARISH CHURCHES
With some building stone present or previously recorded

Broomhill (Camber)
Bulverhythe
Hastings, Castle
Ore, Old St Helens
South Heighton

Pelham tower with spire constructed of Hastings Sandstone (Top Ashdown Sandstone, Sandrock). Chiddingly Church.

# 4. OTHER STONE BUILDINGS*

| 4.1 SELECTED RELIGIOUS HOUSES (11th to 16th century) | 4.2 SELECTED CASTLES, COUNTRY HOUSES and OTHER ANCIENT BUILDINGS | 4.3 SELECTED 18th and 19th CENTURY CHURCHES with date of initial construction | |
|---|---|---|---|

# 5. PARISH CHURCHES adjacent to the SUSSEX BORDER
(Recorded on the Atlas maps)

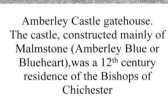

**WEST SUSSEX**

Arundel, Blackfriars (Friary)**
Boxgrove Priory**
Chichester, Greyfriars (Friary, Old Guildhall)**
Dureford Abbey
Shulbrede Priory

**EAST SUSSEX**

Battle Abbey**
Bayham Abbey
Lewes Priory**
Michelham Priory
Robertsbridge Abbey

**WEST SUSSEX**

Amberley Castle
Arundel Castle
Bramber Castle
Cowdray House
Goodwood House
Marlipins (Shoreham-by-Sea)
Parham House
Petworth House
West Tarring, Archbishop's Palace
Wakehurst Place
Wiston House

**EAST SUSSEX**

Bateman's
Bodiam Castle
Camber Castle
Firle Place
Glynde Place
Herstmonceux Castle
Hastings Castle
Lewes Castle
Pevensey Roman Fort and Castle
Winchelsea Court Hall

**WEST SUSSEX**

Chichester-
　St John 1812
　St Pancras 1750
Coolhurst 1833
Duncton, Holy Trinity 1866
Duncton, RC. 1866
Highbrook 1884
Horsham -
　Roffey, All Saints 1878
Haywards Heath 1863
Lancing College Chapel 1868
Lower Beeding 1840
Lowfield Heath 1867
Loxwood 1898
Mannings Heath 1881
Milland 1880
Partridge Green 1890
Selsey 1865
Southwater 1850
Turners Hill 1895
West Lavington 1850
Worthing, Christ Church 1841

**EAST SUSSEX**

Brighton, Stanmer 1838
Crowborough 1839
Eastbourne -
　Holy Trinity 1837
Hastings, Ore 1858
Hastings -
　United Reformed Ch. 1857
Netherfield 1854
Offham 1858
Polegate 1874
St Leonards-on-Sea -
　St Mary Magdalene 1852

**HAMPSHIRE**

Blendworth (lost)
Buriton
Chalton
Havant
North Hayling
Petersfield
South Hayling
Warblington

**SURREY**

Alfold
Burstow
Charlwood
Chiddingfold
Haslemere

**KENT**

Appledore
Ashurst
Cowden
Hawkhurst
Lamberhurst
Newenden
Sandhurst
Stone-in-Oxney
Wittersham

Amberley Castle gatehouse. The castle, constructed mainly of Malmstone (Amberley Blue or Blueheart),was a 12th century residence of the Bishops of Chichester

Battle Abbey Gatehouse, constructed of Hastings Sandstone (Top Ashdown Sandstone) dates from 1338.

**Note**

\* A selection of important 'Other Stone Buildings', the majority of which have been surveyed, is given for reference. Those designated with two asterisks are recorded on the building stone distribution maps.
In addition to the 316 Sussex Medieval churches, the building stones of Chichester Cathedral are also recorded on the maps.
22 Medieval parish churches, adjacent to, but beyond the Sussex county boundary, have been surveyed and are shown on the building stone distribution maps to provide a more complete coverage along the border zone.

QUATERNARY
Field Flint and Beach Flint
Ferricrete (Iron Pan)
Travertine (Calcareous Tufa)
Erratics

PALAEOGENE (EARLY TERTIARY)
Mixon Stone (Mixen Stone, Mixon Limestone), Hounds Stone,
Bognor Rock
London Clay Cementstone (Septarian Concretions)
Harwich Stone
Woolwich and Reading Ironstone, and Ostrea Sandstone
Sarsen Stone
Upnor Conglomerate, and Upnor Ferruginous Sandstone (Ironstone)

UPPER CRETACEOUS
Chalk
Chalk Calcrete
Quarry or Fresh Flint
Lavant Stone

LOWER CRETACEOUS
Eastbourne Stone (Bourne Stone)
Malmstone - (White and Grey Malmstone, Blueheart, Malmstone Marble)
Carstone (Ironstone)
Marehill Ironstone
Bargate Stone (West Sussex variety)
Hythe Sandstone (Midhurst, Petworth and Pulborough Stone)
Hythe Chert
Sussex Marble (Large Paludina Limestone, Petworth Marble, Laughton Marble)
Weald Clay Sandstone
Charlwood Marble (Small Paludina Limestone)
Horsham Stone, Horsham Stone-slate (Horsham Slab, Ripplestone)
Hastings Sandstone -
    Upper Tunbridge Wells Sandstone
    Cuckfield Stone
    Lower Tunbridge Wells Sandstone (Wealden Sandstone, Sussex Sandstone)
    Ardingly Sandstone
    Ashdown Sandstone, Top Ashdown Sandstone
Sussex Purbeck Stone (Blues and Greys), Sussex Purbeck Marble

**SURREY and KENT**
LOWER CRETACEOUS  Reigate Stone
    Bargate Stone
    Kentish Ragstone

**ISLE OF WIGHT**
PALAEOGENE  Ryde Stone, Binstead Stone, Nettlestone Stone
    Quarr Stone (Featherstone)
    Bembridge Limestone
LOWER CRETACEOUS  Ventnor Stone, Bonchurch Stone

**DORSET**
LOWER CRETACEOUS  Purbeck Marble, Unio Marble, Thornback
    Purbeck Limestone (Purbeck Building Stone)
UPPER JURASSIC  ?Portland Stone

**DEVON**
LOWER CRETACEOUS  Beer Stone
LOWER DEVONIAN  Devon (Blue) Slate

**FRANCE (NORMANDY and PARIS BASIN)**
PALAEOGENE  Calcaire Grossier (Ditrupa Limestone)
MIDDLE JURASSIC  Caen Stone
    Jurassic Limestone, Marquise Stone

**BELGIUM**
DEVONIAN/CARBONIFEROUS
    Tournai Marble
    ?Fumay Slate

- Common alternative names of building stones are shown in brackets.
- Important Varieties are listed for some building stones.
- Other Medieval building stones include reused Roman Brick and Tile, and Marble (Mediterranean) and Alabaster (Derbyshire) for memorials and sculpture.
- Hastings Sandstone includes numerous Varieties of building stone.

# INDIGENOUS BUILDING STONES IN ROMAN BUILDINGS OF SUSSEX

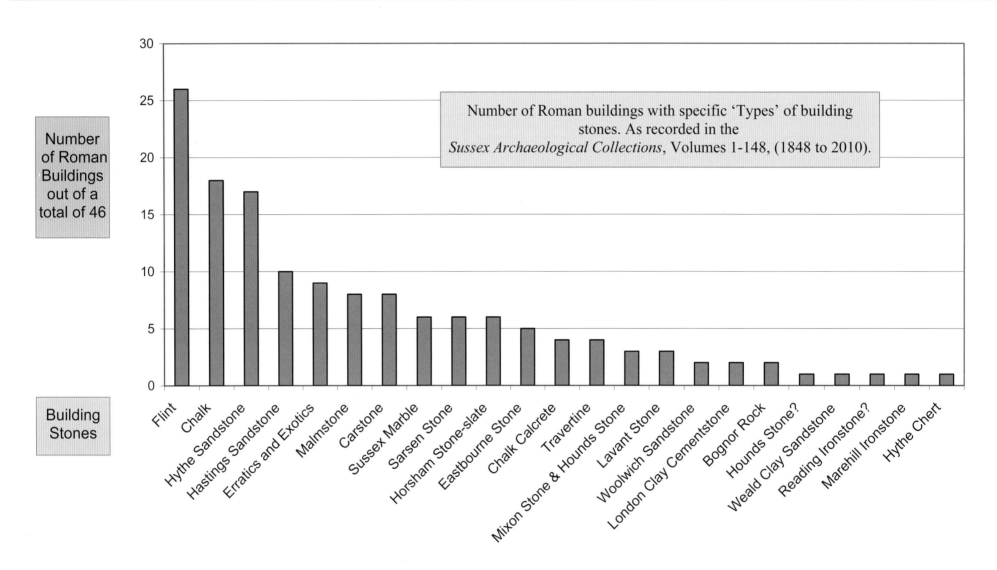

Number of Roman Buildings out of a total of 46

Number of Roman buildings with specific 'Types' of building stones. As recorded in the *Sussex Archaeological Collections*, Volumes 1-148, (1848 to 2010).

Building Stones

## Roman Building Stone Use

The Romans utilized most of the indigenous Sussex building stones, of which Flint, Chalk and Hythe Sandstone were the most important. It should be noted that there may be errors and omissions in identification of Roman building stones, especially in older published reports, leading to a bias in favour of the most obvious ones such as Flint and Chalk.

# INDIGENOUS BUILDING STONES IN MEDIEVAL CHURCHES OF SUSSEX

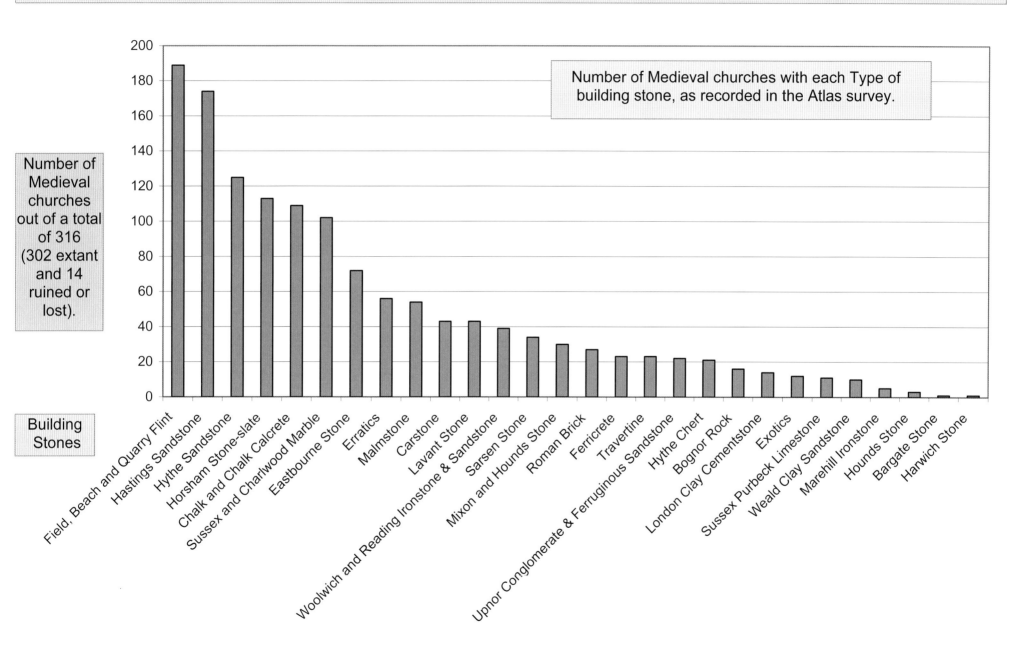

Number of Medieval churches with each Type of building stone, as recorded in the Atlas survey.

Number of Medieval churches out of a total of 316 (302 extant and 14 ruined or lost).

Building Stones

**BRACKLESHAM GROUP**
Selsey Formation
    Mixon Stone Bed (Mixon Stone)
Marsh Farm Formation
Earnley Formation
Wittering Formation

**THAMES GROUP**
London Clay Formation
        (Divisions A to E)
    Whitecliff Member
    Portsmouth Member
        Turritella Bed
    Barn Rock Member
    Bognor Sand Member (Bognor Rock)
    Walton Member
Harwich Formation

**LAMBETH GROUP**
Reading and Woolwich Formations
Upnor Formation

**Left**

Earnley Formation, Bracklesham Bay.

Cardita Bed; a fossil shell-bed of well-preserved bivalve fossils, mainly *Venericardia planicosta*.

**Below**

London Clay Formation, Bognor Regis.

Bed of septarian concretions in grey clay.

**Above**

Bognor Sand Member, Bognor Regis.

Large concretions of Bognor Rock, a hard, calcite cemented sandstone.

**Left**

Upnor Formation, Newhaven. Chalk overlain by ferruginous flint conglomerate and sand of the Upnor Formation.

# CRETACEOUS STRATA OF SUSSEX

## CHALK GROUP

### WHITE CHALK SUBGROUP
Culver Chalk Formation
Newhaven Chalk Formation
Seaford Chalk Formation
Lewes Nodular Chalk Formation
Newpit Chalk Formation
Holywell Nodular Chalk Formation
    Melbourn Rock Member
    Plenus Marl Member

### GREY CHALK SUBGROUP
Zigzag Chalk Formation
West Melbury Marly Chalk Formation
    Glauconitic Marl Member

## SELBORNE GROUP
Upper Greensand Formation
Gault Formation

## LOWER GREENSAND GROUP
Folkestone Formation
Sandgate Formation
    Marehill Clay Member
    Pulborough Sandrock Member
    Rogate, Selham Ironshot Sands and Fittleworth Members
Hythe Formation
    Easebourne Member
      Bargate Beds
Atherfield Formation

## WEALD CLAY GROUP
*(The Weald Clay and Hastings Groups are sometimes placed in the 'Wealden Group').*
4 Sandstone Beds and 3 Paludina Limestone Beds
Horsham Stone Member

## HASTINGS GROUP
Tunbridge Wells Sand Formation
    Upper Tunbridge Wells Sand (*Member?*)
    Grinstead Clay Member
      Cuckfield Stone Bed
    Lower Tunbridge Wells Sand (*Member?*)
    Ardingly Sandstone Member
Wadhurst Clay Formation
Ashdown Formation

## PURBECK GROUP
*(The lowest beds exposed in Sussex belong to the Broadoak Calcareous Member).*
Durlston Formation
    Greys Limestones Member
    Arenaceous Beds Member
    Cinder Beds Member
Lulworth Formation
    Plant and Bone Beds Member
    Broadoak Calcareous Member
    Gypsiferous Member (*Upper Jurassic Age*)

Stratigraphy based on:
Hopson, P. M., Wilkinson, I. P. and Woods, M. A. 2008. A stratigraphical framework for the Lower Cretaceous of England, British Geological Survey, and other publications.

View east from Seaford Head across Cuckmere Haven towards the Seven Sisters. The White Chalk Subgroup is exposed in the cliffs.

# GLOSSARY - ARCHITECTURE

# GLOSSARY OF ARCHITECTURAL AND BUILDING TERMS

**Aisle**
A corridor along the side of the nave of a church, separated by an arcade.

**Apse**
A semi-circular domed recess, usually behind the altar of a church.

**Arcade**
A series of pillars and arches which divide the nave from the aisles.

**Arch**
Upward-closing, curved stonework, rounded or pointed at the apex, around an opening, often supported by pillars.

**Architrave**
The moulded frame surrounding a door or window.

**Ashlar**
Finely-shaped and smoothly-finished stonework, usually laid to course.

**Base**
The lowest visible part of a building or architectural feature.

**Bastion**
A defensive turret or tower on a wall.

**Beakhead**
Stylized bird-head sculpture around a Norman arch.

**Belgian Black**
Black Devonian limestone from Belgium which takes a high polish; used for ledgers in 17th to 19 centuries.

**Billet**
Repeated, raised, round or square-section moulding around a Norman arch.

**Boss**
A carved projection in a ceiling where the ribs meet.

**Buttress**
A pier built against a wall to give additional support.

**Flying Buttress** - A buttress built against a wall as an arch or half arch.

**Cable or rope moulding**
Plaited rope-effect moulding around a Norman arch.

**Campanile**
An ornate bell tower on the roof of a church.

**Capital**
The plain or moulded cap to a column.

**Chancel**
The east section of a church housing the altar.

**Chevron**
V-shaped moulding around Norman arches.

**Choir**
The area of a church between the nave and altar, used by the choir and clergy.

**Classical**
Late-18th century revival of the architectural styles of Ancient Greece and Rome.

**Column**
A vertical pillar in Classical architecture which supports cross members.

**Cobble, Cobblestone**
Small, rounded, tabular stones used for paving.

**Coping (stone), cap stone**
Stone cap used to protect the top of a wall.

**Corbel**
A stone or brick projecting from a wall to provide horizontal support for a beam.

**Cornice**
The moulding at the top of a wall, or the projecting part of a capital.

**Course**
A horizontal layer of stonework.

**Crocket Capital**
A capital carved with projecting leaf shapes.

**Crossing**
The central space in a church where the transept crosses the nave.

**Curtain wall**
The length of wall between bastions in a castle.
A non-load-bearing wall in front of a framed structure to keep out the weather.

**Decorated**
The second phase of Gothic-style architecture dating from c. 1307 to 1350.

**Diaper work**
Diamond or square pattern made on a brick wall using bricks of contrasting colours.

**Dimension Stone**
Building stone which can be accurately carved into square blocks.

**Dog-tooth**
Bevelled or hemispherical projections seen in Norman arch decoration.

**Doric**
The simplest of the Classical Orders of Greek columns; heavy fluted columns with plain capitals.

**Dressed stone**
Stone that has been carefully cut, shaped and smoothed, such as ashlar.

**Dressings**
Ashlar used for quoins, window and door edgings.

**Eaves**
The projecting overhang along the lower part of a roof.

**Early English**
The first Gothic phase of church architecture developed in the 13th century, with pointed arches and relatively thin walls.

**Elevation**
The projection of a vertical plane in a building.

**Fascia**
Flat horizontal stonework under projecting eaves.

**Flagstone**
Stone which may be split into thin slabs and used for paving. Horsham Stone-slate and Purbeck Stone were commonly used in West Sussex.

**Flush work**
Cleaved flints with the split side facing outwards.

**Fluting**
Shallow, semi-circular grooves cut into columns for decoration.

**Freestone**
A homogeneous building stone which may be cut in any direction.

**Galleting**
Small pieces of often-contrasting stone or flint set into the mortar between stone blocks.

**Gothic**
The major style of Medieval architecture from the late-12th to early-16th century, which is distinguished by thin walls, pointed arches and flying buttresses.

**Healing**
An old term used for constructing a roof of stone-slate.

**Herringbone work**
Stone or brick-work laid diagonally, in courses with alternate rows creating a zigzag pattern.

**Ionic**
The second Classical Order of Greek architecture, with fluted columns and scrolled capitals.

**Jamb**
The vertical support of an opening for a door or window to which it is fixed.

**Keystone**
The central, wedge-shaped stone at the top of an arch.

**Knapped flint**
Flint which has been smoothly cleaved to show the interior of the nodules.

**Lacing course**
A course binding the facing to the core of a wall.

**Lancet**
A tall, sharply-pointed window typical of the Early English style.

**Lime putty**
A soft mortar made of lime mixed with sand and water, particularly used for flint walling.

**Lintel**
A long horizontal stone or timber carrying the weight of a wall above a door or window.

**Long and short work**
Late-Saxon style of stonework at the corner of a building, where the rectangular stone blocks are laid alternately, length vertically and horizontally.

**Lychgate**
A covered, often wooden gateway at the entrance to a churchyard.

**Massive Stone**
Stone which has an even texture, so that it can be accurately cut in any direction.

**Mitchells**
An old name used in Sussex for Purbeck Stone paving stones.

**Mortar**
Various mixtures of cement, lime and gypsum, with sand and water, in which stone and brick is bedded.

**Motte and Bailey**
The mound and outer wall of a small Norman castle.

**Moulding**
Ornamental carving on stone, particularly around arches and on capitals.

**Mullion**
Vertical division in a window.

**Nail head**
Norman moulding around arches in the form of a row of projecting pyramidal features.

**Nave**
The main body of a church for use by parishioners.

**Norman**
The Norman style of architecture is often called Romanesque. This style prevailed from the mid-11th to the late-12th century and is characterized by round decorated arches, massive columns and domed vaulting.

**Order(s)**
The three Classical styles of Greek and Roman architecture, Doric, Ionic and Corinthian, each related to the form and decoration of columns and capitals.

**Padstone**
Stone footing for a wooden post to prevent decay of the base due to rising damp.

**Pelham Towers**
Sturdily constructed church towers in central East Sussex dating from the 15-16th centuries built by the Pelham family.

**Perpendicular**
The late phase of the Gothic style of architecture from c. 1327 to 1520, typified by slender columns, large windows and decorative battlements.

**Pier**
A vertical wall support, or area of wall between adjacent windows.

**Pilaster**
A flat-surface pier or column projecting slightly from a wall, typical of the late-Saxon period.

**Pillar**
A small column often used for ornamental effect.

**Pointing**
Smoothed mortar finish infilling the gap between bricks or stone blocks, normally with a downward slope.

**Portico, Porticus**
A colonnaded space with covered roof, forming the entrance to a building. A fine example is the entrance to Goodwood House.

**Putholes**
Gaps in stone walls used to secure wooden scaffolding during construction, e.g. the walls of the churches at Botolphs and West Tarring.

**Quoins**
External cornerstones, which are usually large blocks of high-quality ashlar.

**Rendering**
An external mortar covering on a building to provide strength and protection from the weather.

**Reticulation**

An ornamentation of regular indentations on the surface of stone blocks.

**Rock-faced**

Stone surface with a rough-cut finish.

**Romanesque (Norman)**

Architecture of the Norman period based on the late-Roman style, with rounded often decorated arches and massive piers.

**Roughcast**

A rendering made of cement mixed with gravel.

**Rubble, rubble stone**

Irregularly-shaped stone blocks and cobbles which have not been dressed; they may be laid in random fashion or coursed.

**Rustication**

Stone decoration where the edges are smoothly chamfered to give a 3-dimensional effect.

**Saxo-Norman (Late-Saxon)**

The early type of Romanesque church architecture from *c.* 950 to 1070. Churches have a narrow nave with high walls, external pilasters, small windows, quoins built with long and short work, massive rounded arches and sturdy piers.

**Setts**

Cobble-stones, particularly those cut to a regular size.

**Shaft**

The main part of a column or pillar between the base and the capital. Also, one of several columns in a cluster.

**String course**

A course of horizontal stone, binding a rubble wall.

**Stucco**

A smooth lime-and-sand plaster particularly used on the exterior walls of large houses in Georgian times.

**Terracotta**

A fired mix of fine sand and clay, used for tiles and decorative mouldings, e.g. the Harmer Plaques on gravestones in East Sussex.

**Tournai Marble**

Black limestone from the Tournai area of Belgium which takes a high polish. It was used as an ornamental building stone during the second half of the 12th century.

**Tracery**

Ornamental carving of mullions and transoms in Gothic windows.

**Transept**

Short north-south extensions of a church giving it a cross-shaped plan.

**Transitional**

The transition from Norman to Early English architecture in the late-12th and early-13th centuries. The main feature is the introduction of pointed arches.

**Transom**

Horizontal division in a window frame.

**Tudor**

The architectural style from 1520 to 1558. The arch form has a flattened curve that comes to a point in the centre.

**Vault**

A three-dimensional arch forming the supporting structure of a roof. The barrel or tunnel vault was introduced in Norman times, and the ribbed vault is typical of Gothic architecture.

**Vermiculation**

Stone surface decorated with wavy patterns resembling worm tracks.

**Villa**

A large country residence owned by a wealthy landowner during the Roman period. In more recent times it refers to a large detached house.

**Wealden House**

A large, timber-framed rural house typical of the Weald of Sussex and Kent, often with a Horsham Stone-slate roof and overhanging eaves.

West Hoathly Manor House was built as a dower house in 1627 by the Infields of Gravetye. It is constructed of Ardingly Sandstone with a Horsham Stone-slate roof.

The Old Shop, a 15th c. timber framed yeoman's cottage, Bignor. Infillings of brick, flint and plaster with a Malmstone rubble base.

# GLOSSARY - GEOLOGY

# GLOSSARY OF GEOLOGICAL TERMS

The Geological Formation and Group for each building stone is shown in a coloured box below the chapter heading. Sussex stratigraphy is listed on pages 128-9.

**Alabaster**
A massive form of gypsum, softer than marble, which is easily carved and polished.

**Alluvium**
Sediment transported and deposited by flowing rivers.

**Anoxic**
Lacking in oxygen. Refers to sediments laid down in reducing conditions.

**Anticline**
An upward-closing fold where the strata form an inverted U-shape.

**Arkose**
Sandstone or grit containing feldspar, usually formed in an arid environment.

**Basalt**
A fine-grained, extrusive, mafic (magnesium and iron-rich) igneous rock which forms lava flows.

**Bed, bedding**
Depositional layers of sedimentary rock.

   **Cross or current-bedding**
Beds deposited at an angle, at the front of an advancing sand sheet, by moving water or wind action.

   **Festoon or trough-bedding**
Beds deposited in small scooped hollows. A common bedding structure in Horsham Stone.

   **Flaser Bedding**
Thin discontinuous laminations of finer sediment in a sandstone.

   **Slumped or contorted bedding**
Displayed in sandstone beds where the sand has flowed into complex folds soon after they were deposited.

**Lenticular bedding**
Hollows of ripple-marks filled with coarser sand. Common in the Tunbridge Wells Sandstone.

**Bedrock**
The older (Pre-Quaternary), generally-consolidated rocks which underlie an area.

**Belgian Black (Marble)**
The general name for black limestone from the Devonian and Carboniferous strata of Belgium.

**Benthic**
An organism that lives on the sea-bed.

**Bioclastic**
A sedimentary rock composed mainly of fossil shell debris.

**Bioturbated**
Beds which have been reworked soon after deposition by burrowing organisms.

**Bivalve**
A mollusc (shellfish) with two valves or shells.

**Breccia**
A sedimentary rock composed of angular pebbles.

**Brickearth**
Light-brown clay and silt, which mantles much of the West Sussex coastal plain. It was deposited during the late-Devensian as loess from dust storms, and later reworked by water action.

**Braided river**
A river with numerous intersecting channels which flows over a wide floodplain.

**Calcarenite**
A limestone consisting of a high proportion of comminuted fossil shell debris.

**Calcareous**
A sedimentary rock containing calcium carbonate.

**Calcareous Tufa** (see travertine)

**Calcareous sandstone**
Sandstone containing calcium carbonate.

**Calcite**
The crystalline form of calcium carbonate.

**Calcrete or Caliche**
A hard, calcareous, near-surface deposit which forms in lime-rich soils in semi-arid regions.

**Carstone**
The local name for layers and concretions of hard, iron-oxide-cemented, gritty sandstone within the Folkestone Formation.

**Chalcedony**
The general name for micro-crystalline quartz found as chert and flint. The name is also commonly used for the semi-transparent chert seen in flint geodes.

**Chalk**
A soft, white, coccolith limestone which was deposited in Upper Cretaceous times. The Chalk Group is up to 400m thick and was laid down at a time of much higher sea level than today.

**Chert, pinhole chert**
Chert is the name for a rock made of micro-crystalline quartz. It occurs as intermittent layers within the Hythe Formation of West Sussex, where it is a tough grey rock with a sub-conchoidal fracture. Pinhole chert is a common variety which shows small rod-like cavities from which opaline sponge spicules have been dissolved.

**Clast**
A pebble-size particle within a rock.

**Clastic**
Describes a sedimentary rock deposited as particles rather than by chemical or organic means.

**Clay**
Very fine-grained sediment composed of clay minerals.

**Cleavage**
Parallel planes defined by the alignment of platy minerals along which slate will split. Also applied to fissile sandstone such as Horsham Stone-slate.

**Clunch**

A builders' term for chalk rubble infill. Malmstone and gritty chalk are sometimes referred to as Clunch.

**Concretion**

A large, rounded mass of harder rock within a sedimentary rock. Concretions are often calcareous, such as cementstone, and have generally formed by differential cementation when mineral-rich water passes through the rock.

**Conglomerate**

A sedimentary rock of rounded pebbles within a finer groundmass.

**Contorted bedding** - See bedding.

**Cortex**

The outer white crust on a flint.

**Coombe Rock**

Former term used for superficial deposits of chalky, flinty clay which lines dry valleys and coombes on the chalk downs.

**Cretaceous**

The final geological Period of the Mesozoic, lasting from 145 to 66Ma.

**Crypto-crystalline**

The microscopic texture of chalcedony where the quartz occurs as fine fibres or crystallites.

**Cuesta**

A combined dip and scarp-slope.

**Current or cross-bedding** - See bedding.

**Desiccation or mud cracks**

Cracks left in muddy surface sediment, when a lake or river-bed dries out. Fossil desiccation cracks occur in some beds of the Hastings Sandstone.

**Devensian**

Defined in the UK as the last Glacial Stage of the Quaternary Ice Age from *c*. 73,000 to 12,000BP.

**Diagenetic**

Describes physical and chemical changes, such as hardening and crystal growth which take place in a sedimentary rock after it was deposited.

**Dip**

The inclination of sedimentary strata to the horizontal.

**Dip slope**

The topographic slope formed along a dipping bed.

**Dogger**

A large calcareous or ferruginous concretion formed in sedimentary rocks.

**Dolerite**

A dark-coloured, medium-grained, mafic igneous rock, which typically forms dykes and sills.

**Drift**

The former name for superficial deposits.

**Duricrust**

A hard surface layer in the soil profile formed by precipitation of minerals, e.g. caliche or calcrete.

**Epoch**

A division of geological time shorter than a Period.

**Erosion**

The release of rock or soil by physical agencies such as flowing water, ice, wind and animal activity.

**Erratic**

A rock transported by natural agents out of the area where it was formed. E.g. granite boulders in the raised-beach deposits of West Sussex.

**Escarpment**

The steep slope formed along the eroded edge of strata marking the top margin of a dip slope or plateau edge.

**Estuary**

The wide tidal section of a river in its lower course.

**Exotic**

A rock moved by human agency from the area where it was formed, e.g. former ships' ballast seen in old walls of ports and former ports.

**Facies**

The depositional environment in which a particular sedimentary rock was laid down.

**Fault**

The shear plane along which strata have been displaced by crustal movements.

**Feldspar**

A series of aluminosilicate minerals which contain varying amounts of sodium, potassium and calcium. They are found in many igneous and metamorphic rocks.

**Felsic**

Describes igneous rocks consisting predominantly of feldspar and quartz.

**Ferricrete or Ironpan**

An iron-oxide cemented layer formed in soil profiles or superficial deposits.

**Ferromagnesian minerals**

Minerals rich in iron and magnesium, such as the amphibole and pyroxene group of minerals.

**Ferruginous**

An iron-rich rock such as Carstone.

**Fissile**

Describes a fine-grained sedimentary rock which readily breaks into thin layers along parallel planes.

**Flagstone, flaggy sandstone**

A sandstone which splits into slabs and may be used for paving and roofing.

**Flame structure**

A convolute bedding structure where unconsolidated strata have risen upwards in the shape of a flame.

**Flint**

Found as nodules and sheets in the chalk. It is a type of chalcedony, consisting of crypto-crystalline quartz.

**Fluvial, Fluviatile**

A term for all types of watercourse, although it generally refers to a river environment.

**Fold**

The wave-like structure, from cm to km scale, caused by lateral pressure on strata.

**Foliation**

The typical texture of gneiss, where the minerals tend to lie parallel along a plane.

**Foraminifera**

Small single-celled marine organisms, such as *Nummulites* which have a disc-shaped, calcite shell.

**Formation**

The basic mappable lithostratigraphic division of sedimentary rocks; part of a Group and subdivided into Members and Beds.

**Fossils**
The remains and traces of once-living organisms which have been preserved within a rock.

**Gabbro**
A coarse-grained, mafic, igneous rock composed chiefly of feldspar and hornblende.

**Gastropod**
A single-valve shellfish of the mollusc family.

**Gault**
The clay Formation in the lower part of the Lower Cretaceous, Selborne Group.

**Geode**
A cavity within a rock lined with minerals. In flint it particularly refers to a sub-spherical cavity, which may be lined with chalcedony and/or inward-pointing quartz crystals.

**Geomorphology**
The scientific study of the shape of the land surface.

**Glauconite**
An iron-silicate mineral occurring widely in Palaeogene and Cretaceous rocks as small green grains. It gives the green colour to greensand.

**Gneiss**
A metamorphic rock formed under high pressure and temperature deep within the Earth. It commonly shows banding with different minerals, giving a foliated texture or fabric.

**Goethite**
A hydrated iron-oxide.

**Granite**
A coarse-grained, felsic igneous rock rich in feldspar and quartz, together with mica.

**Greensand**
Sandstone containing the mineral glauconite, which gives the rock a green colour. The Upper and Lower Greensand are rock units within the Lower Cretaceous.

**Greywether**
A former name for a Sarsen Stone.

**Grit**
A sandstone containing discernible coarse grains.

**Groundmass**
The matrix, or fine-grained material in sedimentary rocks.

**Group**
The primary lithostratigraphic division of rocks. A Group includes a number of Formations.

**Head**
Former name for superficial periglacial deposits.

**Haematite**
A commonly occurring iron oxide (Fe2O3).

**Hardground**
A bed of harder, often nodular sedimentary rock formed during a hiatus, or time of very slow deposition.

**Holocene**
The present geological Epoch which began *c.* 12,000 years ago at the end of the last Glacial Stage (Devensian), of the Pleistocene Epoch.

**Hornstone**
An old name for chert, and also a volcanic rock.

**Ice Age**
The last Ice Age comprised numerous Glacial and Interglacial Stages during the Quaternary Period, which lasted from 2.6Ma to the present. During glaciations, ice sheets extended south into present-day temperate latitudes.

**Igneous**
Describes rocks that have formed from molten magma originating in the Earth's crust and upper mantle.

**Interglacial (Stage)**
A warmer period within an Ice Age.

**Involution**
Contorted bedding seen in superficial deposits, caused by freeze-thaw action.

**Iron pan** – see ferricrete.

**Ironstone**
A hard dark-coloured sedimentary rock cemented by iron oxides, e.g. Carstone.

**Joint**
A natural crack within a sedimentary rock.

**Ka**
Thousands of years before the present, e.g. 100Ka.

**Karst**
Landscape formed by limestone dissolution.

**Lava**
An extrusive igneous rock which forms a flow from a volcanic vent.

**Liesegang Banding**
Colour banding seen in sedimentary strata caused by the precipitation of minerals from mineralised water passing through the rock. The bands are often a brown or red colour due to iron-oxide staining.

**Lime**
Quick lime (CaO) is produced by burning chalk in a kiln. Adding water makes lime putty, the traditional lime mortar for binding stonework.

**Limestone**
A sedimentary rock composed mainly of calcium carbonate. Often contains fossil shells or shell fragments.

**Limonite**
The general term for hydrated iron-oxide minerals.

**Lithology**
Describes the type of rock, e.g. sandstone.

**Loess**
A deposit of wind blown dust. Brickearth is a silty deposit of water-reworked loess.

**Ma**
Millions of years before the present, e.g. 66Ma.

**Mafic**
Describes a dark-coloured igneous rock rich in magnesium and iron.

**Marble**
A metamorphosed limestone. The stone industry also use this term for limestones which take a high polish.

**Marcasite**
A form of pyrite (FeS2), which occurs in the chalk as nodules of radiating crystals.

**Massive**
Describes a sedimentary rock which is homogeneous and does not show bedding structures or fractures.

**Matrix** – see groundmass.

**Member**
Subdivision of a sedimentary rock Formation which consists of a number of Beds.

**Mesozoic**
'Middle life'. The Era of Earth history from 252 to 66Ma.

**MIS**
Marine Isotope Stage. Numbered oxygen isotope Stages, which define warm and cold periods during the Quaternary. The present Stage is MIS 1.

**Metamorphic**
A sedimentary or igneous rock which has been altered by the action of heat and/or pressure, within the Earth.

**Micaceous sandstone**
A sandstone with flakes of muscovite mica on the bedding planes which may allow it to be split into flagstones.

**Mineral**
A naturally-occurring chemical compound. Most minerals occur in a crystalline form.

**Mohs' scale of hardness**
A hardness scale of minerals from 1 to 10 (talc to diamond), where a higher-number mineral scratches the surface of minerals lower on the scale.

**Monocline**
A fold where one limb is much steeper than the other.

**Mud cracks** - see 'desiccation cracks'.

**Mudstone**
A consolidated, fine-grained sedimentary rock composed mainly of clay minerals.

**Neogene**
Geological Period from 23 to 2.6Ma.

**Nodule**
A small, hard, rounded, mineralized body in a sedimentary rock, e.g. flint, pyrite and calcium phosphate.

**Oolitic limestone**
A limestone formed in shallow, warm, turbid seas, composed of small, concentrically-layered calcite spheres known as ooliths.

**Orogeny**
An episode of mountain building.

**Outcrop**
The area over which a rock directly underlies or crops out.

**Outlier**
A rock outcrop separated from the main outcrop.

**Palaeoenvironment**
The environmental conditions at a particular time in the past.

**Palaeogene**
Geological Period from 66 to 23Ma.

**Pedogenic**
Processes that occur within the soil layer.

**Period**
A subdivision of the Eras of geological time.

**Petrology**
The scientific study of rocks.

**Phenocryst**
A large crystal in the finer-grained matrix of an igneous rock.

**Porphyritic, Porphyry**
An igneous rock composed of larger crystals or phenocrysts in a finer-grained groundmass.

**Puddingstone**
A conglomeratic variety of Sarsen Stone containing rounded flint pebbles.

**Pyrite, Iron pyrites**
The mineral iron sulphide ($FeS_2$), which commonly occurs as nodules.

**Quartz**
The crystalline form of silica ($SiO_2$) which is the main constituent of sandstone. It occurs in many igneous and metamorphic rocks, such as granite and gneiss. Quartz crystals occur in some flint nodule geodes.

**Quartzite**
A hard quartz sandstone such as Sarsen Stone, and also a metamorphosed sandstone.

**Quaternary**
The geological Period from 2.6Ma to the present, which includes the last Ice Age.

**Ripple marks or ripple structure**
Wave-like bedding structure in a sandstone caused by the movement of water or wind during deposition.

**River terraces**
Remnants of the former floodplain of a river preserved along the valley sides after later river incision.

**Sandstone**
A sedimentary rock made of sand-size particles, normally composed mainly of quartz.

**Sarsen Stone**
A hard silicified sandstone or silcrete found as boulders on the chalk downs, in chalk dry-valley sediments, and in modern beach and raised-beach gravel deposits. They are relics of former beds of Tertiary, Lambeth Group sandstone which have been cemented by silica.

**Scarp, scarp slope**
The steep slope formed by erosion of the edge of an outcrop of resistant strata. A small escarpment.

**Schist**
A coarse-grained metamorphic rock derived from a clay-rich sediment. It has layering or schistosity, denoted by platy or elongate minerals.

**Sedimentary rock**
A rock formed by deposition and consolidation of sediment derived from pre-existing rocks, from biogenic material, or by chemical precipitation.

**Septaria**
Rounded, calcite-rich concretions which are fractured into segments, often with calcite crystals along the fractures.

**Serpulid**
A fossil marine worm, with a calcareous tube.

**Shale**
A mudstone with a well-defined lamination.

**Shravey**
A former Sussex term for Iron Pan and also for flint-rich solifluction deposits.

**Slate**
A clay-rich metamorphic rock with a prominent cleavage, allowing the rock to be split into platy sheets.

**Solifluction**

The down-slope movement of water-charged, near-surface material after seasonal thawing of permafrost.

**Spicules**

Very thin, calcite or opal, skeletal spines of certain sponges.

**Stone-slate**

A sedimentary rock, often a micaceous sandstone, which may be split into large thin slabs. Horsham Stone-slate is the best known example from West Sussex.

**Strata**

Layers of sedimentary rock.

**Strike**

The direction along which an inclined stratum intersects the horizontal plane. The strike direction is perpendicular to that of the dip.

**Structure**

The large-scale features of beds or strata.

**Stylolites**

Jagged lines which generally follow the bedding in limestone and marble, formed by pressure solution with precipitation of insoluble minerals.

**Superficial deposits**

Varied surface deposits formed during the Quaternary.

**Syenite**

A coarse-grained, alkaline igneous rock largely composed of orthoclase feldspar.

**Syncline**

A large down-fold or 'U'-shaped structure of strata.

**Synclinorium**

A regional scale syncline with numerous superimposed smaller folds.

**System**

The general name of a geological Period such as the Palaeogene or the Cretaceous Systems.

**Tertiary**

The original name of the Period of geological time from 66.0Ma to 2.6Ma. It has recently been replaced with the Neogene and Palaeogene Periods.

**Texture**

The small-scale relationship of minerals within a rock.

**Tilgate stone**

Hard beds of calcareous sandstone within the lower part of the Hastings Group. It was commonly crushed for road metal.

**Trace fossil**

Fossil impressions in sedimentary rocks left by animal activity, such as burrows and footprints.

**Travertine or Calcareous Tufa**

An open-textured or banded limestone deposited from calcareous springs.

**Trough or lobate cross-bedding structure**

An intricate cross-bedding structure formed in a sand sheet by numerous advancing sand lobes each of which has internal cross-bedding. Common in Horsham Stone-slate.

**Touch Stone**

Alternative name for Tournai Marble.

**Unconformity**

A break in the stratigraphic record which represents a major interval of non-deposition or erosion between two groups of strata. Often, horizontal strata lie above folded strata indicating an intervening period of earth movement.

**Upper Greensand Bench**

A very gently south-sloping dip-slope of good agricultural land underlain by Malmstone, which parallels and lies to the north of the Chalk Escarpment in West Sussex.

**Vein**

A thin fracture in a rock, infilled by a mineral, usually calcite or quartz.

**Vugh**

A small hole within a rock.

**Weathering**

The breakdown of rock material in situ by the action of mechanical, chemical and biological processes.

**Whinstone**

Former Sussex name for chert. Used in the north of England for dolerite dyke rock.

Chalk cliffs between Brighton and Rottingdean showing alternating darker beds rich in flints. View west towards Brighton.

Bateman's Quarry in Top Ashdown Sandstone (Hastings Sandstone), close to the former home of Rudgard Kipling, near Burwash.

# BIBLIOGRAPHY

# BIBLIOGRAPHY

Antram, N and Pevsner, N. 2012. *Sussex East with Brighton and Hove. The Buildings of England.* Yale University Press.

Ashurst, J. and Dimes, F. G. 1990. *Conservation of Building and Decorative Stone.* Butterworth, Heinemann.

Batten, D. J. ed. 2011. *English Wealden Fossils.* Palaeontological Association Field Guide to Fossils No. 14.

Beswick, M.1993. *Brickmaking in Sussex.* The Sussex Industrial Archaeology Society. Middleton Press.

Birch, R. 2006. *Sussex Stones; The Story of Horsham Stone and Sussex Marble.* Published by Roger Birch.

Birch, R. and Cordiner R. 2014. *Building Stones of West Sussex.* Published by R. Cordiner and R. Birch. (Out of print. Revised, Pdf. version available).

Blair, J. and Ramsey, N. (Eds.) 2001. *English Medieval Industries.* Hambledon Press.

Bone, D. A. and Bone, A. 2000. Lavant Stone: A Late Roman and Medieval Building Stone from the Chalk (Upper Cretaceous) of West Sussex. *Proceedings of the Geologists' Association.* **111**, 193-203.

Bone, D. A. and Bone, A. 2014. Quarrying the Mixon Reef at Selsey, West Sussex. *Sussex Archaeological Collections.* **152**. 95-116.

Bone, D. A. 2016. Historic Building Stones and their Distribution in the Churches and Chapels of West Sussex, England. *Proceedings of the Geologist's Association.* **127**, 53-77.

Clements, R. G. 1993. Type Section of the Purbeck Limestone Group, Durlston Bay, Swanage, Dorset. *Proceedings of the Dorset Natural History and Archaeological Society,* **114**, 181-206.

Clifton-Taylor, A. and Ireson A. S. 1983 (1994). *English Stone Building.* Gollancz.

Cordiner, R. J. 2014. The Variety and Distribution of Building Stones in West Sussex Churches, 950 to 1850 AD. *In: Stone in Historic Buildings: Characterization and Performance.* Geological Society, London, Special Publications, **391**, 121-137.

Cunliffe, B. 1971. *Fishbourne, a Roman Palace and its Garden.* Thames and Hudson.

Dawson, B. 1998. *Flint Buildings in West Sussex.* West Sussex County Council Planning Department.

Down, A. 1988. *Roman Chichester.* Phillimore.

Farrant, J. H. 2001. Sussex Depicted. Views and Descriptions 1600-1800. *Sussex Record Society,* Volume 85.

Godfrey, W. H. and Salzman, L. F. 1951. Sussex Views selected from the Burrell Collection 1776-1791. *Sussex Record Society.* Jubilee Volume.

Guy, J. 1984. *Castles in Sussex.* Phillimore.

Hobbs, M. 1994. *Chichester Cathedral. An Historical Survey.* Phillimore.

Howe, J, A. 1910 (Reprinted 2001). *The Geology of Building Stones.* Donhead Publishing Ltd.

Hughes, A. and Johnston, D. 2002. *West Sussex Barns and Farm Buildings.* Dovecote Press.

Johnston, P. M. 1907. Ecclesiastical Architecture. Civil and Domestic Architecture. Military Architecture. *In*: Page, W. (ed). *Victoria History of the County of Sussex.* **2**. 327-396.

Jope, E. M. 1964. The Saxon Building-Stone Industry in Southern and Midland England. *Medieval Archaeology.* **8**, 91-118.

Lott, G. and Cameron, D. 2005. The building stones of South East England: mineralogy and provenance. *10th Euroseminar on Microscopy applied to building materials. NERC open research archive 11879.* Paisley, Scotland 21-25 June 2005.

Mantell, G. A. 1833. *The Geology of South East England.* Longman, Reese, Orme, Brown, Green and Longman.

Parsons, D. (Ed.) 1990. *Stone Quarrying and Building in England AD 43 to 1525.* Royal Archaeological Institute.

Pevsner, N. and Nairn I. 1965. *Sussex; The Buildings of England.* Penguin Books.

Potter, J. F. 2007. A Review of some Early West Sussex Churches. *Sussex Archaeological Collections.* **145**. 81-96.

Roberts, R. 1988. *Twelfth Century Church Architecture in Sussex.* The Book Guild Ltd.

Salzmann, L. F. 1907 (1973). Economic Industries. In *Victoria History of Sussex* Vol. **2**. 1973. 229-271.

Salzman, L. F. 1952. *Building in England down to 1540: A documentary history.* Clarendon Press, Oxford.

Smith, A. B. and Batten D. J. 2002. *Fossils of the Chalk.* Palaeontological Association Field Guides to Fossils, **2**.

Tatton-Brown, T. 1980. The use of Quarr Stone in London and East Kent. *Medieval Archaeology* **24**. 213-15.

Tatton-Brown, T. 2006. A New Survey of the Fabric of the Church of the Holy Trinity, Bosham, West Sussex. *Sussex Archaeological Collections,* **144**, 129-154.

Venables, E. M. and Outen, A. F. 1969. *Building Stones of Old Bognor.* Bognor Regis Natural Science Society.

Whiteman, K. and J. 1994 (1998). *Ancient Churches of Sussex.* S.B. Publications.

Wolseley, F. 2009. *Historic Houses of West Sussex and their Owners.* Reprinted from the Sussex County Magazine 1926-1936. Country Books, Ashridge Press.

## PUBLICATIONS OF THE BRITISH GEOLOGICAL SURVEY

Aldiss, D. T. 2002. Geology of the Chichester and Bognor District. 1:50,000 Series Sheet 317 and 332 (England and Wales). *Sheet description of the British Geological Survey.*

Arkell, W. J. 1947. The Geology of the Country around Weymouth, Swanage and Lulworth. (Explanation of Sheets 341, 342, 343, with small portions of Sheets 327, 328, 329). *Memoirs of the Geological Survey of Great Britain.*

Gallois, R. W. 1965. *The Wealden District, British Regional Geology.* 4th edit. British Geological Survey.

Gallois, R. W. and Worssam, B. C. 1993. Geology of the Country around Horsham. *Memoir for 1:50,000 Geological Map Sheet 302 (England and Wales).* British Geological Survey.

Lake, R. D., Young, B., Wood, C. J. and Mortimore, R. N. 1987. Geology of the country around Lewes. *Memoir of the British Geological Survey,* Sheet 319 (England and Wales).

Lake, R. D. and Shephard-Thorn, E. R. 1987. Geology of the Country around Hastings and Dungeness. *Memoir of the British Geological Survey.* Sheets 320 and 321. (England and Wales).

Thurrell, R.W., Worssam, B. C. and Edmonds, E. A. 1968. Geology of the Country around Haslemere. (Explanation of One-Inch Geological Map Sheet 301). *Memoirs of the Geological Survey of Great Britain.* British Geological Survey.

Topley, W. 1875. The Geology of the Weald. *Memoirs of the Geological Survey of the United Kingdom.*

White, H. J. O. 1921. A Short Account of the Geology of the Isle of Wight. *Memoirs of the Geological Survey of Great Britain.*

Young, B. and Lake, R. D. 1988. Geology of the Country around Brighton and Worthing. *Memoir for 1:50,000 Geological Map Sheets 318 and 333 (England and Wales).* British Geological Survey.

# INDEX OF PLACES

**Bold Number** indicates a photograph